"This dear man wanted to be an Irish Tenor?
What would have happened to television?
My God!...What would have become of me???"

DICK VAN DYKE

"I've always thought that Carl was everything I would want
to be, except 90!..but he makes 90 look pretty good."

GEORGE CLOONEY

"Funny, touching, and true stories from a living
legend and one of my heroes, Carl Reiner. I know you
shouldn't eat in the bathroom (or wherever Goyim
read), but you will DEVOUR this book."

SARAH SILVERMAN

"A treasure-chest of memories from a treasure of a man.
This book is so wonderfully filled with life, love, warmth,
funny, wisdom, insight, and beauty, it's like having Carl
Reiner himself in your hands to enjoy. Except this you can
keep next to your bedside, and it folds in half better."

PAUL REISER

"I've loved Carl Reiner as a writer, a director, a talk show
guest and a human being. Now I love him as an author."

BILL MAHER

"Crime and Punishment has always been
my favorite book... Until Now!"

MEL BROOKS

"Carl Reiner is at that wonderful point in life where he knows
absolutely everything. Especially, how to tell a wonderful story.
I just love being in his world and this book is the Grand Tour."

JERRY SEINFELD

"Great stories from the great Carl Reiner.
I liked Chapter 29 the best."

ALBERT BROOKS

"At a time when so much of comedy can be cruel and
mean spirited... Carl Reiner is a perfect example of
comedy and kindness mixed with just the right amount
of biting wit to make for a really satisfying read."

JAY LENO

"There is no man funnier, more interesting, insightful or
delightful than Carl Reiner. He is one of my comedy idols,
even though he neglected to mention me on page 264."

JIMMY KIMMEL

I
Remember
Me

I
Remember
Me

Carl Reiner

authorHOUSE®

B
REINER

AuthorHouse™
1663 Liberty Drive
Bloomington, IN 47403
www.authorhouse.com
Phone: 1-800-839-8640

Published by AuthorHouse 3/8/13

ISBN: 978-1-4772-6458-4 (sc)
ISBN: 978-1-4772-6456-0 (dj)
ISBN: 978-1-4772-6455-3 (e)

Library of Congress Control Number: 2012916372

Front cover photo by Oliver DeFilippo
Back cover photo by Michele Reiner
Cover design by Alana Papoy

This book is printed on acid-free paper.

Inviting people to laugh at you while you are laughing at yourself is a good thing to do.

You may be the fool but you are the
FOOL IN CHARGE.

CARL REINER—"MY ANECDOTAL LIFE"

Contents

Foreword

The first time I saw Carl Reiner was when I was six years old. He made me laugh. Our family loved Sid Caesar's show, and my dad, who was a comedy maven, let my brothers and me stay up late on school nights to watch the master. Carl, along with Sid and Howard Morris, were doing a takeoff of those newfangled rock-and-roll singing teams. This group was called The Three Haircuts, and all they did was pose and adjust their cufflinks and sing a silly song. Carl stole the scene just by jumping up and down with a crazy smile on his face. Over and over he would jump, and every time he did, we would laugh and laugh.

As I grew up and started to study comedy—by not only watching television but listening to live comedy albums—I understood that as hilarious as Mel Brooks was as the Two Thousand-Year-Old Man, it was Carl who was feeding him, knowing when to jump in, and knowing when to let Mel go.

Later, as the creator of the great *Dick Van Dyke Show*, and also making an occasional appearance as Alan Brady, once again it was Carl's genius and energy that I was attracted to. Yes, Dick and Mary Tyler Moore were tremendous, as well as Morey Amsterdam and Rose Marie, but it was Carl who gave them all heartbeats.

When I became a working comedian, I appeared on *All in the Family*, playing Rob's best friend. The part suited us well, so Rob and I decided to keep it going. We had just moved from New York to L.A., and Rob really took us under his wing. We were invited to Rob's thirtieth birthday celebration, which was to be a small dinner party at Carl's house in Beverly Hills. I would get to meet him. I was so nervous, I called Penny Marshall,

Rob's wife at the time, and asked her what I should wear. She just laughed and said, "Whatever you want. They're not like that."

We arrived at his lovely home and Carl wasn't there yet. "He's picking up the Chinese food," Estelle Reiner, Carl's lovely wife, told us all. The door opened, and there he was, carrying a carton filled with those little white take-out boxes. Once he put those down, he introduced himself, and I couldn't believe my good fortune at getting a chance to meet a real giant. A giant who gets his own Chinese food. I was thirty when I met him. He made me laugh.

He then announced he was giving Rob his birthday present. He went outside for a moment, and then on a leash, he brought a goat into the kitchen. The frightened, adorable goat started slipping and sliding all over the tiled floor. The more frightened the goat became, the more pellets flew out of his rear. It was like a hairy slot machine that hit a jackpot. Carl was laughing very hard, as were we all. My usual birthday gifts were handkerchiefs and a crisp five-dollar bill. It was a great, fun night, and Carl spent a lot of time talking to me about what he'd seen me do on television, and he was so supportive, charming, and funny. He didn't have an ounce of pretense, and indeed he felt like the uncle you always wanted to have. I've known him for thirty-five years now, and he's never changed.

The last few years, we've had many lunches together, along with a who's who of comedy: Larry Gelbart, Neil Simon, and Norman Lear. The stories were fantastic, and it was Carl who would not only prompt everyone to tell a story that we hadn't heard, but also he never stopped laughing with his beloved friends, filling in missing details if they were forgotten. Sometimes comedians are not generous with their laughter. They tend to sit and listen and nod, like the wise men in *schul*. Not Carl. He loves to make people laugh, of course, but I think more than that, he loves to laugh. When he called to ask me to write this foreword, I was so flattered. From those grainy, black-and-white images of the jumping man to becoming his friend has been a great joy and honestly, an honor.

This book is a great journey as well. It is the not just the story of a show business life; it is the story of a family. From Carl's parents to becoming a parent himself, Carl takes us into moments of his memory as if we were standing there when they happened. The path that funny people take is often a slippery one, and Carl's story is no different. He paints with beautiful colors and details all the fascinating family and friends that Carl touched and has been touched by. We also get an intimate portrait of his relationship with his beloved Estelle, from the first time they met until the moment she passes away. I knew them for a long time and spent many a wonderful evening with them both. Well into her eighties, Estelle was still singing in nightclubs, and Carl was her roadie. Making sure her microphone was right, her ukulele tuned, that we were all seated comfortably, doting on her every need, he never sat down. Once she started to sing, I found myself watching Carl watching Estelle, smiling that proud, loving smile that was on his face for over sixty-five years.

Carl Reiner is not just a funny man who has made us laugh in one form or another for a very long time. He has been comedy's North Star. A constant. I've always looked at his career as one of the best ever and one of the most important. He is one of the great sketch comedians of all time; a fantastic master of ceremonies; a great comedy writer; and as a director, he has given us some of the best comedy films of all time. He is an author, of course, a playwright, and author of wonderful children's books. He has done this for seventy years, never taking his foot off the gas pedal. He knows who he is. He didn't have to be the star. Always willing to be second if it helped the team finish first, Carl has never had an air about him. He is what he is: a nice genius.

Years ago, I was a guest on the game show, *The Ten Thousand-Dollar Pyramid*, and I have to tell you I am the world record holder. Google it, you'll see. In the preliminary round, I was giving the clues to my partner. Names of celebrities appeared on the screen that only I could see, and I had to describe this person in a creative way so my partner could guess who it was. In one minute, you had to guess ten names, and the pace was furious. Sammy Davis Jr. appeared, and I gave this clue: "World's greatest entertainer," and my partner immediately said, "Carl Reiner."

The audience laughed, because they could see the clue, and after I said in haste as the clock ticked away, "One eye, black Jew," she got it. After I thought about it, she's not that far off. I don't know many people who are more entertaining than Carl Reiner. He is a brilliant man, still curious, still interested, and at ninety, probably still can jump up and down like a crazy man. I was sixty-four when I read this book. He made me laugh … and cry.

I Remember Me is the perfect Carl Reiner title. I mean, who could ever forget him?

—Billy Crystal

Preface

I Remember Me offers fifty-five chapters of varying lengths, containing remembrances of things past. It is my theory that these memories are stored in a part of one's brain that does not allow your mind to access them until you are at least ninety years old. Three months ago, I became eligible, and the following is what my mind had stored in my brain.

Acknowledgment

My heartfelt thanks to: first my family, Rob, Annie, Lucas, my grandchildren Jake, Nick, Romy, Livia, Rose and my daughters-in-law Michele and Maud.

And Lawrence O'Flahavan, Alfredo Ritta, Bess Scher, John Clark, George Shapiro, Aaron Davis and Al Pivo.

And our publisher Alan Bower who guided us gently into the light.

CHAPTER ONE

Today, I Am Almost a Man

On January 25 of this year, 2011, I received a letter from a Jill Fiorella, who informed me that she was the granddaughter of Yetta and Max Fishman, who, eighty-five years ago, resided in the Bronx, at 665 East 179th Street on the same floor as my parents, Irving and Bessie Reiner. I remembered the Fishmans! They resided in the apartment across the hall and had a son, Murray, who was my very first playmate.

I learned from Ms. Fiorella's letter that Murray had passed on a few years earlier, and she thought I might like to have an item she had found among Murray's papers.

"In sorting through some of Murray's papers," Ms. Fiorella wrote, "I came across his bar mitzvah speech—it was written so eloquently in such a beautiful handwriting. I knew at once that Murray could not have written it and asked my Mom if she knew who had and she said that it was written by their neighbor, your father, Irving Reiner. I am enclosing a copy of the speech, hoping that it will bring back some fond memories of your childhood. Sincerely, Jill Fiorella."

Ms. Fiorella could not have imagined the memories that flooded back, and they were more than just fond ones—they were revelatory. As soon as I glanced at the enclosure, I knew exactly what it was, and I was amazed and delighted to have it. In my wildest dreams, I could not have imagined that this document existed. Ms. Fiorella correctly assumed that it was the speech my father had written for her father to read at his bar mitzvah, which I learned from a sloppily scribbled date on the back, was held on June 26, 1937. What Jill Fiorella could not know is that the speech her brother made on his thirteenth birthday was, word for word, the very same speech I had delivered at my bar mitzvah one year earlier.

The first two words of this speech, "Worthy assembly," had been emblazoned in my memory. At the time, I remembered thinking how really classy those words were. I had never before heard anyone address a group by saying, "Worthy assembly," and haven't since. The rest of the speech was as flowery as its penmanship.

Ms. Fiorella described my father's handwriting as being "so beautiful," and I concur. Among other things, Pop was a master engraver, and the Old English lettering he used was replete with curlicues and fancy swirls.

As far as I knew, my father had never been a member of a synagogue or ever set foot in one. He was a believer in the Almighty but not a joiner.

A week before my big day, my father visited the Hughes Avenue Synagogue, an unprepossessing house of worship that was located in one of the Bronx's less-affluent neighborhoods. For a nominal fee, the elders agreed to allow my father, a non-member, to rent their *schul* for a Thursday morning bar mitzvah.

That morning, at eight a.m., gathered at the synagogue were my father, my mother, my older brother Charlie, and ten old, Jewish strangers. These mostly bearded men in long prayer shawls were approximately the same wizened group who, four years earlier, had witnessed my brother's coming of age.

Here now, in my father's handwriting, is the short, flowery speech that both my brother and I—and later Murray Fishman—delivered on the day we became men:

Worthy Assembly;

You have afforded me great honor this day when you have come to this Temple of God to take part in our celebration on the day I have become a Bar Mitzvah. I hereby express my deep gratitude for the love and friendship you have shown by this day. May the Lord God of Isreal grant it, that we shall be able to repay ~~them~~ you in accordance with your deeds on the day of rejoicing, and celebration.

II

And to you, my dear Parents, I give thanks of gratitude for that you have brought me up and raised me, to be prepared for this great and honorable day.

May God be with me in my ~~and~~ endeavor to be a good member of society, and a good Jew. Amen.

Now that I read what I had delivered seventy-seven years ago to the "worthy assembly" that had come to celebrate my thirteenth birthday, two things strike me. I don't think that either the writer or the deliverer of the document believed most of what was written. I did not feel at all "prepared for this honorable day," and I had no idea what it meant to be "a good Jew." Certainly, not attending synagogue did not qualify either me or my father for that honor.

On that honorable day, I had the opportunity to deliver the speech twice—first at the synagogue and then at a reception that was held for me in the empty apartment next to the Fishmans'. At the party, my family was joined by my friends Lenny, Davey, Marty, Mutty, Shlermy, and Vic, who were served a slice of birthday cake on paper plates and ginger ale in paper cups. The party lasted for half an hour before all "us guys" left to play a game of stickball in the street, using one of my presents, a "Spaldeeen," the high-bouncing rubber ball my friends had chipped in to buy.

One Saturday morning, soon after my bar mitzvah, I found myself on the verge of losing a battle I had won every week for the past year. After turning thirteen, I became a most-sought-after young Jew. A group of old men who worshiped at a sad little synagogue directly across the street needed my body for the evening prayers. "It is written" that all ritual prayers intoned in a temple will not reach God's ear unless a *minyan*—a quorum of at least ten Jewish men—was present.

Very often, before my bar mitzvah, when a *minyan* was needed, my friends, who all were a year older than I, were often pressed into service. Even after I became eligible, I managed not to be around when an extra body was needed. One Saturday morning, two "men," a ninth and tenth man, were needed for the *minyan*, and I was pressed into service. Besides not wanting to spend my time in a synagogue, I harbored a guilty secret that I have never revealed to anyone—until I wrote the following chapter, whose title tells it all.

CHAPTER TWO

Because of Me, the Prayers of Ten Jews Fell on Deaf Ears

My best friends during my pre-teenage years were, as I have mentioned, Lenny, Shlermy, David, Marty, and Mutty. In their tenth, eleventh, and twelfth years, after a full day attending public school, they spent a good part of their afternoons going to Hebrew school. There, by learning how to read, write, and pray in Hebrew, they prepared for their bar mitzvahs. Happily, my parents did not require that I get this education; however, every day I waited impatiently for my buddies to finish their schooling and come out and play. All became proficient at reading prayers from the holy book they carried to the synagogue every Sabbath. For two years, on Friday nights and all day Saturday, rather than sit alone on the stoop, I accompanied them to the synagogue and hung out with them while they observed the Sabbath and, sometimes, horsed around. Had their parents not been Orthodox Jews, it is likely they would have preferred to spend their weekends in the street playing, rather than in temple, praying.

Often, the six of us were invited to leave the synagogue and not return until we could behave like *menschen*. One old man's admonition has stayed with me through the years. I had been particularly talkative that day and, after not heeding his warnings, the annoyed old man exploded. Speaking with a thick Yiddish accent, he shouted at me, "Hey you! Didn't I once told you to be 'shut up'! How many times must I told you?"

On one occasion, I might have goaded him, just to hear him say, "Didn't I told you to be shut up!"

My days of successfully ducking the responsibility of being tapped as the tenth man were waning. When I was a few months shy of my thirteenth birthday, my father sought out a rabbi who would be willing to teach me the prayers I needed to recite at my bar mitzvah. All I can remember about the rabbi was his long, white beard, his healthy paunch, and the dirty toothpick he took from his vest pocket at the start of each lesson. He used the weathered toothpick to pick his teeth and to point to letters and words in the prayer book. He would tap a Hebrew letter or a word on the page and bid me to pronounce it as he did. I quickly memorized the alphabet and, almost as quickly, learned how to singsong the short but important Hebrew prayer that I had to deliver at the altar before "becoming a man." I never learned to read the prayer, but I memorized it. I was then, and still am, a Hebrew illiterate—and not proud of it.

After my bootleg bar mitzvah, I allowed myself to be conscripted for the *minyan* and spent every Sabbath praying with my religious friends. I feigned reading whatever prayer was being offered by using my ability to "double-talk" Hebrew. That ability stood me well years later when I joined the great Sid Caesar, using French, Italian, and German double-talk in satirizing foreign films on his television show.

My friends were aware that I was praying in gibberish, but they kept my secret. I feared that if the elders discovered this, they would throw me out, leaving me to fend for myself on the weekend. I was happy to be a member of the *minyan*, but I suffered tremendous guilt each time I was the tenth man praying. I knew the old men felt that unless ten adult Jews entreated God with the prescribed holy words, God would not be able to hear them. I worried that because I was not using the Bible's words but Hebrew double-talk, I was keeping the prayers of nine good Jews from reaching God's ear.

I know that the statute of limitations may have run out on my adolescent crime, but not so my guilt.

CHAPTER THREE

The Thirty-Five-Year-Old Silver Filling

(Adapted from the chapter, "Perpetual Papa" in My Anecdotal Life)

Irving Reiner made his living as a watchmaker and, for diversion, played the violin and flute. He was self-taught and mastered both instruments well enough to perform regularly in amateur symphony orchestras—all this before he married my mother. I recall his practicing both instruments on Sundays. Often he would put my brother and me to sleep by playing lullabies on his flute, and he always obliged me when I begged for "one more, one more!" I actually remember my eyelids droop whenever he favored us with a Brahms lullaby.

My father stood five feet three inches tall and would, by any standard, be considered a short person. However, for the first five or six years of my life, he was twice as tall as I, and for the next few years, I continued to look up at him. It was not until my teen years that I became aware I had grown taller than my father. He did have the best posture in our family and possibly in the neighborhood. He strode down the street with his head held high, his shoulders squared back, and at a pace that was quick and decisive. More often than not, his head was filled with some invention he was in the process of developing—the battery-operated clock being one. My mother told of the time she passed him on the street when she sensed he was preoccupied. She playfully said, "Good morning, Mr. Reiner!"

He doffed his hat, mumbled, "Morning, ma'am," and continued on.

My brother Charlie, My Papa and myself

As far as I was concerned, my father always stood ten feet tall. He married my mother, Bessie Mathias, who measured an even five foot two. My brother Charlie and I grew to be over six feet, and we asked our science-minded father how he might explain that.

"It's genetics," he informed us. "You two carry not only genes from your mother and me but from all your forebears."

"Well, who among them was tall?" I asked. "Where did our height come from?"

"From my father, your grandfather!" he stated proudly. "He was almost five foot six."

What my father lacked in height, he made up for in patience, in musicality, inventiveness, and stoicism—a double helping of stoicism.

For as long as I can remember, my father worked at home in the living room of our three-room apartment. He had set up a workbench at the window that overlooked a public school yard. My brother and I slept in the living room on a convertible couch that opened into a double bed. When we became teenagers, our parents decided that all of us would be more comfortable if Charlie and I slept in their twin-bedded bedroom and they shared the convertible couch in the living room.

I was about fourteen when, after school one day, I found myself sitting on that couch and reading the sports section of the *Bronx Home News*. My father was at his workbench repairing a watch and, at one point, I heard him utter a quiet, "Tsk tsk!" There were actually two occasions when I was seated on that couch and heard a "tsk tsk" escape from him. The second time I heard my stoical Pa's "tsk tsk," it was quite a bit louder. I will return to it, as I feel it deserves a chapter of its own.

That first "tsk tsk" was followed by his saying, "Will you look at that!"

Naturally I looked up and saw my father examining a small, metal object that he held in his hand. "You know, Carl, this silver filling," he said thoughtfully, "has been in my tooth for thirty-five years."

He did not seem to be in any kind of discomfort, so I asked the question that any good straight man would: "Pa, how do you know how long that filling has been in your tooth?"

"Because I put it there!" he said, pointing to a bottom molar. "This is the tooth I filled when I lived in Vienna!"

Incredible as it may sound, my father had actually filled his own tooth. Before explaining how this came to pass, he fished out a small hand mirror from his workbench and examined the hole left by the departed filling.

"Now this is something!" he said, grinning.

My father uncharacteristically allowed himself to feel pride in something he did three decades earlier and eagerly told me the story of how circumstances had forced him to take on the dual role of patient and dentist.

When he was a mere fourteen, he received his credentials as a master watchmaker and left his home in Czernowitz to ply his craft at a large jewelry store in Vienna. He was employed there for a few years and dutifully used part of his paycheck to support his aging parents.

He told me how when he was eighteen, he had awakened one morning with a severe toothache. A local dentist examined him and discovered cavities in two of his bottom molars and recommended that relief would come if the decay were drilled out. Without using an anesthetic, the dentist proceeded to drill into the first tooth. My father admitted that, in his life, he had never experienced anything as excruciatingly painful. After the first tooth was drilled and filled and the dentist's drill was poised to start the second one, Pop said that he handed the dentist some money, bolted from the chair, and ran out of the building.

The following morning, the pain was still there but tolerable. It was at this point my father, the watchmaker, decided to become his own dentist.

He visited the public library, found books on dentistry, and from them, learned how to drill out decay, how to prepare a tooth for a filling, and how to compound that filling by using an amalgam with proper amounts of silver and mercury. Not having any anesthetic, he used his delicate jeweler's drill for only seconds at a time, stopping immediately when the pain was less than bearable. It took many hours to complete the work, but he did it.

My father now looked at the small silver filling lying in the palm of his hand, shook his head and sighed, "Thirty-five years is not bad, but fifty would have been better."

Me, Ma & Pa

CHAPTER FOUR

The Louder of the Two "Tsk Tsks"

Not too long after I heard my father mutter "tsk tsk" and learned how capable he was of doing his own dental work, I heard a second and louder set of "tsk tsks." I expected to see him holding another silver filling, but when I looked up, I saw something that would have provoked any regular person to shout, "Holy shit!" or "Damn, damn!" or "Call a doctor!"

Instead of shouting, I saw my father calmly examining his left hand, where the shaft of a small screwdriver had pierced through the tip of his index finger and was lodged up to its hilt. It seems that while reassembling a watch, my father had attempted to screw a small screw into a newly tapped hole, when the screwdriver slipped from the groove. The "tsk tsks" came a beat after the shaft of the screwdriver went right through the fleshy part of his finger. As I looked on, my Pop was already contemplating how best to remove the bloodied tool from his finger. I suggested that he "Just pull it out!" and he quietly explained why he would not "just pull it out."

"If I did that," he explained, "it would just tear more of the flesh."

He then placed a small cutting pliers against his finger and snipped off the lower shank of the screwdriver and then, without causing any more damage, he gently lifted the nub out, after which he deftly applied some drops of iodine to his wound. Instead of screaming or flinching—as I and most mortals would when applying iodine to an open wound—he remained impassive. He deftly placed a small piece of adhesive tape on his finger, clenched and unclenched his fist, popped the jeweler's loupe back in his eye, and went back to work.

My Pop continued to work at his bench for many more years—unperturbed by little accidents or the chattering of children that wafted up from the public schoolyard below his window.

CHAPTER FIVE

Irving Shoots Irving Playing Irving

In 1906, my father bought a beautiful, Bohemian-made violin for five hundred dollars. Today, I understand those five hundred dollars would translate to many, many thousands. At that time, my father was an unmarried twenty-one-year-old who had just immigrated to America from Vienna, where he had worked as a master watchmaker. He had never played the violin but loved the music it could make in the hands of a virtuoso. As a three-year-old, he had watched with envy as his six-year-old brother, Harry, took his weekly violin lesson. My father vowed then that one day he would buy an instrument and learn to play it.

To this end, he bought the violin and two books of instructions, one on how to master the instrument and the other on how to read and transpose music. Within a few years, he mastered all three, reading, transposing, and playing well enough to join a couple of orchestras. One, I think, was conducted by Walter Damrosch and another funded by the City of New York and private charities. These orchestras performed free concerts in the city's parks, concert halls, and public schools. My father spoke of how receptive and grateful the inmates of Ossining Prison were to see and hear a live orchestra playing classical music.

Soon after mastering the violin, my father bought a flute and, once again using books, he learned to master it well enough to be play first flute in these city-sponsored bands.

One of my father's earlier hobbies was photography. As a youngster, he built himself a pinhole camera, and later, as a young adult, he bought a Daguerreotype camera that photographed images on glass plates. On one such plate, the iconic image of President Abraham Lincoln was captured by the great Civil War photographer, Mathew Brady.

At this moment, if I turn my swivel chair 180 degrees and open a small drawer, I can produce four of these Daguerreotype plates my Pop shot almost a hundred years ago. One has on it an image of my mother, Bessie, nursing my one-month-old brother, Charlie.

My father, having the expertise and the equipment, was always considered by friends and family as the designated photographer.

During his young life, he took many photos of friends, relatives, and one that I possess of his co-workers in a large jewelry store in Vienna, Austria.

One day, years later, when someone asked my father for a photo of himself, he realized he had none and went about getting one. He did this by inventing a self-timing device that could be attached to his camera. The hand-crafted metal device contained a watch spring, which he wound to give himself a few seconds to get into place before it triggered the shutter to snap his image. In 1907, he applied for a patent, and while the patent was pending, he learned that six months earlier, a similar device had been developed and patented in Japan.

Pop's still-shining, silver-plated device now sits proudly on a shelf in our den. The timer's spring is still intact, and from time to time, I wind it, just to hear my Pop's invention tick.

Except for photos I took of my father and my mother when in later years they visited us, I have but one good photo of him as a young man. He is seated in a chair, wearing a single-breasted suit, white shirt and tie, and is playing his violin. As far as I know, this is the only picture that exists where my father is both the subject and the photographer.

I feel confident, however, that I can make the following outrageous claim and not be challenged.

I claim that my Pop is the only person on Earth who has taken a plate-glass Daguerreotype photograph of himself while playing a violin and also had successfully drilled and filled his own tooth.

When my father passed away, he entrusted me with the safekeeping of his violin. It was safely stowed in the living room, next to a large, wooden armoire, where it languished for many years. One day, my dear friend, Leon Kirchner, suggested that a musician colleague of his, the eminent violinist and teacher, Eudice Shapiro, could make good use of it. She had many students who needed a fine instrument to play until they could afford to buy one of their own. My father would have been happy to know that dozens of young violinists, in their developing years, had used his violin, including his great-grandnephew-in-law, Daniel Shapiro, who, like himself, has a scientific bent which led him to become a marine biologist and a tenured professor at Cal State University at Monterey Bay, where he teaches ethics and social justice.

My father would have been ecstatic to know that today, the young student who is now playing his violin is his great-granddaughter, sixteen-year-old Livia Reiner. Livia started using it a few years ago and is now playing it in her school orchestra. He would also be surprised to learn, as I was, that tucked in the bottom of her violin case, Livia keeps a copy of the Daguerreotype photo that her great-grandfather snapped of himself.

A few weeks ago, my son Lucas, his wife Maud, and Livia's loving sister Rose, an excellent choral singer and cellist, invited my daughter Annie and I to attend a concert at Livia's school, and all I kept thinking and saying to Annie was, "Wow, would Pop get a kick out of seeing that lovely girl with the long, red hair playing his violin!"

After the concert, when Livia emerged, we started to congratulate her, but she held up her hand and said, "Wait, I'll be right back!"

When I asked where she was going, she said, "I am going to get Irving."

Her family knew what she meant, but it took a second for me to get it. Livia had named the violin "Irving!"

And I thank her for that. Had my beautiful granddaughter not named her violin Irving, I would not have had the pleasure of writing "Irving Shoots Irving Playing Irving!"

The automatic timing device Irving invented to photograph himself

CHAPTER SIX

Meet Mel Brooks, the Man
in the Bay Window

I n 1951, my wife, Estelle, and I and our children took our very first summer vacation on an island in New York's Great South Bay that was called, for reasons I forget, Fire Island. The island was thirty-eight miles long and about three city blocks wide. We first learned of this quiet resort from Mel Tolkin, the head writer of *Your Show of Shows*, who, with his wife Edith, had rented a house there for the summer.

"It's a great place to vacation," he suggested, "especially with kids. Beautiful beach—no cars allowed—and people get to walk around barefoot."

It sounded heavenly, and a week later, Estelle, our children, and I drove to Bayshore, Long Island, parked our Buick in a lot, and then boarded a ferry for the half-hour trip to Ocean Beach, a small town on Fire Island.

Lined up at the Ocean Beach dock were half a dozen eager teenagers and their red metal wagons, who, for a dollar tip, were ready to transport the new arrivals' luggage to their rented homes. We splurged and hired two wagons—one for the baggage and the other for two happy, wide-eyed kids, four-year-old Robbie and two-year-old Annie.

Walking to our summer home, we passed dozens of friendly-faced, barefooted children and adults. I found this, and the absence of cars, wonderfully quaint and calming.

The modest house, which the Tolkins had secured for us and we had rented sight unseen, was located about a half block from the ocean. The Realtor, who met us on the porch, informed us that our new home was one of the few on the street whose rooms had "dwarf petitions." He suggested that in our case, it could turn out to be a plus.

Not knowing what "dwarf petitions" were, I asked, "Why so?" and he pointed to Robbie and Annie, who were getting out of their wagon.

"In the middle of the night, if they're not feeling well or have to 'go potty' and call for you," he explained, "they won't have to scream their lungs out. The ocean is pretty loud, but with no ceilings on any of the rooms, you'll hear them right off."

After learning what dwarf petitions were, I understood why the rent was only eight hundred dollars for the season.

Besides the rooms having no ceilings, we found that the mattresses had lumps, the sheets and pillowcases were unironed, and the dishes unmatched.

One other thing the house lacked was a guest room, but that did not deter Estelle and me from inviting a friend to spend a weekend with us. On that first Saturday, Mel Brooks, twenty-one and single, had been invited by other friends to attend their beach party. His friends' cottage had no extra room or cot, and neither did we, but we had a living room with an alcove that sported a four-foot, cushioned window seat. We offered our window seat to Mel, and he happily accepted it.

That night, as we tucked Rob and Annie in, we forewarned them that if they awoke early and happened to wander into the living room, not to be frightened if they saw a man sleeping in the window seat. We showed them the alcove and the window seat and repeated our warning. "Don't be frightened if you see a man sleeping there."

To show us he understood, Robbie repeated, "A man sleeping there," and little sister Annie nodded and pointed. "A man there?!"

"Yes," I said, "and be very quiet so you don't wake up the man."

At two that morning, a party-weary Mel quietly let himself into the house, took off his shoes, and curled up in the window seat. An hour or so later, two curious children found themselves at the alcove, staring at "the man" they were told would be there. So as not to awaken the soundly sleeping "man," they spoke very softly. Their faces were no more than a foot from Mel's when their whispered conversation was just loud enough to awaken him. Hoping they might go away, Mel feigned being asleep, but when he heard their charming chatter, he could not resist eavesdropping.

Here now is the whispered conversation Mel reported Robbie and Annie carried on sixty years ago:

Annie: "Is dat the man?"
Robbie: "Dat's the man."
Annie: "He the man?"
Robbie: "Yes, dat's the man."
Annie: "Dat's the man?"
Robbie: "Dat's the man."
Annie: "Man sleep?"
Robbie: "Yes, the man sleep."
Annie: "No, man not sleep."
Robbie: "Yes, the man sleeping."
Annie: "Man eye open."
Robbie: "Where?"
Annie: "There—li'l bit."
Robbie: "No man eye closed."
Annie: "No, open, I show."

With that, Annie reached out and, with her forefinger, attempted to open one of Mel's eyelids.

"I'm up, I'm up," Mel said with a grin. "Da man is up!"

Mel then sat up and hugged his young inquisitors.

That morning at breakfast, with the children playing outside, Mel recreated for Estelle and me a verbal transcript of the conversation he had eavesdropped a few hours earlier. Once again, it proves that "out of the mouth of babes" come words that are worth remembering and sometimes, transcribing.

As I think about this event, I can't help but marvel at what those three participants have done since that memorable day in a dwarf-partitioned rental on Fire Island. Here now, for my distinct pleasure, I proudly offer a partial list of their individual accomplishments.

Rob Reiner

On Television:

> Portrayed Meathead in Norman Lear's groundbreaking and air-breaking comedy, *All in the Family*.

Feature Films:

> Directed:
>
> > *Stand By Me, A Few Good Men, This Is Spinal Tap, The American President, When Harry Met Sally, The Princess Bride, Misery, The Bucket List, Flipped, The Beauty of Belle Isle.*

Social and Political Activism:

> Leadership Role in Preschool Education
>
> Health Care for Children
>
> Federal Court Challenge to Give Gays the Right to Marry.

In Life:

> Husband to lovely wife, Michele and father to three fine children, Romy, Jake and Nick.

Romy, Michele, Jake, Rob and Nick

Annie Reiner

Member International Psychoanalytic Association.
Degrees: PhD, PsyD, and Sr. Faculty Psychoanalytic Center of CA
Published Books:
  Psychoanalytic:
      The Search for Conscience and the Birth of the Mind
      Bion and Being: Passion and the Creative Mind
  Children's Books:
      The Potty Chronicles
      A Visit to the Art Galaxy
      The History of Christmas
      The Journey of the Little Seed
  Poetry:
      Presents of Mind, Beyond Rhyme And Reason
      The Naked I
      Mind Your Heart

Annie Reiner

Mel Brooks

Albums, CDs:
The 2000 Year Old Man

I am sorry, but I don't think I am going to continue the formal configuration I used to catalogue Rob's and Annie's achievements. Typing-wise, it is just too wearying. I will simply note that before Mel wrote the screen and stage versions of *The Producers* and the Broadway musical, *Young Frankenstein*, for which he also supplied the music and lyrics, he had earlier Broadway credits and successes, which included sketches and librettos for the following musicals: *New Faces of 1952*, *Shinbone Alley*, and *All American*.

As a writer-producer-director, his theatrical films include: *The Producers*, *Blazing Saddles*, *Young Frankenstein*, *High Anxiety*, *Life Stinks*, *Silent Movie*, *Robin Hood—Men In Tights*, and *Dracula—Dead and Loving It*.

I hope Mel will not be angry that I excluded some of his films. He might be inclined to temper his anger when I add that all of Mel's films are available on DVD and can be purchased or rented at Amazon.com, DirecTV, Hulu, and Netflix. If that doesn't soothe him, then perhaps my including in the appendix an eight-by-ten photo of him sent to me by my former secretary, Sybil Adelman will. She actually asked, "Is the man in this photo Paul Newman or your friend, Mel?"

CHAPTER SEVEN

The Truth about the 2000-Year-Old Man

The truth about this old man is that he does what many old people do: he lies about his age. It was in 1960 when the world first heard this wizened old gent, who resides in the body of Mel Brooks, proudly state on an album entitled *The 2000-Year-Old Man* that he was two millennia old. Now, those of us who can add know that between 1960 and this year, 2012, fifty-two years have elapsed, which would make him two thousand fifty-two years old, or as he continues to insist, "I am two thousand years *young!*"

I contacted Mr. Brooks and told him that I was going to publish his alter ego's real age, two thousand fifty-two! Well, bless him, he laughed and said, "Hold it, buster! Don't make me older than I am. I won't be two thousand and fifty-two until next Thursday."

Actually, I am misquoting him. He did not say "next Thursday." He actually said, "Next *Thoisday*," which he knew would get a bigger smile from me than if he had pronounced it correctly. It did.

I have already covered the genesis of the old gent in the 2003 memoir, *My Anecdotal Life*, but here now are some memories of Mel that only recently popped into my head. They might tickle your fancy, and nothing gives me greater pleasure than seeing Mel's humor tickling as many fancies as possible.

CHAPTER EIGHT

St. Joan of Arc Is Censored by Sir Mel of Brooks

In 1960, ten years after amusing our coworkers on *Your Show of Shows* and our friends at dinner parties, Steve Allen arranged with World Pacific Jazz to record the wisdom of the 2000 Year Old Man for their label. It was during the process of editing that first album that Mel and I found ourselves doing something uncharacteristic—having a serious argument. Our disagreement centered on the final mix and which jokes should be included or excluded.

As you probably know—or if you don't, I want you to know—during our recording sessions, Mel was never aware of what questions would be asked of him. I found that his being unaware of the questions only heightened his powers, and the more difficult the questions, the more brilliant were his responses. Our first session, which was performed for an audience of a hundred friends and family, went on for over two hours—and from it we culled about forty-seven solid minutes. We heartily agreed about those minutes, but there were two extra minutes about which we had different opinions.

If you heard the original release, you might remember the very brief exchange we had about Joan of Arc that ended with my asking: "Sir, did you know Joan of Arc?"

"Know her? I went with her, dummy!"

"How did you feel about her being burned at the stake?"

"Terrible."

I loved Mel's casual delivery of the word "terrible." That exchange got a huge laugh, as did the few lines that preceded it. This comprised the entire Joan of Arc spot. What our loyal public never knew was that there was a longer exchange. We both agreed that the material in question was very funny, but one of us thought that some of it was somehow inappropriate. The following are the bones of contention that caused the contretemps.

After Mel had said, "I went with her, dummy," I said, "Nowhere did I ever see it written that Joan of Arc ever 'went' with anybody."

"Well," Mel said, "Nobody put it in a column—we didn't have newspapers yet."

"How did you happen to meet her?"

"First of all, I didn't know Joan was a 'her.' I thought she was a he—a guy."

"Why would you think that?"

"Well, he had a sword, he wore a helmet and heavy armor—and he rode a big horse. I was like his valet. He was my general."

"Joan of Arc was your general?"

"Not Joan—John! We called him John."

"Oh, I see. You thought it was John because, in French her name was Jeanne d'Arc, and Jeanne is pronounced 'John.'"

"Right, John Dark, but I called him Johnny. All I know—in one second, Johnny was on the horse—then off the horse—then on again... He was some great horseman and a great swordsman."

"When and how did you find out that Joan was a girl?"

"It was after a big battle; he was so dirty and pooped. I said to him, 'Hey, Johnny, let's go find a place where you can take a shower and maybe catch a nap.'"

"And you found such a place?"

"Yeah, an inn, not a fancy one, but as soon as we got to our room, I said, 'Johnny, you're dirtier than me; you take a shower first.' He didn't argue, he just took off his helmet, but when he took off his armor and his pants, I looked at him and said, 'Hey, Johnny, what happened to you?'

You know something, I always liked Johnny, but from that moment on, I *loved* him!"

It was at this point in the routine that I asked Mel how he felt about Joan being burned at the stake, and he said, "Terrible."

We agreed that the material was funny enough, but Mel was

uncomfortable that we were treading on sacred ground. It didn't sit well with him that we were making jokes about a revered Catholic saint. Although we never discussed it, I suspected that Mel's thinking was tempered by the fact that his wife, Anne, was of the Catholic faith. I daresay that excluding the material I cited has in no way hurt the album's success. All five *2000 Year Old Man* CDs are alive and selling.

CHAPTER NINE

Mel Brooks Ate So Many Carrots That...

During the early days of Mel Brooks's television career as a writer on *Your Show of Shows*, he found it almost impossible to get to work on time. "On time" for his fellow writers was ten o'clock in the morning, but most days, Mel walked in at least an hour or two late—a bagel and a container of coffee from the Stage Delicatessen heralded his arrival. He ordered this before he left his house, knowing I would pay the delivery boy the fifty cents, a quarter for the food and a quarter for the tip. One morning, Mel's tardiness angered everyone more than usual. To make him aware how upset we all were and possibly help him mend his ways, I handed the delivery boy not the usual fifty cents but twenty-five cents and a twenty-five-dollar tip!

Mel breezed in ten minutes later, blithely dropped a half dollar on the table, and grabbed for the bag in my hand. I held on to it and informed him that I had given the delivery boy a twenty-five-dollar tip. Without missing a beat, Mel calmly dropped two tens and a five on the desk and snatched the bag from me.

Mel said nary a word about the exorbitant tip he had shelled out but berated the staff for being unable to come up with a punch line for a joke he assumed they had been working on.

"All right, what do you need?" Mel challenged while chomping on his bagel. "Give me the straight line!"

The writers had been working on a joke where a doctor is trying to diagnose why his insomniac patient is having trouble falling asleep.

"So, you can't fall asleep, the doctor asked the man," Mel offered immediately. "Tell me, have you by any chance been eating carrots?"

Groans and hoots escaped from every writer in the room.

"Oh, come on, Mel," our head writer, Mel Tolkin, sneered, "not another old joke about carrots being good for your eyesight."

"No," Mel shot back, "a new one!"

"There hasn't been a new carrot joke since vaudeville," Lucille Kallen offered.

"Because I haven't tried," Mel shot back.

"Okay, try!" Sid Caesar challenged. "Tell me, Doctor, how could eating too many carrots keep someone from falling asleep?"

Mel, acting as if he had been trapped, mumbled, "How could eating too many carrots keep someone from falling asleep?" He then placed his back against a wall, spread his arms as if being crucified, and shouted, "The poor man couldn't fall asleep because carrots make his vision sooo strong that he could see through his eyelids!"

Mel Brooks had taken the old cliché, twisted it gently, and came up with the best new carrot joke of the decade. Needless to say, the room erupted with laughter and I am happy to report that he is still capable of causing eruptions.

CHAPTER TEN

Why Did I Let You Guys
Talk Me into This?

M el Brooks uttered that rhetorical question while riding in the
back of a stretch limo on his way to perform at the Civic
Auditorium in San Francisco. Mel had mumbled that question
many times on the plane ride from Los Angeles. The three guys who did
not answer his query were our intrepid literary agent, Dan Strone; my
manager and beloved nephew-in-law, George Shapiro; and one of Mel's
oldest and dearest friends, me.

George, in attempting to placate our disgruntled friend, reminded
Mel that the American Association of Family Physicians was sponsoring
this prestigious event and how excited they were.

35

"They have never before had anything like this," Dan offered. "There will be over four thousand people at each of your two shows."

"I don't give a shit!" Mel commented.

"They've been sold out for a week!" I chimed in. "These people are dying to see the 2000 Year Old Man."

"Let 'em die!" Mel mumbled.

Better them than me! had to be the unspoken words in Mel's head.

I believe that the clue to Mel's reluctance to perform that night was his fear of "dying" on stage. He doubted his ability to come up with enough great ad-lib lines and jokes that would elicit the kind of laughs these people expected and had paid good money to hear. For the balance of the trip, Mel remained surly and blamed George, Dan, and me for throwing him to the lions.

"Never again," he mumbled over and over. "This is the last time I let anyone talk me into anything!"

"Mel," George reminded him, "for a couple hours of work, you'll be getting a big chunk of money."

"I have a big chunk of money," Mel shot back. "Driver, take me back to the airport!"

Mel's order fell on deaf ears, and we arrived at the arena, where the show's jubilant producer greeted us with the news that they "had to turn people away."

"They're the lucky ones," Mel mumbled too quietly for the producer to hear.

The better the news, the more negative and more vociferous Mel became. He did not want to be in San Francisco, and he said so in as many different ways as he could. At one point, he insisted they refund the money and "get my ass back to L.A."

The producer informed us that the "chunk of money" to which he referred came to two hundred thousand dollars—a hundred thousand for each of us. This news only angered Mel more, and his cursing and fussing intensified as he strode from the limo to our dressing room. Luckily, Mel could stew for only a few minutes before hearing an announcer's voice boom our names over the loudspeakers. There was no turning back—we bounded onto the stage and, for an hour and a half, I asked questions and Mel answered them, while the audience tried desperately not to fall out of their seats. The laughter was loud and continuous. The applause we received as we left the stage was sustained and so apparently sincere that we felt the need to return for an encore.

One down and one to go. We had less than an hour to recharge before getting to bat again.

We both knew it would be impossible to top the reaction we received for that first show, and we were right. We did not top it, but we did something which, by any standards, was a miracle: we equaled it! It was as if the engineers had recorded the first audience's laughter and replayed it.

All of us had family and commitments back in Los Angeles, and after bidding sincere farewells to our happy producers, we scurried to our limo. On the drive to the airport, George, Dan, and I chatted about the performances, while a taciturn Mel sat quietly in his seat and stared out the window. Soon, we all fell silent.

I had asked Mel hundreds of questions that night, and I had one more that I was compelled to ask. I took a deep breath and posed the following: "Mel, be honest. Had you known you would get the reaction you did tonight, how much money would you have asked for?"

Without missing a beat, he answered, "Fourteen dollars."

I knew it, George and Dan knew it, and now you all know it—Mel Brooks is a true artist! He was clearly saying that he would have done it for nothing, but he knew that "fourteen dollars" would get a laugh.

It did, didn't it?

CHAPTER ELEVEN

Nose to Nose, Eye to Eye, and I to Mel

I just jogged my memory which, at ninety, is exciting, since I can no longer jog my legs. I recalled another time and another place where there was no big auditorium, no four thousand screaming fans, and no big chunks of money. There were just the two of us, alone in a living room. I don't know why, but on that lazy afternoon, something possessed me to teach Mel how to speak French, or rather how to speak English with an exaggeratedly phony French accent.

I pointed out that when in a foreign country, if you need directions or help, the natives will be friendlier and more forthcoming if you attempt to speak to them in their language. If, for instance, you asked someone in broken English, "Mister sir—for eat—you can say me—where—is food good?", the person would likely go out of his way to help you.

While explaining to him the advantages of speaking a foreign language when in a foreign country, a two-man comedy bit was born—a bit that only Mel and I knew existed, and now you know.

For the lesson, Mel and I faced each other while I attempted to teach him to speak English with a phony French accent. Using an officious attitude, I started by pointing to my nose and garbled these words: "Mr. Mel, say after me! The nose!"

Which came out: "Meeeestah Mellluh, sayuh ahftah meeuh! Zee nohhze!"

Mel pointed to his nose and replied, "The nose."

"Noh, noh, noh," I said impatiently, "iz not de *noss!* Iz *'zeeee nohze,* zee *nohhhhzze!*" We went through this exercise four or five times, and each time Mel said "nose" clearly, I became more and more agitated and kept repeating it my way. When he finally got close, I gave up and reluctantly went on. I then pointed to my chin and said, "Ziss iss zee tttseeennuh—zee ttttseeennuh—say zee tttsseeeennuh!"

Mel again pointed to his chin and said, "The chin," at least a half dozen times before I accepted his best effort which was "Zuh tsin."

Mel had equal trouble accepting my pronunciation of *the cheek.* "Zee tsssick, I insisted, zee tssssick, zee tsssssick!"

"Zuh sick, zuh sick." was the best Mel could muster.

I half-heartedly accepted, "Suh sick."

Our most contentious confrontation came when I pointed to my eye and said, "Zis iss zeeeee ayyeeeyuh—zeeeee ayyeeeyuh! Zeeee ayyeeeyuh!"

Mel, with his finger resting on his cheek and pointing to his eye, shook his head and said, "That's not the eye!"

To which I calmly informed him, "No, ziss isss how youuuu sayuh, zeeeee ayyeeehuh—zeeeee ayyeeeyuh!"

Mel insisted it was not the eye that I was pointing at, and the more Mel insisted, the more apoplectic I became. To make my point, I shouted my silly pronunciations louder and louder until Mel had enough and stopped me. He then impatiently explained why I was wrong.

With his fingertip resting on his cheek below his eye, Mel calmly stated, "This is *not* the eye."

"Yess, issss," I insisted, "zat issss zeeee ayyeeeeyuh!"

"No, that is just *below* the eye! *This,*" Mel insisted as he pointed to his eye, "*this* is the eye!"

Then, with the tip of his finger, he touched his eyeball. You may doubt that the man actually poked his finger in his own eye just to get a laugh—and from an audience of one! But that is what he did. Seeing the redness in the cornea of his blinking eye and the tears that fell from it made me realize that Mel is cut from a different comedy cloth than most funny men. I challenge you to find a comedian who would poke a finger in his own eye just to amuse one person.

Fortunately, the person Mel amused that lazy afternoon would, one day, in a book of treasured anecdotes, preserve our stupid but precious piece of performance art.

CHAPTER TWELVE

"It's Not the Size that Counts..."
(and other Estellisms)

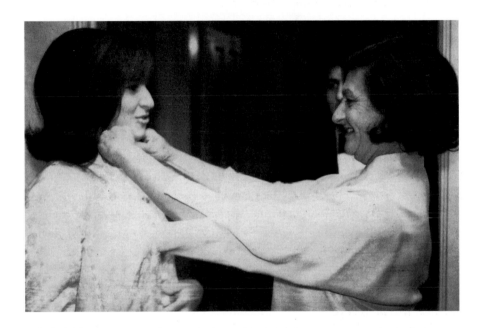

W hen our daughter, Annie, was about to turn sixteen, my wife and I and our eighteen-year-old son, Rob, were seated in the living room, discussing with Annie what kind of a sweet sixteen party she would like and what major gift we might get for her.

Rob, who had strong opinions about most things, and a typical "big-brother-knows-more-than-little-sister" attitude, spoke up. "Hey Annie," Rob suggested, "why don't you get what all your friends got for their sixteenth?"

"What did they get?" I asked.

"A nose job!" Annie wailed. "Rob wants me to get a nose job!"

"Why not?" Rob chided. "Your friends all look great! I hear the guys are chasing after them."

"Hold it, Rob," I chimed in. "Your mom has a more prominent nose than Annie, and look at the handsome guy she got."

At this point, all eyes turned to Estelle, who nodded knowingly and offered this bit of philosophy: "Yes, it is not the size of your nose that counts; it's what is in it!"

Those wise words got a big laugh and tabled the discussion permanently. Annie kept her lovely nose and, judging by the successes she has had in her many endeavors, she made the right decision.

A few years later, when directing *The Jerk*, a film starring Steve Martin, I told Steve what Estelle had once quipped and thought it was very amusing.

Sometime after *The Jerk* and the three more films we did together, Steve called to ask if Estelle would mind if he used her line in his new movie, *Roxanne*. He had adapted it from Edmond Rostand's *Cyrano de Bergerac* and was in the process of shooting it. Estelle was thrilled that Steve wanted to put her words into Cyrano's mouth. And she was again thrilled to be at a preview and see Steve on screen, declaim as Cyrano, *"It is not the size of one's nose that counts—it is what is in it!"*

I wonder if Monsieur Rostand would have hated or loved the liberties that were taken with his text—my guess is that he would have loved it. Steve Martin did, and who doesn't love Steve Martin?

CHAPTER THIRTEEN

Estelle Reiner, One Ahead of Humphrey Bogart

When Rob Reiner was directing the film *When Harry Met Sally* and considering who to cast for the part of an elderly woman who delivers a humorous line, his mother immediately came to mind. Rob knew of his mom's ability to get a huge laugh by tossing off a few well-chosen words.

Both Rob and his mother have been interviewed many times about how she came to be in the now-iconic scene that was shot in Katz's Delicatessen. Estelle's reply when Rob asked her to fly to New York to deliver the one line, was, "Rob, why do you want to spend money to fly me to New York to play an old, Jewish woman when the whole city is full of wonderful actresses who can do that part?"

"Because, Mom, no one will do it as funny as you," was his answer.

And that was it. Rob's mom flew to New York, delivered the line, "I'll have what she's having!", and flew back to California the following day. For the record, the line, which has since become famous, is constantly being quoted—even finding its way as a question on a recent telecast of *Jeopardy*.

In her lifetime in the arts, Estelle has had many great reviews. She had been lauded for her one-woman art shows, her hundreds of appearances as a jazz singer in clubs and cabarets, her seven jazz albums and CDs—but I don't think anything gave her a bigger kick than having smiling people come up to her in restaurants, department stores, or at airports and repeat to her a version of the line she delivered in Katz's New York Deli.

And there have been many, many versions of the line, among them:

"Can I have what she had?"

"I want what you've got."

"Can I have what she's eating?"

"I'll have some of that!"

For the record, the classic line was an ad-lib Billy Crystal came up with during a rehearsal.

A few years ago, the American Film Institute voted the line as number ten in a list of the best hundred lines in modern movies. This year, *People* magazine and ABC conjointly narrowed it down to five, a shorter and even more salutary list.

#1. *Gone with the Wind*
> "Frankly my dear, I don't give a damn!" —Clark Gable

#2. *The Godfather*
> "I'll make him an offer he can't refuse!" —Marlon Brando

#3. *Sudden Impact*
> "Go ahead, make my day!" —Clint Eastwood

#4. *When Harry Met Sally*
> "I'll have what she's having." —Estelle Reiner

#5. *Casablanca*
> "Here's looking at you, kid." —Humphrey Bogart.

Which puts Estelle Reiner one ahead of Humphrey Bogart.

CHAPTER FOURTEEN

Christmas in Kealakekua, Hawaii

Our youngest child, Lucas, was just two years old when we flew to Hawaii for his very first winter vacation. It started a lovely family tradition that continued for many years. I remember this one fondly because our teenage daughter, Annie, accompanied us. In years past, she and her brother Rob had opted to stay home and hang with their friends. Obviously their pals were a lot more fun to be with than parents who were dedicated to raising them to be the best human beings extant—by suggesting that they do things that were, for the most part, boring.

This winter vacation again proved to me that it is possible for children to have a really good time with their parents. We spent our days, as all our fellow vacationers did, eating three beautifully prepared and elaborately served, delicious meals that featured fish with exotic names like ahi ahi—or is it mahi mahi? At his first luau, little Luke's eyes widened as he watched the giant pig being roasted on a spit. It could have been traumatic, but he seemed to be intrigued with the fire and the pageantry.

When we were not eating or napping, we journeyed to the shore that was twenty feet from our door and splashed around in the warm tropical ocean while warm, soothing trade winds wafted the sweet scent of bougainvillea right up our noses.

On Christmas Eve, when we tucked Lucas in for the night, we told him, "Luke, when little boys and girls go to sleep, Santa Claus visits their homes and leaves presents for them—and tomorrow when you wake up, you will see all the presents he left just for you."

Lucas asked to hear the story about Santa and the presents a couple of times before nodding off. What we did not tell him was that the day before, when the four of us drove into town and stopped at Ben Franklin's Department Store to buy some toothpaste, we bought a lot more than toothpaste.

While Estelle and I had scooted up and down the aisles, doing Santa's work—loading up our shopping cart with the toys and knick-knacks, which we hoped would brighten little Luke's Christmas morning—little Luke was outdoors, being kept busy by his sister. Annie's job was to feed coins into the small, mechanical pony that Luke was sitting on and keep the pony rocking until we signaled that our mission was accomplished.

It took almost thirty minutes to gather up enough goodies to make our son's Christmas morning merry and bright.

It might have been the splashing in the ocean or the long mechanical pony ride, but that night, the minute his blond head hit the pillow, little Luke fell sound asleep.

While he slept, the three of us wrapped and tied ribbons to the dozens and dozens of small, inexpensive items we had tossed into the shopping cart. We hoped he would enjoy receiving and unwrapping them as much as we enjoyed buying them. Among the eclectic group of gifts, I remember: a toy soldier, an eraser, a box of Cracker Jacks, a pack of baseball cards, a small pencil sharpener, shoelaces, a chocolate-chip cookie, a box of crayons, a harmonica, a roll of Scotch tape, paper clips, two Tootsie Rolls wrapped separately, a memo pad, a pair of socks and other items.

We placed the dozens of colorfully wrapped presents on the floor between our room and the room that Lucas shared with Annie.

Surprisingly, we were all up before Luke. It was only seven o'clock, but it seemed that we were more excited to see his reaction to the presents Santa had brought him than he was to receive them.

We waited impatiently for him to awaken and soon found ourselves speaking louder than we normally did. It worked, and minutes later we saw a sleepy-eyed two-year-old enter the room and slowly make his way toward us. He took a few hesitant steps and stopped when he was about ten feet from what he must have suspected were the presents Santa had left for him. He stared at the stash that lay before him—slowly looking to the right, then to the left, then up at the three of us, who were looking down at him. We had expected that he would sit right down and start ripping open the packages to see what Santa had brought, but instead he just stared at the colorfully wrapped presents strewn across the floor. A goodly amount or time passed before he looked up, smiled, and asked, "When is next Christmas?"

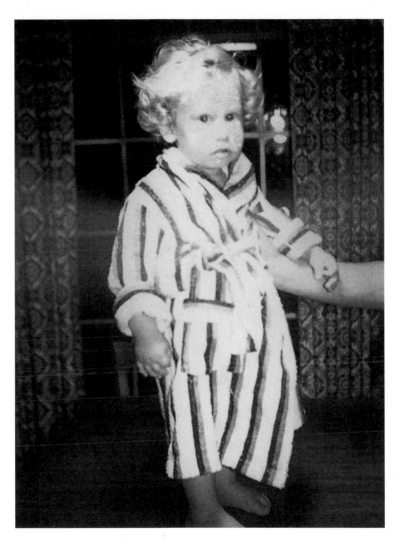

Lucas at 16

CHAPTER FIFTEEN

Our Day in St. Tropez

I n the south of France, nestled on a hilltop, overlooking a healthy grove of olive trees, sits a charming, private domain, or as the French say, "*une domaine privee.*" Sixty-five private homes make up the picturesque enclave called *Castelleras Le Vieux*. It was here in Castelleras, in a comfortable, compact, two-story house, that my wife Estelle and I spent fifteen idyllic summers of our sixty-five-year married life.

A more relaxing summer is hard to imagine. Most years, I used these two months to recharge the batteries I had depleted directing and writing motion pictures. The depletion comes from the concern every director has, from the quality of the script, to the casting of actors, to the finding of locations, to dealing with studio heads, viewing the dailies, suffering through the rough cuts, viewing the final color-corrected print, attending press previews, reading the critics' reviews, and lastly and most importantly, learning of the public's acceptance or rejection of what you hath wrought.

Our problems at Castelleras, while not nearly as heavy, were serious. Each day we had to make what were sometimes daunting decisions. When you are literally a five-minute drive from the quaint town of Valbonne and no more than ten minutes from historic Mougins or twenty minutes from Antibes or Cannes, it is hard to decide what to do. Should we shop at Valbonne's fresh-meat shop and open-air vegetable market and buy food to cook at home, or should we call for a reservation at one of the *Michelin Guide*'s three-star seafood restaurants in Cannes, or should we try to book a table at Roger Verget's world-renowned *Le Moulin de Mougins?* Such was our dilemma.

After vacationing in Castelleras for a half-dozen summers and sampling and enjoying every recommended restaurant in the environs and as far away as Ventimilia, Italy, we settled down. When we did not cook at home, we frequented small neighborhood restaurants— *L'Auberge Fleurie* for *cuisses do grenouille* (frog legs) and *L'Estaminet* for *poulet vinaigre* (vinegar chicken) or *La Chandelerie* for *lapin provencal* (rabbit, provincial style)

Our three children, Robbie, Annie, and Lucas, usually had summer plans that did not include visiting Mom and Dad in France. Our daughter spent parts of some summers with us, as did our youngest, Lucas. He was sixteen the last time he visited us, and for this summer, we also invited his friend Kevin Pinassi, so he would have a buddy with whom to grouse about whatever needed grousing.

Kevin and Lucas were with us when decided to visit some new sights along the coast. We had been driving along, pointing out the famous seafood restaurants and the many pristine beaches, when we saw a sign informing us that St. Tropez was just a few kilometers down the road. Estelle and I were aware that St. Tropez was a nude beach, and sophisticates that we were, we decided not to pass up the opportunity of visiting this much-publicized resort. If nothing else, it was certain to be an educating experience for our teenaged passengers.

We parked the car, kicked off our shoes, and walked to the beautiful white-sand beach. We wore bathing suits and had no intention of shedding them. As we came onto the beach, many young bathers were leaving. All were fully clad, but it was not long before we saw, coming right at us, two very pretty, very bra-less young women. Not a one of us showed any visible signs of having noticed four of the most upstanding and beautiful breasts passing by us. And so the bare-breasted parade continued as we looked for a place to settle. Estelle and I found a spot to spread our blanket, and we sat down. Lucas and Kevin opted to go for a walk, and we agreed that it was a good idea for them to do "a little exploring," and off they went. We told them not to stay away too long, as it was quite a drive back to Castelleras.

The two young men "explored" for at least an hour, and when they returned, they had nothing to report—they actually seemed bored. Their faces were immobile, and their attitude could best be described as detached. When I asked if they were ready to go, they nodded, and the four of us left the beautiful beach at St. Tropez.

For the first few minutes of the drive home, Estelle and I tried to initiate a conversation with the boys, and all we got from them were grunts and monosyllabic responses. None of us was feeling very energetic, the hot Mediterranean sun having sapped a lot of our energy. We all fell silent, but from time to time, Estelle or I would comment on the interesting sights and scenery we were passing, but there were no substantive discussions. Lucas had not said a word for the whole hour we drove. I kept checking the rearview mirror to see if he was awake, and he was. His eyes were open and staring straight ahead. Kevin, however, for most of the way home, napped.

When we drove past Valbonne, I was happy to announce that we would be home in ten minutes. It had been a long day. I made a right turn at the sign that read *Domaine Privee* and headed for the guard gate at Castelleras, where actual guards greeted us every day with a pleasant, *"Bon jour"* or an *"Au 'voir!"*

When we were about a hundred yards from the gate, Lucas spoke for the first time since leaving the beach. Without emotion, and in a slow measured cadence, he quietly delivered these words: "This-was-the-best-day-of-my-whole-life!"

Estelle and I did all we could not to keep from laughing.

Pridefully, I can report that, since then, Lucas Reiner has had at least three more occasions when he must have said that it was the best day of his whole life—and they were: the day he wed Maud and the two days when their daughters, Livia and Rose, came into the world.

A second memory of our summer home in Castelleras just popped into my head. It was of the evening when something provoked my loving wife to a fit of uncontrolled laughter. Estelle had earlier prepared and served a luscious dinner of *poulet vinaigre* to our dear friends, Mel Brooks, Anne Bancroft, and their dear friends, Renee and Harry Lorrayne, who have since become *our* good friends. Harry Lorrayne, besides being the author of dozens of books on magic and memory, is arguably one of the world's greatest sleight-of-hand artists. At that dinner were our son Lucas and his wife, Maud, which brought the count up to eight diners, all of whom sat uncomfortably and uncomplainingly around our very small dining-room table.

After dinner, we repaired from our cramped table to our very-well-decorated, tiny living room that sported two white, plaster-sculpted, cushioned couches and a single club chair. Each couch could accommodate three people. At one sat Anne Bancroft, Harry and Renee Lorrayne; on the other were Lucas, Maud, and myself. Estelle sat in the club chair that closed the semicircle—which left one guest, Mel Brooks, standing and looking about for a place to settle. With his coffee cup in hand, he retrieved a wicker

stool and approached our guests, who were cozily configured in an open horseshoe, facing a white-plaster fireplace. There was little room in front of the fireplace for Mel to put down the stool, so he placed it in the center of the fireplace, ducked under the overhang, and sat on it. With his head up the chimney, he crossed his legs, took a sip of coffee, and for the next several minutes, carried on a conversation as if nothing were amiss. As you might imagine, a headless Mel Brooks casually conversing and sipping coffee would make anyone laugh. We all broke up, but it was Estelle who kicked off the wave of screaming laughter.

It was the first of two events that set Estelle off that night. After the bottom two-thirds of Mel milked all that he could, he emerged from his roost and joined the rest of us in a game of Dictionary. Dictionary, for those of you who have forgotten the game or never knew of it, is played by friends who try to guess the meaning of an obscure word that one player has chosen. Being in France, we sophisticates opted to use a French dictionary. Each player writes that word on a slip of paper, and a monitor reads the invented definitions.

With Renee Lorrayne, Anne Bancroft, Mel Brooks and Estelle Reiner

On this go-around, Estelle was the monitor, and the word someone had chosen was *pourlecher*. She picked up the first piece of folded paper and started to read what one of our players ascribed to be the word's definition. I say *started* to read, for before getting out the first word, her face contorted as she battled to suppress a giggle. She pulled herself together, repeated the word *pourlecher*, and immediately lost the battle. She burst out laughing and made one or two aborted attempts to rein herself in. As often happens, all of us found her struggle amusing and started to laugh—and continued laughing as Estelle attempted to read what someone had written: "To lick all over." "To lick, to lick …" was all she could get out before doubling over. Mel Brooks, for reasons known only to him, found Estelle's laughter so infectious that he stamped his foot, clapped his hands as an almost soundless, high-pitched laugh escaped his lungs. For fear of damaging himself, he bolted out the front door, up a short flight of colorfully tiled stairs, and onto an unlit Castelleras street. Still laughing and desperately trying to stifle himself, he staggered up the street, turned right, and made his way onto the unlit, pitch-black road, risking the possibility of falling into a pothole or off a cliff.

I daresay that being aware, as you are, of the magnificent output of films, musicals, and plays that are attributed to him, Mel did not come to anything but a happy end that laugh-filled weekend.

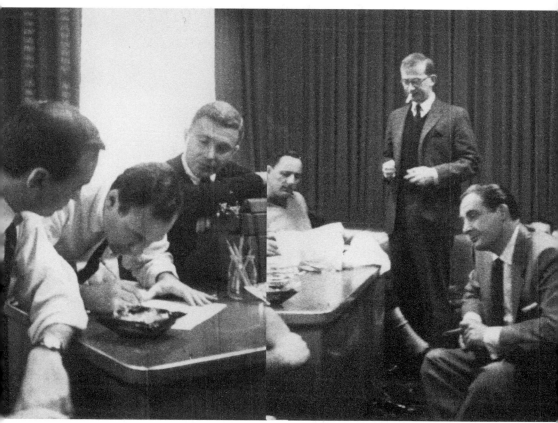

Writers' room - Howard Morris, Mel Brooks, Mike
Stewart, Mel Tolkin, Larry Gelbart, Sid Ceasar

CHAPTER SIXTEEN

The Search for the World's Funniest Number

I am currently a member of a committee that, once a month, is invited to a lunch at the Academy of Motion Picture Arts and Sciences where, by voting, we select which of the newly released films will be previewed for our members.

I had eaten my free lunch (two half sandwiches: one an egg salad on white bread and the other a sliced chicken on rye), recorded my votes, and was ready to leave. As I rose from the impressive, oval conference table, Larry Mirish, the chairperson of the meeting, asked me a question. My short-term memory being fairly good for periods of less than an hour allows me to give you a verbatim account of my conversation with Larry.

"Carl, I have a question for you."

"And I may have an answer for you, Larry—shoot!"

"When you were on *Your Show of Shows*, do you remember doing a sketch about trying to determine what the funniest number is? I never saw the sketch, but a friend of mine said that you might recall what that number was."

"I not only remember the number and the sketch," I boasted, "but I remember the active discussion we had trying to agree on what the number should be."

Larry Mirish's face lit up when he realized he had struck pay dirt. "This is great, go on!" he urged.

I told him that the discussion was in Sid Caesar's office, and present, I thought were writers: Lucille Kallen, Mel Brooks, Neil Simon, Joe

Stein, and our head writer, Mel Tolkin. The sketch in question featured a woman breaking the bank in Monte Carlo by placing a bet on her lucky number on the casino's roulette wheel and winning each time. The sketch was written, and the only thing left to do was to choose the funniest-sounding lucky number for Imogene Coca to call out as she placed her bet. The search went on for at least a half hour, with each writer suggesting a number he or she thought was funny. Imogene, who everyone addressed as *Coca*, was called upon to audition the funny numbers that each writer offered. The candidates were: fourteen, twenty-five, seventy-one, eighty-eight, sixteen, twelve, one, double zero, the ever-popular sixty-nine. Dozens upon dozens of other numbers were tossed up and batted down. So it went and continued to go until someone came up with *the* funniest "lucky" number. I could not remember who that writer was, but if that genius is still alive, he would surely remember that it was he who created the winning entry: "Thirty-two!"

As soon as Coca voiced it, there was no doubt that "thirty-two" was one hilarious number. Every time the birdlike Coca delivered a nasally drawled "Thiiirrrty-twooo!", everyone in the room laughed.

At one point, we were sure that we were punch drunk and that it was weariness that made us all giddy. Some worried that we were—to use the writer's accepted vernacular—"jerking off," but we were not!

On that Saturday night, some sixty years ago, the hundreds of guests who were members of NBC's studio audience and the millions of Americans who tuned in to *Your Show of Shows* laughed every time Coca placed her bet down and chirped, "Thiiiirrrty-twooo!"

No one could explain it. Someone suggested that the audience thought Coca's "Thirty-two" sounded like she was saying "Dirty-doo!" What it really came down to was something a wise comedian once said: "Funny is funny!"

Apropos of nothing, but giving credit to where credit is not expected but due, while I was in the middle of telling the lucky number story and had not yet said what the number was, Larry Mirish suddenly blurted out, "Thirty-two?!"

Larry swore that it was a lucky guess, and I believed him. Why would I not? He was the son of the producer of *The Russians Are Coming, the Russians Are Coming*, the one and only film for which I, as an actor, received top billing. How could I ever doubt that man?

CHAPTER SEVENTEEN

Enter Laughing, Exit Screaming!

My Affair with Shelley Winters, Part 1

O ne morning at breakfast, while reading the *New York Times*, I learned of the passing of actor Farley Granger. I had met Farley during the Second World War, when we were attached to a special-service entertainment unit that was based in Hawaii.

Farley's obituary included the many romantic relationships he had with members of both sexes. And though he lived out his life with a male partner, he acknowledged the satisfying liaisons he had with some of his female co-stars. In his autobiography, he included the short, torrid affair he had with Shelley Winters.

I too had a torrid affair with Shelley Winters, and it was by no means a "one-nighter." Our involvement lasted for two and a half months, but it seemed a good deal longer. At the end, I was bloodied and, happy to say, unbowed. If you are expecting to read a romantic or pornographic account of what went on between Shelley and me, you will be disappointed, but if you are interested in a behind-the-scenes odyssey that involved some of my—and likely your—favorite actors, read on.

It started nine years earlier, in 1967, when I had written my first novel about a young delivery boy who aspires to be an actor. Thanks to the reviews, the book, *Enter Laughing*, had a modest success. The following are not verbatim quotes, but they more or less encapsulate the opinions of some newspaper critics.

"It's okay." —*New York Daily News*
"I've read worse first novels." —*New York Herald Tribune*
"Might enjoy reading it on the beach." —*Women's Wear Daily*
"The graveyard is a very unlikely place for the leading character to have lost his virginity!" —*New York Times*

For the record, I took liberties with the first three blurbs, but the last is an accurate quote from the *Times'* critic.

What I had written in my novel, that the critic found unlikely, I had actually experienced. I was quite unhappy with the criticism, but a week later, I smiled when I read the response it provoked. In a letter to the editor, a doctor of internal medicine at Mount Sinai wrote: "Your reviewer, suggesting that a graveyard is an unlikely place for a young lad to lose his virginity, has not done his research. A graveyard is a very likely place for that event to occur, I can attest to that."

I cherished that admission. The book did get a number of positive reviews, but the single most important review came from my friend, playwright Joe Stein. He simply said, "Carl, this is a dandy book. I think it would make a dandy little play."

And so Joe went ahead and adapted the "dandy book" into "a dandy little play."

The same year he adapted *Enter Laughing* into a dandy little play, Joe adapted Sholem Aleichem's classic, *Tevye the Milkman*, into *Fiddler on the Roof*, the dandiest of all musicals.

Dandy is a word I have never heard anyone use until I heard Joe describe my novel as being that and suggest he adapt it for Broadway. This he did, and in 1962, both *Enter Laughing* the play, and Alan Arkin, its leading player, won Tony Awards. The play ran for more than a year on Broadway, and productions of it continue to be mounted and performed in regional theaters and schools throughout the country.

I just had the niggling suspicion that some of what I have just written I had covered in an earlier book, *My Anecdotal Life*. It was Joe Stein's use of the word *dandy* that alerted me, so I checked, and there it was on page eighty-three. I was reminded by my assistant, Bess, that I had also discussed Joe Stein's proprietary use of the word *dandy* in a eulogy I had written for his memorial service. Joe lived to be ninety-eight.

Recalling Joe's age just triggered a memory of an English play in which two stuffy English gents had the following curt exchange:

"Have you heard? Faversham died!"

"Did he now? How old was he?"

"Ninety-eight."

"Hmm, asking for it, wasn't he?"

Unlike Faversham, Joe Stein was not asking for it. At ninety-eight, his mind was as sharp as ever, and I had spoken to him two days before an unexpected accident caused a fatal fall.

Back to 1967—when Joe and I collaborated on adapting *Enter Laughing* for the screen, we considered a cast of very talented actors, which included Alan Arkin, who was brilliant in the show but was now in his mid-thirties and would not seem credible playing a seventeen-year-old. This gave us the unenviable task of trying to find another genius actor-comedian to fill the role.

After auditioning many actors for the role of David Kolowitz, a Jewish teenager from the Bronx, we engaged Reni Santoni, a twenty-five-year-old of Puerto Rican descent. It was a bit of a challenge for the very talented and creative young man, but he was up for it.

For the important role of Mr. Harrison Marlowe, the aging ham actor, our first choice was Jose Ferrer. Mr. Ferrer was then one of our nation's most distinguished stage and screen performers. He had won worldwide acclaim for his film portrayals of Cyrano de Bergerac and Henri de Toulouse-Lautrec.

I phoned Mr. Ferrer, offered him the role of Marlowe, and held my breath. I did not have to hold it long, as he immediately said that he had no interest in doing a comedy. He punctuated his decision by hanging up his phone—hard! No doubt he would have hung up harder had I told him that the film, *Enter Laughing*, was a low-budget comedy and would be shot in thirty-two days on location in Manhattan. We had planned to build sets in the Bronx's Gold Medal Studio—a studio which had been shuttered for twenty years and we had contracted to be un-shuttered.

I decided to give him none of that information if he decided to pick up my next phone call. He did and was about to hang up again when I did the one thing that will keep any actor from hanging up on anybody—I flattered him, unmercifully and to within an inch of his life!

"Mr. Ferrer," I gushed, "you were so brilliantly funny and entertaining the night I saw you perform at the Stage Door Canteen—I just had to tell you that!"

The silence and not hearing a phone being slammed into its cradle was my cue to continue gushing. "You had me and that whole audience falling off our seats! I had no idea that you sang—and those songs, they were hilarious. Where did you find them, and where did you learn to play the piano like that?"

Jose Ferrer

There was a thoughtful, measured pause before he spoke. "Where and when," he asked, enunciating his Ws, "did you say you saw me perform?"

"At the Stage Door Canteen in New York—about ten years ago, just before D-Day. I was on furlough and wandered into the Canteen. I had never expected to see a serious actor cut up like you did. You had me and my buddies howling. My friend Sol said that you are a fucking genius!"

Whoa, too much, I thought, *better dial it back a bit.*

I was sure Mr. Ferrer was going to hang up on me, and he did, but not before asking for my number. Amid all my slathering, I must have said something that piqued his interest and, two days later, he called and I found that the old adage, "Flattery will get you nowhere!" was wrong. Maybe ordinarily flattery will get you nowhere, but my slathering flattery of his comedy timing got me Ferrer!

Joe—yes, he asked that I call him *Joe*—loved comedians, and he loved comedy and was intrigued with the idea of performing in a comedy. It took a bit more cajoling and the layering on of compliments about his comic instincts, which I truly believed, as I did when I told him what "a ball" he would have working with wonderful comedians and comic actors. What sealed the deal was my listing those who had signed on: Jack Gilford, Elaine May, Don Rickles, Michael J. Pollard, David Opatashu, Janet Margolin, and Shelley Winters.

CHAPTER EIGHTEEN

Enter Laughing, Exit Screaming!
My Affair with Shelley Winters, Part 2

W hen Shelley Winters signed on to play the role of the mother in *Enter Laughing*, she had already collected a shelf full of awards and nominations, among them, Academy Awards for *The Diary of Anne Frank* and *A Patch of Blue* and nominations for *A Place in the Sun*, *Alfie*, and *Lolita*. She had also received a Golden Globe and a British Academy award for her role in *The Poseidon Adventure*. Shelley was also an active member of The Actor's Studio.

Besides celebrating her for her acting, the national and international press exhaustively chronicled her love life and her four marriages. Many articles featured her stormy marriages to Hollywood's ruggedly handsome Anthony Franciosa and to the debonair Italian actor, Vittorio Gassman, with whom she had a child.

Her reputation as a brilliant actress was richly deserved, as was her reputation of being, at times, exasperatingly stubborn, egocentric, self-indulgent, socially inept, and the biggest pain in the ass ever to set foot on a motion picture soundstage.

And true to form, at the first rehearsal of our first day of shooting *Enter Laughing*, I learned that Shelley Winters's reputation as a big pain in the ass was accurate.

The scene we were to rehearse was set in a kitchen. Shelley, playing the mother of an aspiring eighteen-year-old actor, is discussing her son's future with her husband, played by David Opatashu, who is waiting to be served breakfast. As the scene opens, the mother complains of a headache and, while their dialogue is going on, she prepares and drinks an antacid preparation. To keep the scene from being static, I instructed Shelley to busy herself by taking a glass from the cupboard, crossing to another cupboard to retrieve the antacid, cross the room, open a drawer, get a spoon, come back to the table, pour the powder in the glass, and then go to the sink, fill the glass with water, and drink the powder. For the antacid, I chose a Seidlitz powder, the weakest and most palatable product available.

We rehearsed, and it went well enough—she got through her lines and was at the point where she was about to drink the antacid, when I yelled, "Cut!"

"Why did you yell cut?" Shelley shot back.

"Because this is a rehearsal, and I don't want you drinking any more than one glass of this stuff."

"But I have to know how I will react to it when I do it on camera."

"Shelley," I explained, "however you react, it will be an honest one, and we'll use that."

We rehearsed the scene one more time and then shot it. Again I yelled *cut* before Shelley drank the Seidlitz powder, and again she was upset that I did. I explained that we would not use that particular shot because it was a long shot; her drinking would be in a close-up.

Now, with the film rolling and her face in a close-up, she drank almost a glassful and then stopped, spit it into the sink, and sputtered, "This stuff's terrible. I always use Citracal. I have some in my dressing room—somebody go get it!"

I was hoping that this would make her happy. I was working on a limited budget and had much to shoot that day. We did the next take, and all was going well until Shelley gulped down a mouthful of her Citracal and grimaced. "This is warm, I can't drink Citracal with warm water. Can't I get some ice water?"

"Not from the sink, Shelley."

"Well, I can't drink this stuff with warm water!"

I explained that there was no way we can get ice water through the cold-water tap. And that was it—no ice water, no scene! It was up to me to find a way of getting ice water into that glass. Being the son of an inventor, I did come up with a way. I instructed Shelley to place her glass in the sink, right under the faucet, and then turn on the tap and fill the glass. I explained that a glass of ice water will be preset right next to where she set her glass.

"When your glass is filled," I explained, "turn off the faucet and pick up the glass with the ice water. The camera is placed at an angle that excludes the glasses in the sink."

We rolled the cameras, shot the scene again, and Shelley was perfect, that is until she drank, spit, and shouted, "This isn't ice water!"

I don't know how she did it, but Shelley managed to pick up the wrong glass—twice—before getting it right. By the time we completed covering the scene, Shelley had downed at least four glasses of Citracal. Before each take, I told her we have the shot and she did not have to drink any more of the stuff, but she insisted that if she didn't drink it, her performance and the scene would ring false. When I warned of the possible effects of drinking that much antacid, she assured me that she had been "using this stuff for years and never had a problem."

By early afternoon, she had a problem, and her problem became our problem. Work stopped every time she ran to the ladies' room, which was often. We also lost time locating and bringing her the proper absorbent soda crackers whenever she screamed, "Bring me some of my crackers, right now!"

Somehow we managed to film the scene and, to Shelley's credit, one would never know that she delivered that first-rate performance between bouts of vomiting and attacks of diarrhea.

It was on the final day of shooting, at a small theater in downtown L.A., where Shelley Winters and I had our non-consensual "affair."

We had very limited time to film the last scheduled scene of the morning. I needed but one quick shot of Shelley Winters and David Opatashu, seated in the audience and watching the theater curtain rise. All that was required of them was to watch the curtain rise as Jose Ferrer makes his first entrance on stage right, acknowledges some scattered applause, crosses the stage and sits in a club chair. If I got that one reaction shot of the audience, I could move the camera and lights off the stage and after lunch be ready to shoot the action, on the stage. There was one small but surmountable problem—Jose Ferrer had a late call and was not present. I had planned to step in for him, make his off-camera entrance, cross the stage and sit in the club chair just as he would. I told Shelley my plan, and Shelley asked, "Why couldn't Jose do it?"

I told her he was not scheduled to be here until after lunch, and Shelley said, "So why can't we do the scene after lunch?"

"Because if we do, Shelley, it would throw us off schedule."

"For me to react honestly," she said, "I have to see Jose enter, in his costume, and walk across the stage."

I reminded her that she is an actress, a method actress, and that she knows what Jose looks like. I said that I would wear his jacket and walk like him—and she actually said, "I'm sorry, but I cannot work this way."

"This is how I work," I said, "and we haven't the time to work any other way."

"I have! Call me when Jose gets back!"

With that, Shelley turned, left the theater, and went to her trailer, where she remained through lunch and after lunch through the shooting of Jose Ferrer making his entrance on stage.

She remained in her trailer while we reluctantly set the lights and camera to film the parents' reaction to the curtain going up—a shot we should have made before lunch.

When all was ready for Shelley and David to take their seats in the audience, only David showed up. Our good and loyal assistant director, Kurt Newman, informed me that Shelley refused to leave her dressing room. I knocked on her locked door and told her that we were ready to do her scene, and she responded by not responding. I called upon Joe Stein, my co-producer and co-screenwriter, and asked that he try to get our star on stage. He tried and failed. Shelley told him that I had humiliated her in front of the cast and crew and that there was no way she could return to the set.

I thought about what I could possibly do or say that would get Shelley out of her trailer, and, what do you know, an idea did pop! I told Joe to tell her that I intended to make an important announcement to the entire company and that "I did not want Shelley present when I made my little speech, but if she was interested in knowing whose fault it was that they may be losing their jobs because the production was likely to be shutting down, she might want to eavesdrop!"

Joe relayed my message to Shelley, and the following is pretty darned close to what I told the assembled cast.

"Folks," I said, speaking loudly for Shelley's benefit, "we have a problem! A major problem that threatens to shut down our production.

I don't have to tell you that we are working on a very tight budget. We were scheduled to finish this film thirty-two days after starting principal photography—and a problem arose for which I will take some responsibility. I say 'some responsibility' because, as you know, it takes two to tango. My 'co-tango-er,' you may have guessed, is our star, Shelley Winters. When she agreed to do the part of the mother, I promised her something that I had every intention of honoring but I can't. I told Shelley, who, as every man in the world knows, is a very sensuous and desirable woman, that at least once a day, during production, she and I would have sex. Well, I discussed this with my wife, and she simply refused to give me permission to screw Shelley, so I had to renege on my promise. Shelley, I don't know if you can hear me, but if you come back to work, I promise you that, even at the possibility of wrecking my marriage, we will get it on anytime you want—except while we're shooting a scene. How about it, Shelley?"

Throughout my speech, the crowd giggled, but when Shelley sashayed onto the set and hugged me, they exploded.

For the rest of the filming, Shelley remained Shelley—but a mellower, more manageable version of her talented self. She fully captured the essence of a concerned Jewish mother, and she faithfully delivered the actual line my mother said to me after seeing me perform as Donald Meadows in *The Bishop Misbehaves*. She patted my cheek and said, "You were the best one!"

48 Bonnie Meadow Rd. New Rochelle, New York

CHAPTER NINETEEN

Do You Know Any Commies?

I n 1692, by participating in the Salem, Massachusetts, witch hunts, groups of self-righteous do-gooders did bad things to good people. A young girl suspected of practicing adultery would be hunted down by zealots, tried in a biased court, found guilty of practicing witchcraft, have the letter "A" branded on her forehead, tied to a stake, and burned to death.

In the 1950s, the words "witch hunt" were co-opted by our journalists. It was an era when unprincipled politicians and reactionary radio commentators grabbed the headlines and the microphones and attempted to ruin the lives of patriotic American citizens, oft times succeeding. For a blessedly short time, Joseph McCarthy, a junior senator from Wisconsin, chaired an appropriately named investigating committee, "the Army-McCarthy Hearings." The committee's main objective was to identify and silence members of the army who were suspected of being communists or "fellow travelers." His hate-filled words and behavior were dubbed McCarthyism. Fortunately, his career was short and not too sweet. His reign of terror ended in a courtroom, where, after professing his disdain of "Commies and Jews," he attempted to impugn the patriotism of a young army private. The senator had gone a step too far, and the patient, kindly Judge Joe Welch shook his head in sad disbelief and said, "At long last, sir, have you no sense of decency?"

Those words were heard and applauded by the millions of Americans who had gathered at their television sets to watch the proceedings. Among those millions applauding and cheering was a small group huddled in front of a portable, twenty-inch set that belonged to Sid Caesar, the star of TV's *The Sid Caesar Show*. Among the group of "huddlers," besides Sid, were his co-star, Nanette Fabray, his staff of writers and his second bananas, Howard Morris and me. All of us were mesmerized by the hearings, which had been going on for a week.

At that time, most of us were able to discern which proposed legislation or social philosophy or presidential candidate would best serve our country. We forward-thinking Americans were called liberals or progressives, but folks like Joe McCarthy referred to us as "Commies" or "damned Commies." Today, many decades later, liberals are still called liberals, and some are dubbed by the right as "left-wingers" or "socialists" or "not real Americans." One thing, however, is vastly different. Today these abusive speeches and viciously contentious discussions that go on between the right and the left are heard and seen by millions more people—and on giant, high-definition, flat-screen television sets with surround sound.

I believe it is safe to say that our technological capabilities still have not made it easier for the viewers to know whether the opinions expressed by the television news analysts and commentators are their own deeply held beliefs or the "talking point" beliefs held by the corporation's billionaire station owners.

In 1953, my wife and I, with money saved from my salary as a second banana on TV's top-rated show, purchased a new split-level house at 48 Bonnie Meadow Road in New Rochelle, New York. For the next seven years, Estelle and I and our two young children, Robbie and Annie, were living the American dream.

Then, one bright spring morning in 1954, at 8:30 a.m., I was rudely awakened by the ringing of my doorbell. Sleepy-eyed and annoyed that someone would ring our bell this early on a Sunday, I rolled out of bed and managed not to awaken my wife, who was ordinarily a light sleeper. Barefooted and clad in a T-shirt and boxer shorts, I made my way past the sleeping children's bedrooms to the front door. Through a little side window, I saw two rather nattily attired men in dark blue suits. They had pleasant smiles on their tanned faces—their smiles a bit too pleasant for my comfort.

"Yes?" I asked as I opened the door.

"Mr. Reiner?" one asked. "Carl Reiner?"

"Yep, that's me," I answered. "And you are?"

"We're from the FBI," he said, flashing a toothy s   va
credentials. "May we come in, Mr. Reiner?"   C

"Of course!" I countered, smiling. "Come in, gentlemen,   t

"Thank you," the second agent said as they entered. "I hoj   (
waken you."

"Oh no, I was getting up to answer the doorbell anyway   a
ushering them into the foyer.

They accommodated me with a chuckle.

What are they after? I thought. *Or is it* who *are they after?*

My mind was spinning. *How should I play this?* I asked myself.
that's it, a play! I'm in a play, and I'm the lead actor!

Since the two G-men were soft-spoken and ultra-polite, I de
that I would out-soft-speak them and out-ultra-polite them.

"Hey, this is no way to greet guests," I said, indicating my appa
"Would you gentlemen excuse me while I put on some fresh underwe
I'll join you in the living room."

I trotted to the bedroom, where I found Estelle sitting up in bed an
looking concerned. From the whispered conversation, Estelle intuited
that something was wrong. As I casually put on a robe, I told her that
she had nothing to worry about. She might have believed me, had I not
said, "For FBI agents, they sure are polite." When I saw her eyes widen,
I realized she had not known who had rung our bell.

"And they're handsome," I joked. "The tall one is your type, Jimmy
Stewartish."

I gave her a hug and promised, "Everything will be fine!"

I wasn't sure I would be able to keep that promise, but I would try.
On both our minds was the fear that everything we had built in our
twelve years of marriage—our home, our children's security, our way of
life—could go up in smoke. I knew why the FBI knocked at my door—
for the same reason they knocked on the doors and harassed many of our
nation's biggest stars. Information was fed to them by vigilante-citizens
like Lawrence Johnson, a red-baiting owner of a small supermarket in
upstate New York. He was the first to post the names of performers he
suspected were either communists, communist sympathizers, socialists,
or anyone who had joined what he dubbed a "left-wing organization"
like the AVC, the American Veterans Committee, a World War II vets
organization, of which I was a proud member.

The work of these self-appointed "commie hunters" was not in n. They supplied our government's House Un-American Activities committee with names to subpoena for their witch hunts—names at would insure healthy press coverage. Led by committee head congressman J. Parnell Thomas, many prominent Hollywood writers and directors were subpoenaed and asked to answer unconstitutional and possibly incriminating questions. By invoking their constitutional rights and refusing to respond, they thwarted Representative Thomas's plan to humiliate them, but he did succeed in having a group of these left-wing intellectuals sent to jail. The newspapers dubbed them "the Hollywood Ten." and the cast list included Dalton Trumbo, Herbert Biberman, Edward Dmytryk, Ring Lardner Jr., John Howard Lawson, Adrian Scott, Albert Maltz, Alvah Bessie, Lester Cole, and Samuel Omitz.

In his biography, Ring Lardner Jr. wrote that the hours of intellectually nourishing conversations they had, plus the pleasant treatment they received from their jailers, made their incarceration almost tolerable.

These small pleasures were unexpectedly heightened when they next crossed paths with Representative J. Parnell Thomas. This time they met not as inquisitor and defendants but as fellow convicts. The senator had committed a federal crime, for which he received a sentence longer than that of the men he had prosecuted and persecuted. It was reported that the Hollywood Ten treated the facilitator of their incarceration with more civility than he deserved.

What worried me most about my visiting G-men was not knowing what they knew about my wife's political activity. Before we met, Estelle had been active in the struggles for workers' rights, civil rights, and racial equality, and she had once subscribed to the *Daily Worker*. After we married, her role as wife and mother took precedence, and her involvement in radical politics lessened. Truth be told—and I daresay this is the perfect time and venue for it—I first learned about the Major League's blacklisting of Negro ballplayers by reading a sports column by Ted Tinsley in a 1947 edition of the *Daily Worker*. It was there I learned of the exploits of Satchel Paige, Josh Gibson, Cool Papa Bell, and of the existence of a young player, Jackie Robinson, the first black athlete hired to play for the Montreal Royals and later for their parent team, the Brooklyn Dodgers.

These thoughts were in my head as I walked into the living room—or was it "the lion's den" I was walking into?

"Gentlemen, sorry to keep you waiting," I said, bounding in. "How about some coffee?"

"No, thank you," they answered in unison.

"I wasn't offering, I was asking if you had some," I joked. "You guys woke me before I could put up a pot."

They both smiled and actually apologized for the early visit.

"Apology accepted," I said cheerily. "So, now that I'm up, what can I do for you?"

"We just have a few questions, Mr. Reiner."

Their first question actually made me blink. It's not the kind you would expect the FBI to ask first thing in the morning. This may sound like I'm making it up, but the following is an almost verbatim account of their interrogation and my reactions.

"Mr. Reiner, I see you are registered in the American Labor Party, is that right?"

They can't ask me that, I thought. *We have a secret ballot.* But I smiled brightly and snapped back, "Yesiree! That's my party!"

"And we understand, Mr. Reiner, that you voted for their candidate, Henry Wallace?"

"I sure did!" I said proudly. "Didn't you?"

"May we ask why?" one of them asked, neither agent reacting to my audacious question.

"Because he was the best candidate."

"Why do you think that, Mr. Reiner?"

"Well, for one, he was Franklin D .Roosevelt's vice president," I spoke up forcefully, "and he's also a very successful businessman—owns and runs a large strawberry farm. He'd make a great president. Hope you guys voted for him."

The two FBI agents were glancing at one another during my defense of Wallace and then hit me with: "Mr. Reiner, are you aware that there are commies in your television industry?"

I cocked my head, smiled, and thought of how best to answer this blunt but not unexpected question. My inquisitor misinterpreted my blank stare and added, "By commies, of course, we mean communists, reds."

"Communists, of course, I knew that! I just didn't expect that question."

"Well, you're a pretty successful performer and have been on TV for quite a while," the agent pressed on, "so I imagine that you must have worked with a communist or two—"

"Oh, yes, I would say so," I said confidently.

"Good. Mr. Reiner, can you tell us the names of these people?"

"I'm afraid I can't," I answered, smiling sincerely.

"And why can't you?"

"Because I don't know who they are," I explained. "Communist actors don't go around telling you that they're communists. Oh, I know there are communists in our industry; everybody knows that—they're in every industry, but they would be pretty dumb to rat themselves out—and they sure as hell are not dumb."

I had risen to the occasion and delivered an award-winning performance. They may not have believed me, but they did drop the subject. However, they were not finished. They had a whole new set of unexpected and unsettling questions for me to try to parry.

"Mr. Reiner, in 1947," he asked, reading from a note pad, "do you recall hosting a charity event to raise money for veterans of the Spanish Civil War and to honor a Dr. Philip Barsky?"

"Do I recall that? You don't forget one of the most exciting nights of your life!" I answered forthrightly. "I was on fire that night!"

My exuberance had taken them aback. My decision to be the most cooperative, least hostile witness they had ever investigated was paying off. Four arched eyebrows and a short exchange of glances told me that I was on the right track.

"Mr. Reiner, do you recall how you came to host that event?"

"Well, I had the lead comedy role in a Broadway show, *Call Me Mister*—the cast were all former members of the Armed Forces—and someone in the show invited me to emcee this charity event. I don't remember who that was."

I did remember, but I was not about to help them seek out and pester another honest, law-abiding citizen.

"And to be accurate," I continued, being helpful, "I did not host that event. I was actually the emcee."

"Well, Mr. Reiner, as the emcee, were you aware of why Dr. Barsky and these Spanish Civil War veterans were being honored?"

"No, not until someone filled me in," I answered. "On the way to the event, I learned that these veterans of the Spanish Civil War were the surviving members of the fifteen hundred American volunteers who joined a group called the Abraham Lincoln Brigade. They, along with volunteers from many European counties, joined with the Spanish Loyalist Army to battle a rebel army let by General Francisco Franco."

"So you became aware of what you were asked to be a part of?" they asked simply.

"Yes, and I was also aware that General Franco had invited Hitler and the German Luftwaffe to bomb Spanish civilians, and that if there were more brigades like the Abraham Lincoln Brigade, we might have avoided the Holocaust and World War Two."

I had not intended to wax tutorial but, heartened by the weird effect I seemed to be having on my visitors, I decided to do go for broke. When I finished, they would either applaud me or handcuff me.

"Do you know," I continued smugly, "what some people called those American volunteers? Premature Anti-Fascists! And do either of you know who Dr. Barsky is?"

"Yes," one of the agents answered, "Dr. Barsky was a known communist. Did you know that?"

"No, but do you know why they were honoring him?" Without waiting for a response, I barreled on to explain why all of us, including my two inquisitors, owe him a debt of gratitude. How Dr. Barsky, a young thoracic surgeon, had volunteered to perform life-saving operations in crude, makeshift battlefield hospitals. With the aid of a jeep's engine, he had learned to harvest the plasma from blood, a process used in ensuing wars to save the lives of countless servicemen wounded in battle. The more I chattered on, the less able I was able to discern whether I was impressing or depressing them. In making my case, did I ruin theirs? One of the agents held up his hand, indicating that he wanted to say something. I hoped it was *Thank you for your cooperation, have a nice day,* but instead it was another hardball that, thankfully, was right in my wheelhouse. I managed to hit this one out of the park.

"Mr. Reiner, what you've told us is all very interesting, but we don't think you have been quite honest with us. You have not told us the real reason you appeared at that event."

When I dropped my head and sighed, they thought they had me.

"You got me!" I sighed, feigning contrition. "I didn't tell you the real reason because it's—well—embarrassing."

"You might feel better if you told us why you agreed to emcee that left-wing event."

"Because that left-wing event," I continued, smiling sheepishly, "was being held at Carnegie Hall—the greatest concert hall in the world! Every kid in show business dreams of playing Carnegie Hall one day. Well, I can't sing or play the violin or piano, so when this opportunity came along, I jumped at the chance to stand on that great stage. I didn't care what the event was. I tell you right now, if the FBI ever holds a benefit at Carnegie Hall, I'm your guy! I mean it—and you know where I live!"

That did it. They smiled, thanked me for my cooperation, slid into their black sedan, and drove off.

I am happy to report that since that unnerving morning a millennium ago, no one has knocked on my door and asked me if I knew any commies.

CHAPTER TWENTY

Subdue the Rattling

There is something rattling around in my head, and unless I address it, the annoying rattle will distract me from concentrating on "R.T.T. Deeply Loved I.S.," the chapter I am preparing to write next.

The rattle relates to an appearance Mel Brooks made on *The Tonight Show*, way back when Johnny Carson was its host. The memory of the laughter that exploded from me when Mel delivered a blockbuster of a punch line has lasted till now.

I am aware that it will probably not have the same effect on you, but I will tell it to you about it anyway. If it does not make you laugh out loud, my guess is that it will make you smile broadly.

On one of Mel's many appearances with Johnny Carson, Johnny was fascinated to learn of Mel's knowledge of fine wines and of his extensive and expensive collection of rare classics. Impressed with the depth of Mel's oenological interests and his passion for wine, Johnny asked, "Mel, are you capable, as some connoisseurs are, of being blindfolded, sipping a fine wine, and then telling us its color, its vintage, and what company bottled it?"

Mel, proud of his discerning palate, grabbed the mask, placed it over his eyes, and commanded, "Start pouring!"

Johnny brought forth a bottle of red wine, poured a small amount into a stemmed glass, and handed it to Mel. Mel then deftly swirled the wine around in the glass, brought it to his nose, sniffed it, took a small sip, let the wine sit on his tongue, swallowed it, and announced, "What we have here is a classic red wine, a heady Chateau Haut Brion, 1944."

The audience was poised to applaud, but Carson shook his head and said, "No, it's not that."

"Not a Chateau Haut Brion, Johnny, or not a 1944?"

"Neither," Johnny assured him.

"Hmm, I don't understand…wait!" Mel said, holding up his hand. "You may be right. Let me have that wine glass."

Mel then took a second sip and with utmost confidence offered, "It is not a heady Haut Brion, and it is not a red wine—it is a fruity pinot blanc '51, a white wine."

"No, Mel."

"Not a white—wait a minute—wait a minute!" Mel said, taking another sip. "Is this beer? Did you slip me a beer in a wine glass? This is beer, isn't it? A Bud Light!"

"No, Mel, it is not."

"A Miller Lite?"

"It's not beer!"

"Not beer?"

Mel then took another sip and asked, "Is it Chiclets?"

Johnny and the studio audience roared with laughter, as I imagined the whole country did at the inability of a great connoisseur to discern the difference between a vintage red wine and a cube of sugar-coated gum.

Did I guess right? Are you smiling broadly?

CHAPTER TWENTY-ONE

R.T.T. Deeply Loved I.S.

This is a love story. Not only did R.T.T. deeply love I.S., but R.T.T. loved many people, and many people loved him. I.S. are the initials of my dear wife's brother-in-law, Ira Shapiro, the father of George Shapiro, my nephew-in-law and theatrical manager. George is one of the finest human beings I know, so fine that I have to restrain myself from making this piece about him. He deserves a chapter of his own and, unless he commits a heinous crime or forbids me to write about him, I will keep my options open.

R.T.T. was our pet German shepherd, who we called Rinnie. He was named after Rin Tin Tin, the most popular canine movie star of his day. I am happy to say that our Rinnie had a long and full life, so full and eventful that I felt a need to document it.

Besides Ira Shapiro, Rinnie had great affection for my wife, Estelle, my son, Robbie, my daughter, Annie, me, and for a short time, our youngest, Lucas.

Rinnie was born in 1955 and passed away in 1968. He came into our lives because Robbie, who was six at the time, had fallen in love with the star of a black-and-white television show, *The Adventures of Rin Tin Tin.*

Our family had just moved to New Rochelle, and my wife and I had decided that the only thing missing to make our new, split-level home complete was a dog. When Robbie heard this, he screamed, "A Rinnie dog! Get a Rinnie dog!"

My wife and I agreed that a German shepherd was perfect, as we would be getting both a pet and a watchdog. No one was more excited about bringing a dog into the house than I was. Estelle and her family always had dogs in their lives. My father, being a watchmaker who worked at home in our small, three-room apartment, never entertained the idea of owning a dog or any pet.

I had once found a tiny kitten on the street and brought it home. It was the first and only pet I ever had. I had asked my mom if we could keep the "kitty cat" and she answered with a noncommittal, "We'll see."

I felt that my mother saying "We'll see," and then feeding the kitty cat a scrap of liver boded well. A few moments later, kitty cat hopped up onto on my father's favorite chair, deposited a neat mound of liver-based poop on the seat and kitty was back in the street.

I had never owned a pet for more than half an hour, so I was more thrilled than anyone in our family about bringing a dog into the house. I immediately contacted a farm that bred German shepherds. It was located in Pound Ridge, a two-hour ride upstate. My wife suggested that I wait for the weekend, when the whole family could be involved in picking out our new pet, but I could not wait. The breeder had informed me that only two pups were available and that he had potential buyers for them.

Estelle questioned the wisdom of my driving up to Pound Ridge at this hour, but I felt it would be worth it just to see Robbie's face light up when he saw a Rin Tin Tin lookalike dash into the house.

I was met at the farm by a charming man who made a point of introducing the puppies' parents to me. These animals were mighty impressive—their coats were shiny, their markings were distinctive, and their ears stood upright. The breeder then took me to where the weaned puppies were kept and said, "Take your pick—or take the one who picks you."

Had I ever seen a six-week-old German shepherd pup before, I would not have been so disappointed. These two pups looked nothing like the handsome animals I knew they would become. When I saw their droopy ears flopping up and down, I knew exactly what Robbie would say—and he did say it: "That's not a Rinnie dog!"

I sped home with information about the heritage of our pup, who was now curled up in the back seat. I kept reaching behind me to pet his droopy ears and to keep him informed. "Hey, Rinnie, just a few miles more…"

I kept calling him *Rinnie*, even though I knew that on his pedigree papers he was dubbed, Blake of Dornwald and was sired by the impressively named Pfeffer Von Berne.

When I arrived home, the family was gathered in the den, ready to welcome their new dog. Annie was smiling and clapping her hands when the puppy bounded in, and a disappointed Robbie reacted as I knew he would. "That's not a Rinnie dog!" he complained. "He's not a German shepherd."

Annie 6, Rinnie 1, and Robbie 8

I insisted that he was, but Robbie kept alluding to his droopy ears. "Rin Tin Tin's ears stand up," he whined. "His ears are hanging down—he's not a shepherd!"

The poor kid was in tears, and nothing his mother or I said would convince him that when the dog was a little older, his ears would stand up. I told him that I met Rinnie's mom and dad, and their ears stood straight up, but Robbie would not be consoled. As far as he could see, I had brought home a mutt!

After six weeks, one of Rinnie's ears stood up, but it was not until the morning my son awoke to see a "two-standing-up-eared dog" walk into his bedroom that he accepted our pup as being a bona fide Rinnie dog.

When Rinnie was full grown, we built a run in our back yard that sported a custom-made doghouse with a front porch. He actually used it, but both Rinnie and the family preferred that he live and sleep in our house. When duty called, he would slip through the doggie door we had installed in the kitchen and relieve himself in our fenced-in back yard.

One summer morning, at about two or three o'clock, I awoke to the sound of very loud, insistent barking. I did not think it was Rinnie, as I had never heard him bark so loudly and continuously. But it was him, and he seemed to be in some sort of distress. I ran onto the back porch and saw Rinnie, yapping and pawing at the base of the fence between our property and my neighbor's. It was not like Rinnie to get into a fight with another dog, but that is what he appeared to be doing. The other dog, however, was not barking but cowering and hissing.

I shouted for Rinnie to come, but he did not heed. To assess what the problem might be, I walked out into the yard, wearing boxer shorts and a T-shirt. As I got closer to the fray, I saw that Rinnie had not cornered a dog, but a black cat with a white tail. He had the poor cat pinned against the wire fence and kept nipping at it. I came to within fifteen feet of Rinnie and his hissing quarry, when I realized that his quarry was not a cat but a skunk—a frightened skunk dousing her enemy with a generous amount of her spray.

In my travels down country roads, I had smelled the pungent odor of a dead skunk, but nothing came close to the toe-curling stink that this live skunk was emitting.

I grabbed Rinnie by the collar and started to drag him away. For my rescue effort, the grateful skunk lifted its tail and gifted me with the last few squirts from her odious collection.

I dragged the stinking Rinnie onto our screened-in porch, shouted, "Stay! Sit!" and he summarily disobeyed both commands.

He just kept shaking his head as he paced back and forth, behaving as if he was aware that he stunk to high heaven.

Showering was my first priority, and when I dashed though the house on my way to the bathroom, my usually soft-spoken wife screamed, "Phhhheeeewwwww! Caaarlll, you're stinking up the house!"

I showered three or four times, and after each soaping, scrubbing, and rinsing, I checked to find that the nauseating aroma of "Eau de Skunk" persisted. Never having met anyone who had been sprayed by a skunk, I had no idea what the antidote was or if there was one. I put on an expendable pair or boxers, wrapped my offending shorts in a plastic bag, tossed them into a garbage can, and then went about tending to Rinnie, who was behaving as if he was trying to get away from himself. I led the sad animal to the backyard, and after hosing him down and shampooing him with doggie soap, I worried that Rinnie and I might stink of skunk for the rest of our lives.

I phoned our vet, and he gave me the antidote. To fill the prescription, I drove to the to the Scarsdale supermarket and bought a dozen quart jars of Campbell's tomato juice.

I worried what Rinnie's reaction would be to having tomato juice poured all over him and was happy to find him totally acquiescent. He behaved as if he knew that a tomato juice bath was the accepted antidote for skunk stench.

After doing the best I could for Rinnie, I got into my tub and had my first and last tomato juice bath. I no longer smelled from skunk, but it was a day or more before Rinnie and I started to smell less like marinara sauce and more like ourselves.

I have two more memories of our gentle, loving Rinnie, and both of those occurred when our family moved to Los Angeles.

In 1959, when Rinnie was a playful four-year-old, I was hired to appear in *The Gazebo*, an MGM film that starred Glenn Ford and Debbie Reynolds. It was our family's first trip to L.A., and my agent had rented us a comfortable, three-bedroom house on North Alta Drive in Beverly Hills—a house that I was particularly excited to inhabit, as it belonged to one of my favorite character actors, Akim Tamiroff. Before Mr. Tamiroff came to Hollywood, the Moscow Art Theater hailed him as a Most Honored Artist.

One of the cast members in *The Gazebo* was a pigeon who played the part of Herman. Herman is importantly involved in the denouement of the movie, and if you are curious about how he is involved, you can rent the film, but I must advise that it is not regarded as a "must-see film"—and I had an undistinguished supporting role.

Many trained pigeons were needed to essay Herman—there were walking Hermans, pecking Hermans, and a flying Herman. Most of them had their wings clipped, and I adopted one of those. The children enjoyed getting a new pet and renamed him Kingfish, after a character on *Amos 'n Andy*, a popular, albeit politically incorrect, radio show of the day. For a short while, they paid him some attention, but the novelty of feeding and petting him soon waned, and I ended up being Kingfish's sole caretaker.

Kingfish lived in a corrugated carton that sat on a bench in the pool house. To insure that Rinnie could not get at the bird, I cautioned everyone to keep the men's dressing-room door closed at all times.

For the record, one morning, Annie had gone to look in on Kingfish and found that Kingfish had laid an egg. It was then that we changed Kingfish's name to Sapphire—Sapphire being Kingfish's wife on the *Amos 'n Andy* program.

That summer, our New Rochelle neighbors, Millie and Jerry Schoenbaum, who were visiting from New York, joined us for lunch and a swim. I had not briefed Jerry about keeping the men's-room door shut and discovered my goof when I glanced toward the pool house and saw Rinnie with his head in the corrugated box and his tail wagging. I shouted his name and rushed to the cabana, expecting to find a dead pigeon, but instead, I found a naked one.

Sapphire was naked because Rinnie had been nibbling at the poor bird, who was trying to defend herself. With jackhammer speed, Sapphire was pecking at the nose of the pervert who was trying to undress her. Rinnie knew he was doing wrong because he stopped the moment he saw me.

I had no idea what Rinnie had in mind, but he seemed to be playing a game with Sapphire, a game Sapphire obviously hated. It was miraculous that Sapphire was not harmed. Rinnie had obviously not nipped her hard enough to draw blood. It seemed that each time he closed his teeth on her, she hopped away, leaving her plucked feathers in his mouth.

In a few weeks, after placing Sapphire's carton on a high shelf out of Rinnie's reach, our naked clipped-winged pet recovered. Not only did her feathers grow back, but so did her wings.

It was Rinnie who was instrumental in our discovering that Sapphire had regained her ability to fly. I had taken her carton from the high shelf and placed it on the bench when Rinnie strolled in and immediately poked his head into Sapphire's carton. The panicky bird flapped her wings furiously, flew out of the cabana, soared high in the air, and alighted on the weather vane atop our house.

Sapphire sat on that weather vane for days. We worried about her starving to death. She knew of no other home but ours, and we all felt responsible for her survival. Every morning, Estelle tossed bird feed on the back lawn, and every morning, Sapphire flew down, pecked at the seeds, and when sated, flew back to her perch. This ritual kept on for a few days, until one morning while Sapphire was having her lunch, Rinnie strolled out into the yard. As soon as Sapphire spotted her nemesis, she flapped her wings and soared back to her safe haven.

The very next day, we looked up, and Sapphire was gone. We liked to believe that she had chosen to join one of the flocks of pigeons that regularly flew by our house.

The setting for the last and my favorite tale of Rinnie was the foyer of our home in Beverly Hills. The year was 1966, and it was six years after moving here from New Rochelle. The whole family was excited about a visit we were about to receive from one of our favorite relatives, my wife's brother-in-law, Ira Shapiro. Ira was just one of those good souls who was happiest when he was doing things to make others happy.

One of the others he always made happy was Rinnie. After every family dinner, whether at Grandma Minnie's apartment in the Bronx or at our house in the suburbs, Ira would take Rinnie for a walk. The two took dozens of leisurely, twenty-minute strolls on Wilmot Road in New Rochelle and on the Grand Concourse in the Bronx. Sadly, those walks were discontinued when I signed on to write and produce *The Dick Van Dyke Show* and had to relocate in California.

Ira had arranged to fly out from New York and visit with the West Coast contingent of his family. This included his son, Georgie, who was working at the William Morris Agency in Beverly Hills and Rinnie, his walking buddy, who was now getting on in both regular and dog years. It had been six regular years since Rinnie and Ira last saw each other.

At eleven, Rinnie was still a fine-looking specimen. Even though his hearing was impaired and his back hips ached, he still had a regal air about him. His appetite remained intact, and thankfully, so did his teeth. Strangers often remarked about how white they were. I thanked them and took credit for their healthy condition. I would tell them about the article on dental hygiene I had read in some doctor's waiting room. It claimed that the number-one cause for tooth loss in animals was an excessive buildup of plaque. Armed with this information, each night as we watched television, Rinnie would rest his noble head on my lap, and with my dental tool, a Roosevelt dime, I would scrape the plaque from his teeth. I was actually disappointed when I completed the job and could find nothing to scrape.

Considering Rinnie's age and the fact that he had not seen Ira for six years, we anticipated that he might not welcome Ira with the same level of enthusiasm he did when Ira took him for his nightly stroll. And we were right—he did not greet him with that same enthusiasm.

When the doorbell rang, Estelle and I, our young son, Lucas, and Rinnie all came to the door to greet George and Ira. I opened the door, and when Ira stepped into the room, Rinnie did not welcome him as he had years earlier. Instead of wagging his tail and waiting impatiently for Ira to attach a leash to his collar, a howl escaped Rinnie's throat, a howl the likes of which I had never before heard come out of him—or any dog. It was a prolonged, deep-throated, extended, wolflike howl that he continued to emit while pressing his body against Ira's legs and encircling them. The howling sound that Rinnie produced was much like a human wail—a legato wailing that to this day, I can impersonate almost perfectly. I plan to recreate this sad-happy wail for the audio recording of *I Remember Me*.

Here is how one might spell the air-piercing howl:

"AAAAAAAAAAAWWWWWWWWWWRRRRRRRRRRR"
"AAAAAAAAAAAWWWWWWWWWWRRRRRRRRRRR"

I may, in other stories, have exaggerated or even invented a bit, but everything I have written about Rinnie up to now is on the nose. And for the record, Rinnie's nose, until his last days, was always cool and damp.

In his last year, Rinnie's coat still shone, his teeth still sparkled, his appetite was good, but he started to have hip problems. Prednisone was prescribed for his condition, and it worked, but only for a couple of months. He was no longer able stand on his back legs, which made his bowel movements difficult. I would support his haunches whenever he had to go or when he had to negotiate the five steps down to the back yard. We considered having a contraption built that we had seen fitted to a dog who had lost his back legs in an accident. Considering his age, and there being no hope that his condition would improve, our vet recommended that we put him to sleep.

A few days later, with me supporting his back legs, Rinnie walked into the vet's office. If not for some graying around his muzzle, he still looked as young and regal as he did back in New Rochelle.

I sat and watched as a white-coated assistant helped Rinnie walk out of the waiting room. Before leaving, Rinnie suddenly stopped, sat down, slowly turned his head and looked back at me with, what I can only describe as a hangdog expression.

I thought, *aaaaaaaaaaaaaaawwwwwwwwwwwwwwrrrrrrrrrrrrr.*

Awhile after Rinnie's death, I chanced to be looking up something in the *Encyclopedia Britannica* and came upon a section that featured every breed of dog extant. My eye was caught by a photo of a German shepherd, listed as Pfeffer Von Bern, who, I thought, our Rinnie very closely resembled. And why shouldn't he? On Rinnie's pedigree papers, he was registered as Blake of Dornwald and grand-sired by Pfeffer Von Bern, *the* Pfeffer Von Bern, who, according to the encyclopedia, was the world's finest example of a German shepherd, whose genes informed the breed and who sired the world's most famous and awarded German shepherds of the modern era.

So there it was, the reason our Rinnie Von Reiner seemed to have a royal mien about him—he was of royalty! To his credit, he never behaved like anything but a good dog. And that is exactly what he heard us tell him almost every day of his life: "Good dog!"

Estelle Lebost at age 2

CHAPTER TWENTY-TWO

Estelle, B.C. and A.C.

E stelle B.C. (Before Carl), whom I refer to in the chapter heading, was born Stella Lebost on the fifth of June, 1914 and weighed in at four pounds. Her three siblings, Sylvia, Sidney, and Eddie, were respectively ten, eight, and six years older and, from all accounts, they treated her as their pet. When she was four, Stella's brothers, whose athletic abilities she admired, had devised a contest where they placed their little sister in the middle of a field and tossed a tennis ball back and forth over her head. Whoever threw the ball closer to the top of her head was declared the winner. She remembered enjoying the experience and never once worried about being struck. The influence her brothers' athleticism had on her was palpable. In later years, by playing handball, softball, and tennis with them and their friends, she developed skills that stood her in good stead for the rest of her life. When we played tennis, our friends would comment that Estelle served a tennis ball "like a guy!" "Like a guy" is how she tossed a ball—or anything that needed tossing. It was traditional in Estelle's family to toss items. If someone said "pass the salt," a salt shaker would likely be tossed—and caught.

Her mother, Minnie, made me privy to some of Stella's gifts that started to manifest themselves early in her life.

- At the age of four, little Stella soloed, at the altar of the White Plains Catholic Church, singing the hymn, "Jesus Loves Me," a capella.
- At thirteen, she had taught herself to play the ukulele and entertained her friends. One summer afternoon, at Rockaway

Beach, while singing and playing her uke for friends, the manager of Bronx radio station WBNX heard her sing and liked what he heard. For three consecutive Saturday mornings, he paid Stella five dollars to play her ukulele and sing her songs. A positive audience reaction resulted in the manager offering her a daily fifteen-minute program, which she declined, explaining that she had used all of her repertoire and had no time to learn new songs, as she was getting ready to start high school.

+ In her late teens, Stella and her brother Sidney entered a ballroom dance contest and won first prize—a gold cup.

+ At Bronx's James Monroe High School, Stella won another first prize for taking dictation faster than all the other contestants.

+ In a citywide high-school art competition, Stella was awarded still another first prize, this time for her still-life drawing of a yellow, ceramic bowl filled with fruit. (Hanging in my breakfast room is a painting she did of this same subject.)

+ In her youth, she was often teamed with one of her brothers and played in men's doubles handball competitions.

Estelle a few years later

So this is the Stella who became my wife, Estelle, with whom I shared a productive and loving sixty-five-year union. Our pairing was an unlikely one, a coupling that no professional matchmaker or Internet dating service would ever have recommended or dared to have set up. I am sure you would agree with this assertion—if you knew just one thing about us. And here now is that one thing, which will kick off part one of multiple addenda.

Part 1
"The One Thing"

From March 20, 1922, the year of my birth, until sometime in 1932, Estelle, nee Stella Lebost, and I lived in the Bronx. She and I resided with our families in apartment buildings that were but a few blocks apart, but Estelle and I did not meet until ten years later, in July of 1942—and not in the Bronx.

At that earlier time, when we resided in adjoining neighborhoods, I was referred to as a skinny *"melink,"* even though I was, by any account, a fine-looking lad who sported a head of dark, wavy hair. Had we met at that time, Estelle would not have given me a second glance, or for that matter, a first one. I, on the other hand, would have done more than just glance at her—I would have ogled her, as I would any pretty girl with great legs, a curvaceous body, and gorgeous gazonkas. "Gazonkas" was the word my friend Marty often used to describe our friend Lenny's sister Theresa's ample bosom.

You might ask how I could know of Estelle's physical charms, not having met her, and how I could assume that she would not have given me a second glance. It is easily explained when you know that we actually met seven years later at an adult camp called Allaben Acres. Allaben was a vacation resort in New York's Adirondack Mountains, where I was a member of the social staff. For the heady salary of ten dollars a week, I performed in variety revues, hosted game shows, and at the Saturday night socials, was expected to dance with the unescorted female guests. Estelle had hired on to work backstage as the assistant scenic designer.

After we had spent our first days together, it became clear that my initial premise was right. Had Estelle and I met in our old neighborhood, I would, no doubt, have ogled and drooled, and she would have totally ignored me, as any normal twenty-year-old woman would have, had a twelve-year-old pubescent passed by. It was at Allaben Acres that I learned of the almost eight-year difference in our ages. I cannot tell you how happy I am that we did not meet in our old Bronx neighborhood! Had we met then, it is unlikely that I would be sitting at my computer and chronicling the history of our coupling.

PART 2
OUR FIRST ENCOUNTER

When I arrived at Allaben Acres, I had two things on my mind: doing well as an emcee and sketch actor and getting laid—the latter being my first priority. I don't mean to present myself as a lothario, for if truth be told—and that is what I am attempting to tell—up to then, I had been romantic with but three women. I had been deeply in love with all three but bedded only one.

My first afternoon at Allaben Acres was an exciting one. I met the top banana, Bernie Hern, who described some of the sketches we would be performing in the variety revues. Bernie was a talented comedian whose politically left-leaning monologues were funny, original, and loudly appreciated by our audiences.

Before hiring on as Bernie Hern's second banana, I had been a serious actor. In two seasons as a resident member of the Rochester Summer Theater in Avon, New York, I had performed leading roles in twenty-two legitimate plays. After my second summer at this rustic, open-air theater that was built between two empty grain silos, I was hired to tour with the Avon Shakespeare Repertory Company. That the word *Avon* appeared in my first two incursions into professional theater, I took as a good omen. Little did I know how good an omen or what a pivotal role the Bard of Avon would play in my young life.

Bernie Hern was my first comedy mentor, and I am grateful to him for that and beholden to him for acting as the best man at my one and only wedding.

Estelle and I were married by the clerk at New York's City Hall. Bernie and his wife, Mary, were our two witnesses, and when the clerk asked, "Is there anyone present who knows of any reason that these two should not be joined in holy wedlock? Speak now—" Bernie raised his hand.

"Any reason?" The comic, could not resist asking, "Well, I know a—uh..."

"Yes?" the flustered clerk asked, staring at Bernie.

Bernie thought for several seconds, shook his head, and then waved his hand and said, "Never mind, not that important—go ahead, Judge!"

What better way to start a marriage than with a big laugh. After we left the justice's chambers, the four of us started to laugh, and we continued to laugh all through our wedding breakfast.

It is interesting to note that my wedding took place in Manhattan at 100 Center Street, in the very same building that housed the first acting class I ever attended. I was all of seventeen when I enrolled in the free WPA government-sponsored drama program. For those who loudly advocate "getting the government off our backs," I say, I am here because my government invited me onto its back, and for that, I will be eternally grateful.

My very first day at Allaben Acres, and days before my first encounter with the one who was destined to be my wife, I found myself seated on a veranda after dinner, chatting with a tall, pretty girl. I don't remember much of what we talked about, but I do remember that her name was Claire Faust—yes, Faust was her actual surname. I had no doubt that Claire Faust would make an exciting sexual partner, and I felt that her name being Faust boded well. Did not Mephistopheles offer Faust a wish? Could I not act the devil and offer this female Faust a wish, and if her wish were to sleep with me, I would most certainly grant it.

For an hour or so, Claire and I sat on a canvas settee with our feet resting on the porch railing. She was friendly and asked a lot of questions, which I answered while checking out her long legs. I concentrated on the four inches of bare calf that were visible between the tops of her socks and the bottoms of her slacks. When I complimented her on her colorful socks and commented on how very white the exposed portion of her calves was, I learned that this young lady was not only pretty but perceptive.

"Look," she said simply, "I am here for the day, and even if I were staying, I am not interested in starting any kind of relationship. My life has been a roller coaster ride, and I am just getting over a bad hump."

I confess that the words *bad hump* might not be verbatim, but I could not resist. Actually, Claire did tell me that she had recently broken up with her boyfriend.

"If you are looking for a companion," she suggested, "a friend of mine is due here soon, and you might want to introduce yourself to her. Her name is Stella, Stella Lebost. She's a terrific gal."

PART 3
STELLA AND CARL'S ACTUAL MEETING

Stella Lebost and I met in the resort's grand ballroom during the first Saturday night dance. The large room was filled with guests dancing to the soulful music of Sidney Bechet and his orchestra. If by chance you have forgotten or perhaps never knew of Sidney Bechet, he was, besides being a virtuoso of the soprano saxophone, one of the trio of history-making New Orleans musical pioneers who introduced Dixieland and jazz to the world, the others being trumpeters Jelly Roll Morton and Louis "Satchmo" Armstrong.

Our company's scenic designer, Paul Petroff, and I were standing just below the bandstand and chatting about my forthcoming duties as an emcee, when he stopped and waved to someone.

"Hey, Carl," he said, looking past my shoulder, "my new assistant is walking toward us—she was supposed to be here last week. Her name is Stella Lebost."

Stella Lebost, I thought, *she's the terrific gal Claire Faust told me about…*

"Stella doesn't know anybody here," Paul said. "Ask her to dance—be nice to her!"

Those last four words were words I never forgot. With his suggestion, *be nice to her,* ringing in my ears, I turned to see who it was he wanted me to be nice to—and what I saw approaching us was a smiley-faced girl with a really fine figure. I thought, *I would like to be nice to her!*

Paul introduced us, and I did what I was instructed to do. I started being nice to her. I told her that Claire Faust had said we should meet, and I was happy that we did. As far as asking her to dance, that was the last thing in the world I wanted to do. I was never much of a ballroom dancer. I was, however, a good jumper. I could jump three feet in the air and make my legs move crazy fast. I had no trouble dancing to make people laugh, but keeping the beat and staying in rhythm had always been a challenge for me. Tonight, however, the gods were smiling down on me! As I took her hand and led her onto the floor, the music stopped, and a ten-minute break was announced.

I feigned disappointment and, by affecting a credible English accent, I channeled my favorite actor, Ronald Colman, and suggested "we retire to the patio and breathe some of your exhilarating, American mountain air."

Stella welcomed my suggestion, as the ballroom was stifling hot. Although my British accent was impeccable, I suspected Stella knew I was not a worldly Beau Brummell but a naive Bronx bumbler.

I remember Stella and me sitting side by side on a canvas glider and each, in turn, asking all the obligatory questions that would necessarily come up on a first date—and this was, by any description, a first date. It was then I learned that Stella was sometimes called Estelle and that her mother preferred calling her that. I thought, *If her mother prefers Estelle, then I prefer Estelle*, and from that day forward, I called her Estelle. I was happy not to have to call her Stella, because Stella was the name of the tragic title character in the tearjerker film, *Stella Dallas*. Stella was played by Barbara Stanwyck, a gifted dramatic actress but just not my type. Decades later, when assembling footage for the Steve Martin film, *Dead Men Don't Wear Plaid*, I used clips of Barbara Stanwyck in *Double Indemnity*, and I found her to be more attractive than I did when I was a callow youth.

I have a fair ability to dredge up details from my long-term memory, and some of the words I now attribute to Estelle may not be totally accurate, but the words I used to court her seventy years ago are almost verbatim, and forthwith, you will see why I can make that claim.

In telling Estelle my life story, I opted not to linger on my earlier days working as a delivery boy in the millinery and dress trades. Instead, I described fully my tour of our southern colleges as an actor with the Avon Shakespeare Repertory Company. I proudly listed the roles I played and the plays in which I appeared: Orlando in *As You Like It*, Antipholus of Ephesus in *The Comedy of Errors*, Claudius the king in *Hamlet*, and Lucentio in *The Taming of the Shrew*.

Estelle seemed impressed by my résumé and did what I had hoped she would: ask if I would recite some of Shakespeare's words. I happily obliged—not with words I had done on tour but with snippets of speeches from *Romeo and Juliet*—a play more appropriate for my purpose.

I moved close to Estelle, rested my chin on her shoulder, and quietly whispered Romeo's words into her ear.

"But soft, what light through yonder window breaks? It is the east, and Juliet is the sun. Arise, fair sun, and kill the envious moon, which is sick and pale with grief," segueing to:

"Ah, see how she leans her cheek upon her hand—Oh, that I were a glove upon that hand, that I might touch that cheek."

Estelle seemed to enjoy my edited and whispered version of the balcony scene. She did not pull away or ask me to stop, so I continued by sighing, "Ah me…" just as Juliet had.

"She speaks!" I responded as Romeo. "Oh, speak again, bright angel, for thou art as glorious to this night, being o'er my head, as is the winged messenger of heaven, who stares into the white-upturned, wondering eyes of mortals who fall back to gaze on him, as he bestrides the lazy pacing clouds and sails upon the bosom of the air."

I am not sure of the sequence of these speeches or of the exact words, but I do remember quoting one or two of the star-crossed lovers' more famous exchanges:

"What's in a name? Would not a rose by any other name smell as sweet?"

"Juliet, call me but love and I shall be new baptized."

After rereading the above, I know I have misquoted Shakespeare but, on that balmy evening, whatever words I whispered into Estelle's delicate, well-sculpted left ear had an even more positive effect than I ever dreamed they would have.

PART 4
SHAKESPEARE DID IT

My rendering of the Bard's poetic prose into Estelle's accepting ear softened her heart enough to accept a few gentle kisses from me—and an invitation to go for a walk.

We soon found ourselves strolling, hand in hand, on a path that led us into the woods behind the dance hall. We walked, or more accurately hiked, over a long stretch of unfriendly terrain, hoping to find a setting more romantic than the busy-bodied hotel patio. Miraculously, deep in the hills of the Adirondacks, while looking for a neat patch of lawn to stretch out on or a friendly tree to sit under, we came upon a log cabin, a dilapidated, abandoned, real log cabin!

Estelle didn't have anything in her eye except me

It was here in this rustic, one-room, Lincolnesque abode that Estelle and I spent every free moment of every day of the two idyllic months we worked at Allaben Acres. It is hard to believe, but our hideout was so well hidden from view that no one in the camp knew of its existence—neither the owners nor any of the guests—and we were not about to tell anyone about our precious discovery. Every time we made our way down the gully and approached our love nest, we feared that interlopers might have appropriated it. As far as we were concerned, this land and cabin were ours! We had found it, and we were its legal squatters. For the fifty-five blessed days we spent at Allaben Acres, no one contested our proprietary rights. The rough-hewn structure became the first and most treasured of the many abodes Estelle and I shared for the next sixty-five years.

PART 5
HER UNSUSPECTED TALENT

Among the many things I learned about Estelle at our secret lair was of her deep interest in the arts and her being a graduate of New York's National Academy of Design. I learned too that she loved jazz and the blues and enjoyed nothing more than listening to recordings of great jazz artists—in particular, Billie Holiday. Estelle spoke of how thrilled she was to have seen Billie Holiday perform at a Fifty-Second Street New York jazz club. It was there that she first heard "Lady Day's" moving rendition of "Strange Fruit."

I later learned that "Strange Fruit," the powerful, socially significant song about lynching, was written by our staff songwriter, Lewis Allen, nee Abel Mirapol, who taught English at the Bronx's Dewitt Clinton High School.

One Saturday night after the performance of our weekly musical revue, Estelle's unsuspected talent came to light. Sidney Bechet and his band, besides playing the overture and providing the music for our weekly show's song-and-dance numbers, also performed a Dixieland medley that featured a solo on his signature soprano saxophone. The thrilling mix of soaring notes he produced invariably brought down the house. When the show was over, Bechet and his band had a need to unwind, which they did in an empty, garage-like shed that abutted the dining hall. After playing for our comedy revue, featuring songs like "Oh, You Can't Make Love in a Bunk for Eight," these gifted jazz men were in need of a show tunes antidote.

To hear some of the finest Dixieland jazz improvisations outside of New Orleans, the cast and crew and other music aficionados crowded into that shed. I, who was not yet a jazz buff but a dedicated Estelle buff, found myself at her side that memorable night.

Sidney Bechet, after leading his band in performing a couple of wildly exciting Dixieland classics, including "When the Saints Go Marchin' In," switched gears and began rendering a slow, sensuous introduction to "Lover

Man." Estelle was, by nature, reserved and shy, but for some reason, on this night, her shyness fell away, and she started to sing. It seemed as if she had channeled Billie Holiday and delivered a spot-on rendition of Billie's iconic classic. Bechet and his band members did not react. None of them looked up to see who was bending and caressing those sweet, pure notes; they just continued playing. When the song ended, Bechet's trombonist, the great Sandy Williams, lowered his mouthpiece, looked at me, and then slowly enunciated the following four words: "Dat lady should reeecaawed!"

Fifty-six years later, in 1996, Estelle did "reeecaawed" "Lover Man" and include it in her first album, which was appropriately titled, *Just in Time*.

PART 6
SUMMER SCHOOLING

Estelle Reiner at The Gardenia

At age thirteen, I announced at my bar mitzvah, "Today I am a man!" which I have already documented, but it would have been more appropriate had I waited to say those words after my two-month learning experience at Allaben Acres. In that summer, thanks to the following staff members: Bernie Hern, the "mentoring *mensh*" of a comedian, who taught me about political humor and how to perform sketch comedy; and Vivien Rifkin, the gifted concert pianist who convinced me that, with proper coaching, I was capable of singing the lead roles in productions of Earl Robinson's *The Ballad for Americans* and George Kleinsinger's *I Hear America Singing.*

My heartfelt thanks and undying gratitude would have to go to Paul Petroff, who suggested that I "be nice to" his new assistant. Had I not heeded his advice, I would not have developed, among other things, the social conscience that ultimately became part of my psyche.

It was from Estelle that I learned about the progressive forces in our country and their struggle to spotlight the inequities that existed in the world and how these injustices might be corrected. Underlining the theme of chapter nineteen, "Do You Know Any Commies?", I learned at Allaben that people who were called "left-wingers" were not the ogres that the reactionary commentators constantly pilloried on their radio programs.

In those days, and probably today as well, when two people meet at a resort and spend their days and nights together, the most oft-asked question by one of the romantics is, "Will I see you in the city?"

I was a politically naive young man, and thanks to Estelle, who I continued to see in the city, I slowly learned to distinguish the good guys from the bad guys and my ass from my elbow.

PART 7
"WILL I SEE YOU IN THE CITY?"

When the summer ended, Estelle and I went to our respective homes in the Bronx—I to my parents' three-room apartment, located at the corner of 180th Street and Arthur Avenue, and Estelle to her mother at the Pickwick Arms, an English-style architectural gem that was located at 3224 Grand Concourse, off Mosholu Parkway. In order to visit Estelle, I had my choice of riding on two separate bus lines or traveling by subway.

Either way, it took at least thirty minutes to get from 180th Street to 203rd Street, but it was worth it. After seeing someone for sixty consecutive days, twenty-four hours a day, it was difficult to adjust to communicating by phone or seeing each other only once a week.

We were both in the process of looking for jobs. Estelle had been trained as an architectural draftsman and was trying to reconnect with her old firm. I was frantic about finding a job, because greeting me when I returned home was a letter from the government that started with the word "Greetings!" and went on to inform me that I was eligible to be drafted into the army. It was 1942, and while I was blithely entertaining the guests at Allaben Acres and falling in love, our nation was at war with Germany, Italy, and Japan.

My brother Charlie, who was three years older than I, had been drafted and was seeing action in North Africa as a member of the Ninth Division, Thirty-Seventh Infantry of the First Army.

While at Allaben, I had written him that I was seeing a wonderful girl, and it might be something serious. In a return letter, my caring brother said that he was happy for me, wished me luck, and enclosed a packet of government-issue rubbers "just in case…!" He also found it necessary to inform me that if I wanted to re-order, the packet of three cost a dime.

When I was called up, I was hoping to be assigned to Special Services, where I would be able to use my talent as an entertainer. I knew my chances would be improved if I were a member of a theatrical union like Actors' Equity. To be eligible to join, I would have to have acted in a Broadway show or at least contracted to do so.

I bought a copy of *Show Business*, a theatrical newsletter that listed the names of shows that were casting, and the only casting that day was for a musical, *The Merry Widow*. I learned too that they were auditioning singers for the chorus. I was due to report to the draft board in a week and had little time to look further. In discussing it with Estelle, we agreed that being a member of Chorus Equity, while not as prestigious as being a member of Actors' Equity, would be better than having no theatrical credentials.

Armed with the knowledge that I had successfully sung the "Ballad for Americans" at Allaben Acres, I auditioned for and secured a role in the chorus of *The Merry Widow*. I loved the Franz Lehar operetta, as did my father, who often played the recordings of its great songs on our phonograph—a crank-winding RCA Victrola.

By not informing the producers that I had received my "Greetings" from the US government, I was hired as a second tenor. I rehearsed for one week before saying farewell to Estelle and starting out on what was scheduled to be a sixteen-week cross-country tour.

On the third week of the tour, while performing in Philadelphia, the draft board ordered me to report for a physical examination. My need to sing in the chorus of *The Merry Widow*'s fictional country of Moravia was superceded by our non-fictional country's need for me to train as an army air force radio operator.

The army's accelerated plans gave Estelle and me no opportunity to say a proper farewell. A few unsatisfying phone calls were all we could manage before I was shipped to Fort Dix, New Jersey.

After a few days of indoctrination, the army decided that I could best serve my county if I were sent to Miami Beach, Florida. There, three times a day for two weeks, while waiting to be assigned, a platoon of fellow inductees and I marched up and down Collins Avenue. We started from the hotel where we were billeted and marched ten blocks to the mess hall where we were fed.

It was here along the Florida coast that my training as an actor was first put to use. Somehow—probably because I told him—our sergeant in charge learned that I had been a performer and chose me to bark out the cadence for our ten-block march to the mess hall. Three times a day, as we strode proudly to and from our daily chow, I sang out at the top of my lungs, "Hut-tup-threep-forp, hut-tup-threep-forp, hut-tup-threep-forp!"

After two weeks of marching and eating in a sunny resort town, the army brass ordered our platoon transferred to a bleak army base in Missouri. It was at Camp Crowder, the historic Southern installation where, while in the process of learning to become a telegraph operator, I collapsed and lost all contact with my family, my old buddies, and my new best friend, Estelle.

PART 8
A YEAR OF SPARSE CONTACT

The week before my collapse at Camp Crowder, I had little time to do anything but eat, sleep, study, shower, shit, and memorize Morse code. To become a member of a two-man communications team, I had to learn to use a telegrapher's key and how to operate a portable generator. By cranking the two handles of this hundred-pound, compact generator, I created the electricity needed to tap out our coded messages.

My partner and I took turns being telegrapher and power maker—while one tapped the other cranked. To keep our operation hidden from the enemy, we were instructed to lie face down while we did these jobs.

My fateful day started at seven o'clock on a bright, sunny morning. Over the barracks' loudspeaker we heard: "Temperature sixty-five degrees! Uniform of the day: summer khakis and windbreaker!"

A windbreaker was a light, zippered jacket, commonly known as an Eisenhower jacket. When we started our five-mile trek to the training area, the sky was cloudless, and a balmy breeze was at our backs. Most of us chose not to wear our windbreakers and had tied them around our waists. By two o'clock, the temperature had dropped precipitously, and the pleasant, balmy breezes turned into bone-chilling gusts of icy wind. In seconds, my taut, hundred-sixty-pound body had gone from profuse sweating to teeth-chattering chills.

I had started this day dragging a portable generator though a craggy field and ended it dragging my fever-racked body to an infirmary. There, I was handed a washcloth and a bar of soap and was ordered by a disembodied voice to "Take a shower!"

I remember standing in a large, multi-nozzled shower room and trying to undress. I remember staring at the washcloth and the soap that I held in my hands and wondering what I was supposed to do with them—and that was all I remembered.

Sometime later, I was told by an orderly that I had fainted under the shower while trying to take off my pants.

I do remember waking up disoriented and lying in a bed that was not in my barracks but in a place that looked much like a hospital ward. I had no idea how I had gotten there or how long I had slept. I recall wondering why I was in a hospital and thinking, *Who was that man in white reading from a clipboard that is hanging from my bed?*

The man left before I could question him, but I thought I might clear up the mystery if I could read what was on the clipboard. I managed to scoot down and retrieve the chart. Through bleary eyes, I made out my name and the words, "Pneu, Right Lob," which I took to be my medical problem. The word *Right* conjured up an image of Britain's wartime prime minister, who was addressed as "the Right Honorable Winston Churchill." I thought, *I have pneumonia of my Right Honorable Lob!*

I laughed when I realized that it was not my right "Lob" that had pneumonia but my right lobe—a lung lobe. I learned from the male nurse that what I had was a severe case of pneumonia and that I had been unconscious for two weeks.

When the haze cleared, I thought about my mother and father and wondered if they were worried about having received no mail from me. Fortunately I wrote to them only once a week, and in my last letter, I informed them that I was training to be a radio operator. I expected that this news would make my parents happy. My father was a radio buff, and in 1927, he hand-crafted our first radio.

I could hear my mom saying, "It is good that Carl is a radio operator.

Radio operators don't shoot at people, so why would anyone shoot at Carl?"

Estelle and I had little contact during my stint with *The Merry Widow* and less after my induction. We met to say our farewells, and while our summer romance was memorable, there was a danger that our relationship was, as a Cole Porter lyric once suggested, "great fun but just one of those things!"

PART 9
DRIFTING FURTHER APART

After I successfully concluded a three-week physical recovery program at Camp Crowder, Missouri, some army functionary determined that I was well enough to ship to the army base at Laramie, Wyoming. It was here that my military skills would be re-assessed, and I would be re-assigned to a job that would better serve our nation's war effort.

During a three-week stay at Laramie, I had an experience that provoked me to write and post a letter that could easily be the stupidest, most thoughtless, hurtful, selfish, ill-advised, and potentially life-altering thing I ever did.

I remember very little about my new buddies at this Laramie base, but I do remember one of them saying that a couple of girls at the university had invited him for an afternoon of horseback riding and asked if he would like to bring a friend. Rather than dozing on my cot or sitting in the day room, reading magazines, I opted to go horseback riding.

The closest I had ever come to riding a horse was when I was a very young boy and "the pony man" came to our Bronx neighborhood. For a nickel, he allowed us to sit on his pony and have our picture taken. For a dime, he let us stay on him while he walked us down the block and back.

The two things I remember clearly that sunny day in Laramie were the white horse I was to ride and the girl with black hair who was to be my date. The horse's name was Whitey, and the girl's name was Lois, and both were beautiful. Whitey was tall and broad; Lois was of medium height, and until she invited me to follow her to the corral, I was unaware of what an extraordinarily broad derriere she sported. It was firm and mesmerizingly attractive—as was her ample bosom.

Lois was obviously a skilled horsewoman, who, with no effort, mounted her brown steed and waited for me to do likewise.

She assured me that Whitey was "the gentlest horse in the stable" and bid me to "mount up!"

She smiled while I impersonated the cowboy star, Randolph Scott, and attempted to mount my steed as I had seen him mount his—and miraculously, I did.

So far so good, I thought, as Lois led our party of four out of the corral and onto a rocky trail. Whitey and I brought up the rear, and from the way I handled the reins, Whitey knew that he had a novice sitting on his back.

While Lois and the group went up a steep hill, Whitey and I went around it. The harder I pulled on the reins, the more resolute he became. I shouted up to Lois, but not loud enough to be heard over the sound of clopping hooves. Whitey had something in mind, and after minutes of unsuccessful pleading and tugging on the reins, we came to a stop beside a small, black watering hole. The watering hole was ostensibly a mud hole that still contained a shrinking pond of water some twenty feet from the bank. Whitey's thirst had brought us to the mud hole, and as he stepped into it, his hooves started to sink into the mud. By the time he arrived at the shallow pond, his legs were half submerged. As he lapped at the water, he kept sinking further and further. All I could think of was a movie I saw where people got caught in quicksand and were sucked under—I was terrified of meeting that fate. Whitey must have seen that movie too, because he suddenly stopped drinking and tried to pull his legs out of the mire. The sucking sound Whitey's legs made as he tried to free himself was my cue to "abandon horse!" To save my life and maybe his, I relieved him of my weight by dismounting. I started for the shore and, for the first two or three steps, I struggled mightily, but with each succeeding step, it became easier to pull my feet out of the mud.

When I finally made it to the shore, my shoes, socks, and khaki pants were covered in black, oily mud. I had no idea where Lois and the rest of the party were, and I shouted for their help. It was Lois who deduced that Whitey had taken control of my life, and she returned to rescue the two of us. Lois actually waded into the mud hole and was able to grab Whitey's reins and coax him out. Whitey was now a half-black horse with a white mane, and I was a red-faced soldier with black khaki pants. Lois was very sweet and actually apologized for choosing Whitey to be my mount. She thought that because he was old and docile, he would give me no trouble. She had no idea how inept I was. I had fooled her by mounting Whitey a la Randolph Scott.

My buddies and I spent almost two weeks in Laramie, waiting to be re-assigned. During those fourteen days, I saw Lois almost every night. I had told her that I had a girlfriend, and she said that she did not have a boyfriend, but she would like it if, while I was in town, we could be friends. And that is ostensibly what we were—until a couple of days before I left Laramie.

Lois being very proper and I being guilty about having feelings for someone other than Estelle, kept Lois and I from starting any kind of physical relationship—until one moonlit night when we kissed. It was a goodnight kiss and not a very long or passionate one, but it did engender enough feelings to keep me awake that night. Lois was unlike any girl I had ever met, and I started to think that I might be in love with her. The feeling persisted and grew to the point where I felt that she was the one and only for me. Physically, we behaved ourselves and did nothing more than teenage-type petting—but I was smitten!

Never having had the capacity to have more than one girlfriend at a time, and tortured by the fact that I was now in that predicament, I acted! I did the heinous thing I described in the first paragraph.

I sat on my bunk and wrote the stupidest, most thoughtless, hurtful letter I ever wrote or ever will write to anyone—and I mailed it! Estelle's response on learning that I had fallen in love with someone else was embodied in a cold, curt note. It contained no anger, no vitriol, but it managed to summarily dismiss me from her life. As I illustrated earlier, Estelle had a knack for using a minimal amount of words to get maximum effect. In a few short sentences, she managed to make me feel like the shit that I was.

I fought to regain my equilibrium, as Lois and I had but a few more days together before my unit was shipped out. Some of us were assigned to Georgetown University to attend their School of Foreign Service. We were to study French and hopefully become interpreters.

On the train ride to Washington, DC, my guilt about Estelle abated, and my thoughts returned to Lois and what a lovely person she was. In particular, my thoughts returned to her mesmerizingly attractive derriere. I was planning to write her a letter, but instead I wrote her a poem that was inspired by her broad backside. I titled it "Ode to the Buttocks Bountiful." I did not save a copy of it or remember anything but the lines, "You will ere remain, 'Queen of said terrain.'" Not my best work.

I sent the ode to Lois and learned by return mail that she was flattered and thrilled that I would write such a humorous and loving poem about what she considered her worst feature. This made me like her all the more.

Lois and I corresponded for a short while, and with each letter, I realized more and more how little we had in common. Her letters were about her love of horses and the open plains, and mine were about New York, Broadway, and its theaters. I felt that she may have had deeper feelings for me than I for her, and she proved it by traveling from Laramie to the Bronx just to visit my parents. I learned of this from my father, who told me that a very pretty girl named Lois had dropped in on them just to say hello and tell them what a good son they had raised. My father said, "She seemed like such a fine person. Your mother and I had quite a nice chat with her."

Lois and I never wrote about the visit she paid to my folks, but it may well be that it gave her closure to a relationship she knew had ended.

Writing this may have done that for me.

PART 10
CANCELING THE CLOSURE

The day after settling into the lower bunk of a double-decker bed in the Georgetown University dormitory that I shared with three of my closest strangers, the privates first class, Charley Straight, John O. Benson, and Phil Wool, I started to think about Estelle Lebost, and the more I thought about her, the greater was my desire to see her. Not knowing how she would receive a letter from me, I decided to find out. I figured that the worst that could happen is that she would tear it up, and the best, she would read it and answer it. My letter was a friendly, straightforward one, telling her that I was now in Washington, DC. My writing that letter turned out to be one of the best decisions I would ever make.

Estelle answered my letter, and after a few more written exchanges and many long phone conversations, she agreed to my visiting her in New York as soon as I was eligible for a weekend pass.

Our first meeting was in her mother's four-room Bronx apartment, and it was a blissfully joyful one—as was our second meeting and the next half dozen. It was during one of these visits, while cuddling on the living room couch, that I said simply, "I love you, and what do think about us getting married?"

And she said, "I love you, and I think it's a good idea."

Two weeks later, we were joined in matrimony by the preoccupied city clerk at New York City's Town Hall, and we spent an idyllic night in the Honeymoon Suite of Manhattan's elegant St. Regis Hotel.

For the next seven months, while I was at historic Georgetown University on O Street, learning to be a French interpreter by day, at night I was in a sublet apartment on P Street, learning to be a husband.

Corporal and Mrs. Carl Reiner

Each morning as I left my honeymoon haven to return to the university, our wizened, old Jewish landlord, Mr. Jacobs, reminded me to lock the front door and then instructed me on how to lock it properly.

"Listen," he'd say, "after you lock it, prove it! Always prove it!"

He would jiggle the doorknob to show it was locked and then jiggle it again and say, "Lock it and prove it! Always lock it and prove it after you lock it!"

I do not think there was a luckier or happier soldier in the whole US Army than I—until the day I was called into the captain's office and threatened with a court-martial for "flagrant disobedience."

The night before my captain threatened me with a court-martial, our platoon had been remanded to quarters because a soldier had disobeyed the order that forbid alcohol to be brought into the dormitory. Estelle was due to leave Washington that following day, and I could not see myself spending my last honeymoon night with the boys instead of with my bride.

That night, when the officer came to my cot to do a bed check, he found not me in my bed but my blanket covering a stuffed barracks bag. Earlier, I had slipped out the back door of the dormitory, traversed the university's soccer field, scaled a wrought-iron fence, raced to our apartment on P Street and into my wifes arms.

It was a short but lovely night, and before dawn broke, I made my way back to the dorm, only to learn from a bunkmate that my dummy did not fool the bed-checker.

Our captain ordered me to his office and asked questions that, for the most part, I answered truthfully. I told him that it was the last day of my honeymoon and how anxious my new wife and I were to see each other that night. I told of my sneaking out of the dorm, traversing the soccer field, and scaling the fence. Here, without changing tone, I lied and said that I had second thoughts about scaling the wall. I knew that had I been caught, I might never get to see my wife. I also knew I would never be able to sleep, so I just kept walking around the soccer field until it got light.

"You're telling me, that you didn't spend the night with your wife… you spent it walking around the soccer field?" the captain asked, looking me squarely in the eye. "Are you asking me to believe that?"

"Yes, sir, I am asking you to believe that."

"Well, you are asking a lot—and don't ever ask again," he barked. "Dismissed!"

I saluted the captain, and when returning my salute, he allowed me to see the subtle grin on his lips. I later learned that he too was a newlywed and had listened to my story with an empathetic ear.

Our months at Georgetown and our weekends in New York afforded Estelle and me the opportunity to get to know each other, and the more I discovered about her, the more dear she became to me. I assume it was so with her, because she never said otherwise.

After graduating as French interpreters, the army assigned my buddies and me to Camp Crowder, Missouri, where little or no French is spoken. It was the army's plan for the French interpreters to go to a signal corps school and become members of a signal battalion. Ours was not to reason why; ours was but to do and learn to type.

Being stationed in Camp Crowder was another fortuitous happenstance for Estelle and me. By arranging for a leave of absence from the war plant where she worked as a three-dimensional draftsman, she was able to stay with me until I was assigned to a unit.

For two whole, wonderful weeks, in Neosho, Missouri, she and I were able to spend our nights together in the tiny front bedroom of a cramped, three-room railroad flat. The bathroom, being in the hall, required the two couples who had rented the back rooms to walk through our room whenever nature called. To insure our privacy, the landlord slung an opaque gauze curtain on one side of our bed. Estelle and I were so happy to be together that this invasive inconvenience, instead of depressing us, amused us.

The sad day finally arrived. Estelle went back to New York to work at the Sperry Rand Corporation. The three-dimensional blueprints she drew were of submarine and airplane parts for neophyte assembly workers who were not equipped to read regular two-dimensional drawings. Estelle, a schooled artist, was, along with a dozen of her coworkers, the first Jewish, African American, or female workers ever to be hired by the famous Rand Corporation. It took Hitler and a world war to get this race-, religion-, and gender-bigoted firm to accept the tenets of our constitution.

For the next year and a half, Estelle and I wrote to each other at least once a day—sometimes twice or thrice—and once, in my case, fifteen times. Yes, and on one particular Monday, Estelle received seventeen of my letters—the fifteen I wrote on that one day and two strays that had not been delivered the previous week. Each of the fifteen letters was at least four pages long. Estelle's letters to me were always four to six pages. If anyone cares to check the volume of our correspondence, you have but to fly out to L.A., come to my home, and examine the cartons in my bedroom that contain bundles and bundles of our letters. Estelle saved all of mine, and I carried all of hers back from overseas in my bulging duffel bag.

I think I became a writer because of my need to tell Estelle who and what I cared about, what bugged me and what I found funny.

Even though Estelle is gone, I still have that need—so I tell you.

25th Anniversary

ART
KLETTER

CHARLIE
RUGGLES

NANETTE
FABRAY

DELLA
REESE

OLIVIA
de HAVILLAND

MOREY
AMSTERDAM

PEARL
BAILEY

EFREM
ZIMBALIST

ANGIE
DICKENSON

JIM
BACK

Z
G

THE CELEBRITY GAME

CHAPTER TWENTY-THREE

The Game Show Shows

There was a period in my professional life, immediately after my days as a second banana to the great Sid Caesar on *Your Show of Shows* and before my life-changing experience as a writer-producer of *The Dick Van Dyke Show*, when I happily accepted invitations to appear on game shows—as either a panelist or host.

I had appeared on the legendary *What's My Line?* and the less-legendary *I've Got a Secret*, but I believe the first one I ever guested on as a panelist was titled *The Name's the Same*, hosted by Robert Q. Lewis. The show's premise was simple: by asking a contestant non-direct questions, two other celebrity panelists and I tried to discover what famous person bore the same name as the guest. My fellow panelists were Joan Alexander, a gifted Broadway actress, and Bill Stern, a famous sports broadcaster and newspaper columnist.

On one particular telecast, we were trying to guess the name of a contestant who, we learned after a series of questions, was a "baseball player," "a center fielder," and "played for the New York Yankees."

It was Bill Stern's turn to either ask the next question or say the name of the famous person. Before Bill could answer, we stopped for a commercial. It was clear to Joan, to me, to the studio audience, and to the entire sports world that the man's name must be Joe DiMaggio. I looked to Bill Stern, expecting to see a confident, smiling man, but instead, I saw a panicky, sweating man who smiled at me, and without moving his lips, whispered, "What the fuck is his name?"

For a split second, I thought he was putting me on. How could he not know the name of one of the greatest baseball players of all time? I knew that Bill Stern was not a kidder, so I quickly whispered, "Joe DiMaggio," and not a moment too soon. Our host called on Bill, and Bill, smiling broadly, asked the contestant, "Is your name Joe DiMaggio?"

The audience applauded, as did Joan and I. Bill smiled and graciously acknowledged us all.

There was an explanation, and after the show, Bill felt a need to provide me with it. He thanked me for helping him out and said that he had been sick all week and was still running a fever.

I had always enjoyed listening to Bill Stern's inspirational stories on his radio show. He would spin a dramatic yarn of someone who had a tragic beginning but by luck and pluck, managed to become a huge success. Ironically, at that time, Bill was the undocumented subject of his own show.

A few months after the show was canceled, I learned that Bill Stern had checked into a rehabilitation center to conquer his longtime addiction to drugs. He developed the addiction after breaking his leg and taking the painkillers that were prescribed for him.

I felt a kind of kinship to Bill—perhaps it was because, on the show, we both sported snazzy toupees.

In 1964, I was asked to host a new CBS game show that I thought had real potential. It was called *The Celebrity Game* and had a simple premise. Two contestants would try to guess how eight star panelists would advise them about certain domestic problems, such as: "What would you do if you hated your mother-in-law's expensive but ugly wedding gift?" or "Should you tell your best friend that you saw her husband out with an attractive woman?"

The contestants would win small cash prizes if they guessed what the majority of the celebrities had advised. Each week, among the eight celebrity panelists were some I had known and some I was thrilled to meet. If you are old enough to remember, you will be as impressed as I was with this following roster of performers who, sixty years ago, were among our panelists: Gloria Swanson, Oscar Levant, Basil Rathbone, Sal Mineo, Nancy Sinatra, Eartha Kitt, Betty Hutton, Steve Allen, Edgar Bergen, Martha Raye, Vic Damone, Art Linkletter, Ida Lupino, Joseph Cotten, Zsa Zsa Gabor, Jan Murray, Ann Southern, Steven Boyd, Frankie Avalon, Mel Brooks, George Hamilton, Hedda Hopper, and Ronald Reagan.

Each week, eight of these stars sat in a two-tiered semicircle directly opposite the desk where the contestants and I were anchored.

Of all the celebrities, the one guest on whom I could depend to get big laughs was Zsa Zsa Gabor. She had a genuine gift for saying just the thing that would make the audience and all the celebrities roar, all but Oscar Levant, the brilliant concert pianist, Gershwin interpreter, and world-renowned wit. He would never crack a smile. One time after the entire audience had laughed uncontrollably, I asked him, "Oscar, how, when everyone is doubled over, laughing their heads off, can you just sit there and not laugh?"

"Carl," he said sadly, "it's been so many years since I've laughed, I'm afraid if I opened my mouth, dust will fly out."

I remember that line getting one of the biggest responses ever!

Groucho Marx, Eden Marx, Paul Lynde, Shelley Winters, Franie Avalon, Dale Robertson, Zsa Zsa Gabor, Jim Backus, Gisele MacKenzie

And now, if I may, a word or many words about *The Celebrity Game*'s most successful alumnus, Ronald Reagan, whom I met for the first time at Tony Curtis's home. It was in 1960, the year our family migrated to California, and Mr. Reagan was then president of the Screen Actors Guild of America. He was as charming and witty then as he was during his years in the White House and just as fiercely dedicated in helping his very wealthy friends become even wealthier. It was here, when chairing a meeting of actors to discuss the subject of their film residuals, that I had the first intimation of Ronald Reagan's political philosophy. There were two Guild proposals being discussed about residual pay for actors who worked pre- and post-1968. One plan would have guaranteed that older actors, who were most in need of financial aid, would get it, and the other plan would insure that Mr. Reagan's former employers, personal friends, and benefactors, General Electric, Twenty Mule Team Borax, and the large studios would legally be able to financially screw all Screen Actors Guild members—all, that is, but its president.

I am painfully aware that as I deride a man who has had an airport, a library, and an aircraft carrier named after him, I may be losing readers—but I probably lost them when they read chapter nineteen, "Do You Know Any Commies?"

I have two more bones to pick with our late, much-beloved president, and I may as well pick them now.

Bone number one has to do with a piece of legislation that Herbert Hoover worked on before he became our thirty-first president. It was in 1927, when Mr. Hoover was the secretary of commerce, that he proposed and helped pass a bill insuring that the airwaves belonged to the people and not the broadcasters. The regulation limited airtime for commercials to three minutes of every hour or ninety seconds for every half-hour. For decades, the writers and producers of radio dramas and comedies had ample time to tell their stories, with minimal interruptions.

After President Reagan was sworn in, one of his first priorities was to thank the heads of the major corporations and the top film studio executives for their energetic efforts and financial support in helping him to get elected. To show his gratitude, President Reagan supported a bill that deregulated the amount of minutes per hour that advertisers could use to sell their products. In a very short time, the networks' half-hour comedy shows, which had used twenty-six and a half minutes to tell their stories, were now trying to tell a story in twenty-two minutes. Recently it was chopped to twenty minutes.

On most networks, we are now able to now watch strings of commercials that peddle high-fiber cereals, incontinence pads, health insurance, full-figure brassieres, Odor Eater foot pads, an eyelash separator, Hamburger Helper, an erection-enhancing cream, toe fungus lotion, Cheez Whiz in a spray can, a lawyer who handles cases for victims of mesothelioma—all this without having to be interrupted by any kind of entertainment.

If you enjoy watching these commercials more than you do a good comedy or drama, then you are one lucky guy or gal! And you lucky guys and gals can thank President Ronald Reagan for that. He has gifted our country with a healthy chunk of entertainment-free television!

CHAPTER TWENTY-FOUR
Gotta Go for a Walk

The bright September day in 1953 when Estelle, our two young children, and I moved from our four-room apartment in the Bronx to a brand-new split-level house in New Rochelle was one of the most exhilarating and exhausting days of my life.

From high noon, when we stepped across the threshold of our new home on Bonnie Meadow Road, we were busy, busy, busy, and we remained busy, busy, busy until a little past midnight, when we became tired, tired, tired. We remained so until two thirty a.m., when we became utterly exhausted, exhausted, exhausted—or, as I might have described it in French, *fatigue´, fatigue´, fatigue´* or *au bout de ma force, au bout de ma force, au bout de ma force!*

We were so full of all the above that we could not open another carton or hang another curtain or stack another cupboard or fill another utensil drawer or hang another painting. Only Madeline Kahn as Lili Von Shtupp in Mel Brooks's *Blazing Saddles* singing "I'm Tired" to describe how spent she was after a night of unromantic sex, would come close to describing how bone-weary Estelle and I felt. It was one of the few nights in our then-decade-long marriage that we opted to go to bed without brushing our teeth. We had just laid our heads on our pillows after an inept attempt at a goodnight kiss, when something in me—I believe it was my overly tired funny bone, made me sit up and announce, "Honey, I am going for a walk!"

"A walk? Now?"

"Yes, now!" I said, tossing off my side of our coverlet. "I gotta go."

"Honeeey," she whined, "it's two in the morning!"

"I know, and that's why I gotta go! I won't be able to sleep unless I go for a little walk."

"That's crazy! You're dead tired! Just close your eyes, and you'll fall right off!"

"Honey, don't try to talk me out of it. I am going for a walk."

"Caaarlll, you are not actually going to get up, put on your shoes and socks, and go for a walk?"

"I am not putting on shoes or socks, but I am going for a walk!"

And with that, I stood up in bed, stepped on my pillow, and warned, "And don't try to stop me!"

I then stepped over her head, made a left turn, walked three short paces, down the length of our king-sized bed, made another left, walked four paces across the foot of the bed, turned left, took three paces to my pillow, stepped on it, stepped over Estelle's head again, and continued my stroll around atop our bed until she stopped laughing, which was after my eighth or ninth go-around.

No doubt about it: a good laugh can be relaxing. For the next few hours, Estelle and I slept like babes—until our babes, who slept like four-and six-year-olds, came into our room to ask if breakfast was ready.

CHAPTER TWENTY-FIVE

Father Walsh: Jesuit
Private Reiner: Non-Jesuit

This morning when I checked my calendar, I noticed that on the twenty-fourth of this month, I am scheduled to speak at the Paley Center, where I am the subject of a symposium sponsored by Georgetown University.

My stay at Georgetown University in 1943 immediately conjured up two memories. One I have shamelessly described as being "the most theatrically triumphant day of my career," and the other is my memory of Father Edmund A. Walsh, the dean of the School of Foreign Service, with whom, on the day following my "triumphant day," I had a brief, heart-stopping encounter.

On the next few pages, I plan to chronicle some of the dramatic events that occurred during the eleven months I spent at Georgetown University.

When I, and three hundred other members of Company E, marched onto the two-century-old Catholic campus, we had no idea what the army had in store for us. We all were duly impressed by the architectural magnificence of the buildings and the beautifully kept grounds. Our group, a specialized training unit, was led into an imposing nineteenth-century structure, where we would meet in Gaston Hall to hear lectures delivered by lay and Jesuit instructors. It was on Christmas Day, in this hallowed hall, that I stood at the very same lectern used by our distinguished professors and delivered what I have earlier described as "the most theatrically triumphant day of my young career." But more about that later.

The army had ordered that I, and three hundred other anxious soldiers, be housed in the university's dormitories, fed in their dining halls, and educated in their classrooms.

The small dormitory room to which I was assigned accommodated two bunk beds, four footlockers, and three total strangers, whose names, I learned, were Charley Straight, John O. Benson, and Phil Wool.

Of the three strangers, John O. Benson was the strangest and most memorable. He was chubby and so soft-spoken that we had to strain to hear his stories, but it was well worth straining to hear him describe his job as a "vat man" at the Hellman's mayonnaise factory. One evening, before lights out, John O., with no visible emotion, related the following.

"I loved my job at the Hellman factory," he began. "I sat on a high ladder and looked into a giant vat where they mixed the mayonnaise, and when I saw any impurities, like big blobs of something that shouldn't be in the vat, I scooped it out with my long-handled, aluminum shovel and plopped the impurity in a waste barrel. The job took a lot of concentration. I could never look away or let my mind wander. I worked for Hellman for almost a year and never had no problems—until this one day when I see something lumpy floating in the mayo, something that had no business being there—it was near the back of the vat. So I go up a rung on the ladder and reach for the lump—but my foot slipped and my spoon started to fall.

"I made a grab for it and missed, and both me and my spoon fell right in the vat of mayonnaise. I can't swim, but I can do the dog paddle, but it's hard to dog paddle in mayonnaise. I yelled for help, but no one came. I went under once, but I dog paddled my way up. If my supervisor had not come by to check the vat and seen me drowning, I wouldn't be here to tell you this story. My supervisor got a pole and pulled me out. Boy, was I was full of mayonnaise! I had mayonnaise everywhere, in my eyes, in my ears, up my nose, under my collar, in my pockets, in my shoes, in my socks—there was no place on me without mayonnaise in it. I always loved mayonnaise, but after almost drowning in it, I lost my taste for it. Now, when I order a BLT, I say 'hold the mayo!'"

John O. and I slept on the top bunks, and Charley Straight the company bugler, slept below me. I originally had a bottom bunk, but I made the switch after the first morning, when Charley climbed down to play Reveille and stepped on my face.

Charley, a dedicated bugler, practiced every free moment of every day. If he were not such a good person, he might have been strangled to death. The last line in Irving Berlin's song, "Oh, How I Hate to Get Up in the Morning," said it all. "And then, we'll get the other pup, the guy who wakes the bugler up."

Charley had one unusual talent that made him the envy of every serious drinker in our company. Once a week, Charley would get stinking drunk—and he did it with less than eight ounces of tap water. It was hard to believe, but our master bugler was also a master self-hypnotist. It would take him less than half an hour of slow sipping and self-hypnotizing to get his eyes to unfocus and his speech to slur. My bunkmates and I decided that whether he was really drunk or just pretending, he was doing no harm to his liver.

I will now attempt to describe what I have shamelessly heralded as the most theatrically triumphant day of my young career.

A week before Christmas, our commanding officer, Captain Dixon, the one who chose not to discipline me when I went AWOL during my honeymoon, called me into his office. During my stay at the University, I had made a few successful appearances at the USO in town, and the captain had seen one of my performances. It was also noted in my file that I had been an actor/emcee in civilian life. Knowing this, the captain thought I might be the one to cobble together a variety show to present at Gaston Hall on Christmas Day. I was thrilled to be asked and immediately went to work. I knew of three or four talented soldiers in our unit, one a guitarist-singer, Eddie Riley, who sang a show-stopping rendition of "Paper Doll."

"I'd rather have a paper doll to call my own,
  than have a fickle-minded real live doll." (Johnny S. Black, 1915)

Also in our outfit there were four soldiers who sang old standards in close harmony, a baritone who could belt out an operatic aria, and an accomplished pianist who could accompany the baritone and also play some Chopin or Gershwin. That would be our Christmas extravaganza, four acts and me as emcee and comedy-monologist. Armed with *chutzpah* (colossal nerve), I hunkered down and prepared for the big day.

As part of my act, I would offer my fairly good impressions of motion picture actors. As show day drew near, I decided that instead of doing my standby impersonations, it might be more fun if I did impressions of our Jesuit teachers and instructors. There were three I was able to mimic, and I knew that would be well-received. One was Father Verhoosel, a hip Jesuit priest who wore his clerical hat at a jaunty angle, and when in his office, could always be found with his feet on the desk and a racing form in his hand. He spoke with a thick Belgian accent in a deep monotone that he produced from the back of his throat. It was difficult to understand what he was saying, but his sonorous, room-filling voice was comforting.

I was able to do a spot-on impression of Professor Coutinho, a Portuguese professor who, we were told, helped to create Portugal's Falangist government. Professor Coutinho was a political scientist who, early in his career, we heard, had spent time in Paris with one of the architects of the Russian revolution—a dear friend and fellow Marxist, Vladimir Lenin.

Many of our group of three hundred students leaned to the left, and when they heard that Professor Coutinho knew Lenin personally, they could not wait to hear what the famous revolutionary was like—and the first question asked was, "What was Lenin like?"

With his high-pitched, nasal voice, in short, staccato, Portuguese-accented sentences, Professor Coutinho almost answered the question. He did not tell us what Lenin was like, but rather what he liked. For literally ten minutes, Professor Coutinho spoke of their meeting at a little Paris bistro and what Lenin liked to have with his coffee. In great detail, he described the "little chocolate nougats" Lenin ordered every day. The professor was not certain we knew what a chocolate nougat was and took a goodly amount of time describing what the nougat looked like, how it tasted, what it was made of, and how fine was the chocolate that was laced through it.

After hearing more than we needed to know about chocolate nougats and Lenin's love of them, one of our group interrupted the professor and asked if he might tell us more about "Lenin the man."

"Lenin was nice man, very nice man!" the professor happily replied. "I call him Vladimir. Vladimir was little taller than me but had smaller hands. He was smart man, *very* smart man—had good ideas—many good ideas...also a short, pointy beard—from photographs you can see what kind beard..."

From our session with Professor Coutinho, I was thoroughly convinced that Lenin was smart, nice, not too tall, and liked nougats—and our Professor Coutinho knew everything there was to know about those cute French pastries.

To this day, I cannot see a chocolate nougat without thinking of Professor Coutinho and his good friend, Vladimir, the "very nice man."

By show time seated in Georgetown University's staid Gaston Hall were the Georgetown student body, the three hundred soldiers from Company E, a few dozen priests, professors, and teachers, and a smattering of State Department officials, all primed to enjoy our Christmas offering.

Generally, performers are nervous before walking out onto a stage, but on this night, because I was also the producer of the show, it was not nervousness I was feeling but rather a numbed excitement. I knew that the acts I had gathered would do well, but I had no clue as to how "the powers that be" would react to material I had never before performed.

Would those who control my fate smile and find me funny, or would they frown and find me a perfect candidate for a court-martial?

Just as I had foreseen, all the performers on the bill did great. I was particularly heartened by the cries for encores that each of our musical acts received.

My army buddies were very supportive and laughed loudly when I did my impressions of our professors, and I was relieved to see that most of the faculty who knew the men at whom I was poking fun were either smiling or laughing. After I delivered my impression of Professor Coutinho, I walked off into the wings to appreciative applause and did not return for a bow. Instead, I ran around to the back of the stage, and after the applause had petered out, I made my appearance, not as myself but as someone whose gait and body language I hoped they would recognize—and they did. A hush fell over the auditorium, a hush that hid the collective thought, *Oh no, he's not going to do an impression of him!*

The "him" they never dreamed I would have the guts to impersonate was the dean of the School of Foreign Service, the Reverend Father Edmund A. Walsh.

Once a week, all the university's students were present in this very hall when Father Walsh delivered a lecture on geopolitics, a subject on which he was the preeminent scholar. Our dean was a frequent visitor to the White House or State Department, where he was asked by top government officials for his opinion on the geopolitical problems that were besetting Europe and the world.

At Gaston Hall, we often heard him expound on his "Theory of the Heartland."

"Whoever controls the heartland," he insisted forcefully, "controls all of Europe and therefore, all of the civilized world! That is why it is imperative that the United States use its military might to seize this territory before the Russians do!"

It did not concern him that the Russians and Americans were fighting side by side to rid the world of Hitler and Nazism. Under no circumstance could Father Walsh accept godless Russia as his ally.

As one might expect, some outraged student fed Father Walsh's statement and position to the *New York Post*. Back then, the *Post* had a liberal bent, and its headline screamed, "Government Sponsored Fascism at Georgetown!"

It naturally caused quite a brouhaha.

Nonetheless, on that Christmas afternoon, I strode to the lectern, approximating Father Walsh's mien, and behaved as if I were looking at an audience who had respectfully greeted me by standing up. I nodded benignly and uttered a spot-on impersonation of Father Walsh's deep, well-modulated voice, instructing them to "Please be seated!"

I was greeted by a gasp and a few guarded chuckles. The gasp was from those who were shocked that I would dare to make fun of our revered dean. The guarded chuckles were from those who were aware that rows full of clergy and teachers were in the balcony, looking down at them. To laugh at jokes that skewered Father Walsh would not be the most politic thing to do—and that's what we did. I skewered, and they laughed!

Pitching my voice to Father Walsh's register and using his mellifluous tone and cadence, I launched into a version of his lecture on the "heartland," ending with: "While it may have been true, that 'Whoever controls the heartland controls all of Europe,' there is a newer and truer truth emerging about the heartland! I have just this night been informed by a ranking member of our State Department that adjacent to the heartland, two new territories have been discovered. They are the liverland and the onionland. On our blessed Earth, was there ever anything more compatible or gastronomically mated than liver and onions? I daresay not! It does the heartland good and will bring everlasting happiness to our homeland."

You will have to take my word for it, but the laughs that this silly parody engendered were seismic, way beyond what it deserved. No doubt that austerity of Gaston Hall, the constituency of the audience, and the suicidal nature of the undertaking were, in great measure, the reason for its success.

I spent the rest of that day accepting and enjoying the accolades I received from my buddies. At night, as I lay in my bunk, I took great pleasure recalling the images of Father Verhoosel, Professor Coutinho, and the many men of the cloth, seated in the balcony, pounding on the railing and laughing uncontrollably at my impression of Father Edmond J. Walsh. Had their dean been present, I doubt they would have allowed themselves to act as they did.

I am, at this moment, reliving and once again enjoying this very special day in my life.

The morning after my performance, I was asked to report to Captain Dixon's office, where I learned that Father Walsh had requested that I visit his office—"immediately!"

Of one thing I was certain: nothing good could come from this visit.

Father Walsh was not smiling when I entered his office. He sat behind a huge, antique desk that was as cold and impressive as he was. He nodded politely and invited me to sit in the wooden chair opposite him. I waited as he straightened some papers and then neatly slipped them into a drawer. His first words, delivered in his hypnotically mellifluous voice, were: "Private Reiner, I was told that you put on a little show last night—a Christmas entertainment, I understand. Is that right?"

"Yes, sir."

"And who, may I ask, requested that you put on this, um— entertainment?"

"Our captain, Captain Dixon asked me if I could get some performers together and do a little Christmas show for our company."

"A little Christmas show, I see." He nodded and then stared at me for too long before asking, "Private Reiner, do you plan to, uh, put together any more of these—little shows?"

"No, sir, I do not."

"I see," the Father said, peering into my soul. "Well, should you change your mind, I would appreciate it if you would check with me first! Will you do that?"

"Yes, sir."

"You may go, Private Reiner!"

I had dodged a bullet. I breathed a huge sigh of relief. I had fully expected to be kicked out of Georgetown, re-assigned to an infantry unit, and never again see my wife or my folks.

At the end of the year, my buddies and I graduated Georgetown's School of Foreign Service as French interpreters, and after being re-assigned and trained as teletype operators, we became members of the 3117th Signal Battalion and shipped to Hawaii, where, to this day, very little French is spoken.

Such are the ways of the military. They move in mysterious ways, but somehow they do get the job done!

1943 Georgetown University

CHAPTER TWENTY-SIX

The Deaths of Jackie Cooper
and His Priceless Pet

After awakening each morning—which can be anytime between eight and eleven, depending on the quality or seductiveness of the old movies on late-night television—I make my way to the breakfast table and read the morning papers. I check the obituaries, and if my name is not listed, I'll have breakfast. I make a point of checking the ages of the deceased, to see if they are older, younger, or the same age as I. Of course, like most people, I am heartened to read the names and history of the living centenarians. Not too long ago, I learned that an old friend, Norman Corwin, the revered radio dramatist, had passed away at 101. A few weeks earlier, I had called to wish him a happy birthday, and we talked about his brother, who made it to 102, and his father, who lived to be 110. I challenged him to do better than his dad and go for 111, and he said, "I'll do my best."

And his best was a not-too-shabby 101 and five months.

Earlier this year, I had read in the *Los Angeles Times* that Jackie Cooper had passed. He was just short of eighty-nine, a couple of months younger than I. I did not consider Jackie a close friend, but we were very close acquaintances and even closer neighbors—our homes in Beverly Hills being less than a block apart. Two incidents immediately came to mind. One involved our involvement in the 1964 presidential campaign, and the other was about an arowana he had bought. An arowana, I learned, was a rare and exotic tropical fish.

About twenty years ago, we met on our street in Beverly Hills, where he excitedly told me about his having spent fifteen hundred dollars to purchase this arowana and asked if I would be interested in seeing it.

Who would not be interested in seeing a fifteen-hundred-dollar fish? My older brother, Charlie, was a tropical fish fancier but had never bought anything but guppies and never paid more than a quarter for a pair.

The tank that held Jackie Cooper's exotic fish was in the living room of his impressive two-story brick house, located at the corner of the famous Rodeo Drive and Elevado, the less-famous cross street.

I had never before heard of this breed of tropical fish, and it was different than any I had ever seen. It was about a foot long and had a big, flat head that was shaped like a triangle.

About a year after visiting Jackie Cooper's home and seeing his weird pride and joy, we happened to meet again, and he invited me to see how large his arowana had grown. He explained that the fish's growth depended on the size of the aquarium it lived in—and Jackie had built an especially large tank that allowed his flat-headed friend to grow to be almost three feet long. Jackie happily informed me that his fifteen-hundred-dollar fish was now worth fifteen thousand dollars, and he had been offered as much by the curator of an aquarium—an offer Jackie rejected.

The tank "Mr. Flat-head" now swam in was about ten feet long, three feet wide, and had been mounted in the center of a handsome bookcase that housed beautifully leatherbound classics.

Each day, the arowana, when not sleeping, would glide lazily up and down the length of the tank, make a slow U-turn at each end, and continue to swim hundreds of similar slow, graceful laps.

Not long after Jackie had proudly exhibited his fifteen-thousand-dollar pet for me, we met at a Rite-Aid drug store, where he informed me that his precious fish had died. I asked him what had happened, he shook his head and said, "Automobile accident."

I might have laughed, had I not seen the sadness in his face. He was definitely not trying to be funny.

He sighed resignedly and explained that a drunk driver who was barreling down Rodeo Drive jumped the curb and ran up onto his lawn. The car's bright lights shone through the living room's bay window and directly into the eyes of the startled flat-head. The poor, panicked fish had sharply turned away from the blinding light, so sharply that he broke his back and died instantly.

Jackie said his rare, tropical fish ended up "looking like a floating number seven."

Sometimes I wish I was not such a passionate disbeliever in a hereafter. It would be nice to envision a heaven where my very close acquaintance, Jackie Cooper, might reunite with his flat-headed pet—and possibly Wallace Berry, with whom, as a child actor, he co-starred in *The Champ.*

During the 1964 presidential campaign, Jackie and I, along with other forward-thinking Democrats, Henry Fonda, Barbara Rush, Jackie Cooper, Joan Staley, Tippi Hendren, and Eddie Fisher, volunteered our services to help elect Lyndon Johnson and his running mate, Hubert Humphrey and keep the country from falling to Richard Nixon and William E. Miller. To this end, we agreed to fly to a half dozen or more large cities and speak at rallies on behalf of these candidates. I was the nominal master of ceremonies, who succeeded in getting a few laughs before introducing Jackie Cooper and Henry Fonda. They, in turn, made very convincing speeches on why it would be a disaster if we did not elect our guys. Eddie Fisher was our closer and never failed to excite and entertain the crowds by singing a number of his hit songs … always melting the audience with his rendition of "Oh My Papa."

On the way to one of our venues in St. Louis, the public relations folk thought it would be newsworthy and a great photo opportunity if, while in Missouri, we made a detour, stopped at Independence, and visited our much-loved former president, Harry S. Truman.

Harry Truman was always considered to be a straight-shooting, no-airs man of the people, but we were all surprised to discover how down-to-earth he really was. After his term in office, he went back to his modest home in Independence, Missouri, and resumed the life he and his wife, Bess, had chosen for themselves.

Our group was driven down a narrow street of unprepossessing homes, where we saw some folks standing in their yards with non-manicured lawns and chatting with their neighbor over a picket fence. At the fence of the modest two-story frame house that was adjacent to President Truman's home, a man wearing overalls and clutching a hoe chatted amiably with a similarly clad neighbor.

It was clear that President Truman's home stood out from the rest of the houses on the street, in that his was set back at least twenty or thirty feet deeper that the others, and the front lawn was greener and neatly mowed.

We were told by our publicist that Mr. Truman was not well and did not feel up to hosting us for a visit, but he would greet us at the front window for a very limited time. As we made our way up the path to the house, we saw him standing at the window, clad in pajamas. As we approached, the former president opened the window, smiled, and welcomed us. We told him how thrilled we were to meet him and, at someone's suggestion, we four Hollywood visitors launched into an a cappella rendition of the song, "I'm Just Wild about Harry." We sang a full chorus at the top of our lungs, and when finished, we waved to the president, who smiled warmly, closed the window, turned, and walked away.

I was happily shocked to discover that a photo of that event magically surfaced and was presented to us … which I proudly present to you.

Harry Truman looking out at us from his window: Barbara Rush, Carl Reiner, Henry Fonda, Jackie Cooper, Joan Staley, Eddie Fisher and Tippi Hedren

CHAPTER TWENTY-SEVEN

Barry Lebost Chats with My Badly Toupeed Albert Einstein

My hairline had started to recede when I was in my first Broadway show, *Call Me Mister.* The first hairpiece I bought was a small strip of hairy lace that successfully replaced the hairs that once defined my widow's peak. Each year, the lacy hairpieces became fuller and fuller until, by the end of my days on *Your Show of Shows* and *Caesar's Hour,* I had a full-blown toupee sitting atop my head. I am proud to say that the toupees I had made for me were the least-detectable ones in all of show business. I may sound as if I am blowing my own horn or blowing a horn that nobody wants to hear blown, but I will blow it nonetheless.

I have known many actors who wore what they thought were natural-looking, undetectable toupees, and back then, the biggest joke about undetectable toupees was that there was no such thing. To illustrate with a joke of that period:

A man walks up to another man, stares at his forehead for a while, then says, "Sir, I hope this isn't impolite, but are you wearing a toupee?"

"I am!"

"Really? You know, you can't tell!"

In my time, I have had many people act surprised when I told them that I was wearing a toupee—and I told everyone. On *The Tonight Show,* I chatted with Johnny about why I had decided to wear or not to wear my hairpiece when I came on his show. I told him I wore it whenever I felt like appearing younger and handsomer than I was.

I cannot tell you how many letters I received from viewers asking me where they could get a hairpiece like mine, one that "looks so natural." Actually, I can tell you how many letters I received from viewers—it was at least a dozen. I informed these viewers that to insure your toupee doesn't make you look like you're wearing a dead animal on your head, have your toupee maker use one-third the hair he usually does, keep the hairpiece fresh by wearing it only for very special occasions, and then decide that your talent is not enhanced by wearing false hair.

What I finally decided was that it is a lot easier to live life with the hair that grows from your scalp, however sparse it may be.

It was fifty years ago that I handed out that piece of solicited advice—but if one has the inclination and the money, there are a myriad of hair-replacement centers and qualified physicians who will accommodate your need to look even handsomer than you are.

The last time I donned a hairpiece was in the film *Ocean's Thirteen*, where Saul Bloom, the character I essayed so adequately, wore a white wig—not to look younger or handsomer but to hide my character's identity.

I actually supplied the white hairpiece, which, many years earlier, I received as a gift from a Cleveland wigmaker who professed to be a fan of my work on television. He wrote to say that he would be grateful if, in return for the two wigs, I would honor him with a "personally autographed" photo of myself—a pretty lopsided trade, wouldn't you say? I never dreamed I would ever use those hairpieces but happenstance intervened, and I ended up using both of them. One, as I said, in the big-budget *Ocean's* films, shot in Vegas and the hills of Rome, the other, in a no-budget film, shot in my home in the Hills of Beverly.

Barry Lebost, whose name is borne in the chapter title, is my late wife's nephew and my children's first cousin. Sixty years ago, my brother-in-law, Eddie Lebost, and his wife, Sylvia, flew to Maine and adopted Barry when he was a few days old.

They had no idea that this cute little bundle they brought home to their Bronx apartment would someday accomplish the following:

+ At age six: Test the explosive potential of a Fourth of July cherry bomb by tossing it into a bathtub filled with water.
+ At age fourteen: Experiments with illegal substances.
+ At age eighteen: Grow up to resemble Elvis Presley.
+ At age twenty-three: Use an electric fan to demonstrate to

close relatives a plan to harness wind as a viable source of energy, and convince those close relatives, cousin George and Uncle Carl, to invest fifty thousand dollars to finance construction of a giant wind turbine.

+ At age thirty: In 1979, construct and install the Lebost Wind Turbine on the roof of a New York University building to demonstrate how wind power can heat water tanks and illuminate light bulbs.

Barry Lebost astride the Lebost Wind Turbine

You may well ask what all the above, while interesting, has to do with wigs and toupees, and I hasten to respond. This Barry Lebost fellow has recently written a book, which is titled *The Universal Properties of Acceleration (Did Einstein Look the Wrong Way?)*.

In the book, the author presents a cognitive analysis of gravity and how it affects the environment and why it is the principal architect of the universe and why acceleration and gravity can be, and are, misinterpreted. A new theory called ACRET states that the surfaces of the planets are invisibly accelerating toward outer space and demonstrates how Albert Einstein's Principle of Equivalence guides observers "to look the wrong way."

But more on that later. We return now to how and why my old Cleveland-bred wig came out of retirement.

In addition to writing *The Universal Properties of Acceleration*, Barry also wrote an imagined conversation he and Einstein had about gravity and equivalence and arranged to have the conversation between Einstein and himself filmed. Barry would play himself and, having heard the credible German accent I used in *Dead Men Don't Wear Plaid* when playing Field Marshal Wilfred Von Kluck, he wisely offered me the role of Einstein. It was an offer I could not refuse, but I did hesitate when I saw the wig he expected me to wear. From a shop that sold Halloween costumes, he had purchased a wig that looked like a floor mop.

Luckily for Barry, I fell asleep that night guiltily mulling over my indecision. At six thirty, my overactive "muller" awoke me, and I remembered the two white wigs that my fan, the Cleveland toupee-maker had sent me—and wondered if one of them might help me to become Einstein.

I retrieved the wigs from a hall closet and successfully distressed one of them to match old Herr Einstein's natural dishevelment. From the second wig, I snipped off a sideburn and fashioned it into a scraggly mustache.

That afternoon, a crew arrived and managed to transform the corner of my living room into a corner of Professor Einstein's office.

With shelves of handsomely bound books as a backdrop, Barry Lebost and the ghost of Einstein engaged in a spirited and enlightening discussion on gravity. A small sample of it follows:

BARRY LEBOST

"Mr. Einstein, I believe I have found something that you have always been looking for: the proof that gravity and inertia are the same, not approximate, not equivalent, but exactly the same."

ALBERT EINSTEIN

"I always knew that inertia and gravity were exactly the same, but I could not prove the "exactness." True exactness would mean that the surface of the planet is exactly the same as an accelerating spaceship. It was my original concept because the feeling and sensation a person would have while accelerating at the speed of gravity inside a space vehicle would be exactly the same as the feeling a person would have while standing upon the surface of our planet. But logically, this does not appear to work, because it would also mean that the surface of the planets were accelerating upwards into space…just like the floor of the spaceship… the diameter of the Earth would be getting larger faster and faster. I had to give up this idea of exactness and go with my second choice, which I called Equivalence. Equivalence allowed me to stick with inertia, but just a numerical equivalence of it."

BARRY LEBOST

"Dr. Einstein, a hundred years after you devised the principle of equivalence, I found the proof for exactness. Your first choice had been right. You did not have to settle for equivalence to make space-time curved exactness was essentially perfect all along."

The conversation goes on, and Barry makes the point that Einstein's original theories of the universe both expanding and accelerating, which Einstein doubted and amended, were proven to be correct after all.

I am aware that the imagined discourse between Einstein and my nephew-in-law may be of limited interest to many of you. I, however, am utterly fascinated by it—but by no means do I understand it.

I just realized how far afield I have gone, just to give closure to the history of my life as a toupee wearer.

Since writing those last words, I have become privy to a most exciting development in the life of innovator and inventor Barry Lebost. He and his wife, Alice, spent an evening with me and his cousin Annie, my daughter, where we learned of his new invention, a mosquito-trapping device that is designed to reduce generations of mosquitoes in localized areas. In May of 2012, the US Patent Office issued him a patent for this device, which effectively targets gestating mosquitoes that are about to lay their eggs. This very, very inexpensive device made of cotton mesh, in effect, eliminates the potential of millions of mosquitoes to be born (in subsequent generations).

According to figures from 2008, WHO, the World Health Organization, estimated that there were 250 million malaria cases including 855,000 deaths. Africa accounts for 90 percent of the world's cases. Before 2008, WHO guessed that there were 500,000 cases and 1 million deaths.

The product Barry Lebost created, Evarcha, is designed to wipe out these generations of potential disease-carrying mosquitoes in localized areas in the most economical fashion possible—and most importantly, without using poisons, insecticides, or gases.

Barry Lebost is my kind of guy!

CHAPTER TWENTY-EIGHT

Major Maurice Evans
Cannot Play a Butler!

One of my happy experiences in what we in show business call show business was my meeting and working with Steve Martin. At this juncture in Steve's career, he was a tremendously successful stand-up comedian, having toured the country and performed at venues that held as many as forty thousand screaming fans. Steve is a most gifted and civilized human being. I daresay that I've had the good fortune to work with quite a few performers who were almost as gifted and civilized. I consider myself to be one lucky, talented director.

I felt that way when I was hired to direct *The Jerk*. I have been told that discerning critics and moviegoers consider *The Jerk*, written by Steve, Carl Gottlieb, and Michael Elias, to be one of the funniest comedies ever made. I cannot disagree.

During the filming of *The Jerk*, because Steve and I rode to work together and discussed what would be shot that day, one of my favorite gags was conceived and born. Steve came up with an idea that tickled me so that, as soon as we arrived on the set, we rehearsed it and shoehorned it into the schedule.

To remind those of you who saw the film, and inform those who didn't, Steve, playing Navin Johnson, a naive farm boy going out into the big world, is being given an important piece of information by his daddy.

"Son," his daddy says, showing him a can of shoe polish, "this here is Shinola, and that," he says, pointing to a pile of manure, "is shit!"

When challenged, an unsure Navin makes his old man proud when he demonstrates that he can distinguish shit from Shinola.

It occurs to me that some of our younger readers may never have heard the phrase, "You don't know shit from Shinola!" Well, now that you have, please feel free to use it whenever some wrong-thinking people need enlightening—like some right-wingers who argue that our country and its citizens would be better off if we got rid of or privatized Social Security and Medicare.

Back to Maurice Evans and *The Jerk*. In the film, there was a role of an elegant English butler who tends to the needs of a newly rich farm boy who lacks all social graces. Our casting agent excitedly called to say he had the perfect actor to play the butler. I blanched when he told me that the actor was Maurice Evans—the distinguished English stage star who, during the war, was *Major* Maurice Evans, my commanding officer. It was Major Evans who had arranged for me to be transferred from the Signal Corps to his Army Entertainment Unit in Hawaii. How dare I ask this great man to play a lowly butler?

I flashed on a sketch Sid Caesar and I had done on *Your Show of Shows*, where a great Broadway star, played by Sid, drinks himself into oblivion and, after years in the gutter, is given a last chance to return to Broadway in the role of a butler. It is a bit part, and he has but one line: "Dinner is served!" His three failed attempts were: "Dinner is severed!" "Dinner is ser-ver-ved!" "Dinner is Sever-ied!"

Maurice Evans's agent informed me that there were many actors he could recommend, but Mr. Evans requested that he submit him and said he was certain I would want him. I explained to the agent why I was reluctant to offer him a role so beneath his stature. However, upon hearing that Maurice Evans wanted the job to keep his guild membership and his eligibility for the medical benefits our union provided, I acquiesced.

The day Major Maurice Evans arrived on the set, I stopped all work, requested the full attention of the actors, grips, electricians, craft services, and studio personnel, and made them aware of how honored we were that Major Maurice Evans had joined us that day. I informed them that he was my commanding officer during the war, in charge of a company that produced dozens of shows that entertained our troops in the Pacific. I also announced that Major Evans was the first actor in modern times to have produced and starred in a five-hour, uncut version of Shakespeare's *Hamlet*—a performance I had the privilege of seeing on Broadway. It was gratifying to hear the healthy response the major received from the crew.

Great actor that he was, Major Evans was as dedicated essaying the role of Steve Martin's butler as he was performing *Hamlet*.

During the course of the production, Major Evans bade me to call him Maurice, but I could not bring myself to address my former commanding officer as anything but sir or Major Evans—the army had trained me too well.

Some thirty years ago, at his memorial service, I had the opportunity to salute Major Evans one last time.

CHAPTER TWENTY-NINE

Albert Brooks Channeled
Harry Houdini

I purchased and read Albert Brooks's first novel, *2030, The Real Story of What Happens to America* and agree with the critics who lauded it. I, among millions of others, know of Albert Brooks's many extraordinary talents, but thanks to my son, Rob, who was Albert's friend and teenaged schoolmate, I was privileged to be present when he exhibited a talent we had no idea he possessed.

Since then, I have seen Albert Brooks perform on many television shows, including Johnny Carson's. Many years ago, on the week I filled in for Johnny as the show's host, Albert was booked as one of my guests. He arrived that night dressed as a white-faced, Marcel Marceau-type street mime, but instead of doing what mimes do, walking against the wind or attempting to escape from a glass box, this white-faced clown proceeded to behave like a nightclub comic and rattled off a string of mildly funny one-liners. The studio audience did not quite get what he was doing, but the band did. We all laughed hard and long enough for the audience to figure out what Albert was doing and joined the party.

When he was just sixteen, the talent he displayed in our living room and the reaction he provoked was of such a nature that I not only remember it to this day but say without equivocation that in my life, there are but a handful of times that I ever laughed as hard. I say that knowing you are aware I have spent many an hour with the other hilariously funny Brooks—the great Mel.

To set the scene: in our living room full of friends, Robbie announced that his buddy, Albert, was going to demonstrate his art as a Harry Houdini-like escape artist.

Albert then requested that I take my handkerchief and fold it so it formed a triangle and then fold it twice more and use it to tie his wrists together. I did so and placed the folded hanky over his wrists, but before I could start making a knot, Albert said, "That's perfect! Now that my wrists are securely tied, would you stuff a Kleenex into each one of my nostrils!"

With the hanky draped loosely over his wrists, I placed tissues in Albert's nostrils. Immediately his breathing became labored, and through his tightly clenched teeth, he mumbled almost incoherently, "You see I can't breathe, and my wrists are securely tied. I am going behind the drapes and free myself in five seconds."

It sounded like: "Ysee, cnna bre—n m'rits r'scooly ty. 'm gona git hine de drays n freem fsecns."

And with that, Albert ducked behind the drapes, and for a good five minutes, not seconds, he moaned and gasped for air, all the while thrashing about violently behind the drapes. The more he moaned and sounded like a man suffocating, the more Estelle and all of our guests roared. I started to lose it when I heard him begging between the gasps and groans that people not help him. I actually left the room because I was laughing so hard, I feared I would damage myself. I peeked into the room a couple of times, hoping he would free himself and make it safe to return. Finally, he fell to the ground and lay face up, gasping for air— the hanky still lying limply over his wrists while he begged for someone to untie him. I obliged by lifting the hanky from his wrists, and as soon as I did, he rubbed his wrists as if he were trying to get circulation back into them. Still gasping for air, he begged me to remove the tissue from his nostrils, and as soon as I plucked them from his nose, he noisily started sucking air into his lungs and thanking me for saving his life.

It was a night to remember.

I daresay that this momentous event might never have been chronicled, had I not fled to the kitchen to keep from dying of laughter.

CHAPTER THIRTY

D. D. Eisenhower, M. Twain, H. Holbrook, and Me

If you guessed that the D.D. in the title stood for Dwight David, the M. for Mark, the H. for Hal, and the Me for Me, you have guessed correctly.

In an earlier chapter, I mentioned that at various and sundry events, I was often invited to perform as a master of ceremonies, but none of those sundry events could hold a candle to the elaborate dinner party and show I hosted in Washington, DC, to celebrate President Dwight David Eisenhower's seventy-fifth birthday. The party was held in the Grand Ballroom of the White House, and the show featured the Lennon

Sisters, Rudy Cardenas, the world's greatest juggler, and Hal Holbrook, performing his transcendent recreation of Mark Twain.

I was more than a little nervous during dinner and more than very nervous while awaiting my cue to step to the mike and make my opening remarks. The cue would come from Merriman Smith, President Eisenhower's press secretary and one of Washington's most knowledgeable and trusted journalists. It was from Mr. Smith I learned that President Eisenhower's dinner guests were Mexico's head of state, El Presidente Manuel Alvarez Mateos, and El Presidents's wife.

Over the loudspeaker came a well-modulated voice announcing my name and crediting me with being one of the stars of *Your Show of Shows* and the creator of *The Dick Van Dyke Show*.

I opened my turn by launching into a speech where I explained the Soviet Union's view on the current disagreements between our two great nations—which I delivered in Russian double talk.

On *Your Show of Shows*, Sid Caesar's brilliant double-talking in foreign languages was the basis of our movie satires. Audiences enjoyed hearing someone spouting a raft of Russian-, Italian-, or French-sounding gibberish and following it with some mundane English words or phrases.

The guests at the head table were laughing, or at least smiling, while our president was deep in conversation with his Mexican counterpart. At one point, I noticed President Eisenhower beckoning Merriman Smith to join them.

Sometime later, in the Green Room, I learned from the press secretary that President Lopez Mateos had told Eisenhower that he did not understand Russian and asked what I was saying. Our president said that he did not understand Russian either. Merriman Smith then explained that I was a comedian and talking Russian double-talk. Having no idea what double-talk was, El Presidente was totally taken aback. He saw most everybody in the room laughing and assumed that most Americans understood this Russian double-talk. He was duly impressed.

After accepting some appreciative applause, I introduced the lovely and popular Lennon sisters, whom the audience loved, and then Rudy Cardenas, who juggled his way to an ovation.

My introduction of Hal Holbrook was effusive and completely sincere. I ask your indulgence for a paragraph or two, as I explain why I felt so strongly about Mr. Holbrook—and still do.

In 1957, when our son, Robbie, was ten and our daughter, Annie, was eight, their mother and I bought tickets to *Mark Twain Tonight*, a live theater performance starring Hal Holbrook.

It was a magical evening that began the moment we stepped into the lobby of New York's century-old Manhattan Theater. The walls of the quaint playhouse were in desperate need of a fresh coat of paint, and the threadbare carpeting was crying to be replaced. The distinct but not unpleasant mustiness in the air transported me back in time—and that was only the beginning of the time transportation that I experienced that night.

From the time I read *A Connecticut Yankee in King Arthur's Court*, I had been an annoyingly vocal fan of Mark Twain. I was then a young chap of thirty-eight and a cast member of *Your Show of Shows*. A copy of the book was in a bookcase on one of our sets, and I picked it up and read it. As a kid, I had read a modified version of it and had also seen a fairly insipid film adaptation that starred Bing Crosby.

I was amazed to discover what a magnificent work it was. I was completely overwhelmed by Twain's ability to entertain me as he enlightened me about how humans, governments, and societies behaved and evolved since the Middle Ages.

Most of my confreres had read and enjoyed this classic, and my proselytizing for them to read it again made me a giant pain in the ass.

Being gifted with a complete set of Twain's work that sported his autograph on the title page of *Innocents Abroad*—and having been awarded the Mark Twain Prize for Humor in 1960 has quieted me down some.

When the Manhattan Theater's house lights dimmed and Mark Twain walked out onto a cozy living room set, I was rapt. Every actor attempts to inhabit the character he or she portrays, but that evening, Hal Holbrook did not inhabit Mark Twain; he *became* Mark Twain. The longer he was on stage, and the more he spoke, the more I believed that Mark Twain had returned from the beyond just to do one more performance—for us.

Backstage, after our show, Merriman Smith informed us that President Eisenhower was on his way to visit with the cast. I could not wait to call my brother, Charlie. During the war, Charlie had fought in eleven major battles, some under General Eisenhower's direct command.

When the president arrived backstage, the Lennon Sisters, Rudy Cardenas, I, and Hal Holbrook were lined up in that order. A smiling, very appreciative president bent down and shook hands with each Lennon sister as he complimented them. He then told Rudy Cardenas how impressed he was with his juggling, then turned to me, smiled, and said some kind words that I barely heard. I was too busy thinking, *I am shaking hands with our president— Five-Star General Dwight D. Eisenhower—one of the greatest military leaders of all time!*

When the president moved to the end of the receiving line where Hal Holbrook stood, I saw his demeanor change. Our president behaved toward Mark Twain's impersonator as all of us had behaved toward him, deferentially. I saw President Eisenhower actually defer to Mark Twain—such was the power of Hal Holbrook's transformed appearance and transcendental performance.

One thing that gives me a great deal of satisfaction is being able to recommend something to friends that I know would bring them pleasure. Back then, everyone who took my advice and went to see *Mark Twain Tonight* thanked me—some profusely.

When *Mark Twain Tonight* came to Los Angeles, I of course recommended the show to Dick and the members of *The Dick Van Dyke Show*. They all went to see it and did what all perceptive people do, raved about Hal Holbrook and his reincarnation of America's greatest wit.

At Desilu, the studio where we filmed *The Dick Van Dyke Show*, Andy Griffith also shot *The Andy Griffith Show*. I knew that Andy, who was a gifted monologist, would get a big kick of Holbrook's performance and recommended that he see it. Andy said that he would love to but had no time to go to the theater. I insisted that he owed it to himself not to miss this once-in-a-lifetime event.

Andy was adamant, as was I. We actually got into what I knew it would be—a deadlocked argument, so I just handed him fifty dollars and said, "Andy, you can use this money to buy tickets and have a great time, or you can keep the money and feel guilty—your choice!"

To brook any further discussion, I turned and walked away.

If you guessed that Andy used my money to secure tickets to the show and thanked me profusely for forcing him to have "one helluva fine night," you would have guessed right.

If you guessed that he repaid me for the tickets, you'd be two for two.

CHAPTER THIRTY-ONE

Guilt by Association with Myself

Rose and Livia

Tonight, as I walked around the block, I had a most disquieting thought. I may very well not be the wonderful person everyone thinks I am. By *everyone*, I mean the hundreds of thousands of people who have told me so. Perhaps I am being too hard on myself, but to learn the truth—to discover whether or not this self-guilt I felt today was justified—I have decided to put myself on trial. To ensure that I get a fair trial, I will act not only as the defendant in this courtroom case but as my own defense counsel, the prosecuting attorney, and as the presiding judge. I will also assume the roles of eleven members of the impartial jury, leaving one seat for the reader to fill. I trust that after weighing the facts, every intelligent and literate jurist will vote his or her conscience and find for the defense. And so…

"I, Judge Reiner, with three raps on the space bar of my keyboard, bring this open-minded court to order! Prosecutor Reiner, we are ready to hear your opening statement."

"Thank you, Your Honor. Gentlemen and gentlemen of the jury, this will not be a difficult case for you to adjudicate. It involves a grandparent who, by committing an unconscionable act of extreme hedonism, has abdicated his right to be called a loving, caring Grandpa. For the benefit of that quizzical-faced member of the jury, the word 'hedonism' means 'selfishness.'"

"Thank you Mr. Reiner. Now, sir, as the defense counsel, you may proceed with your opening statement."

"Thank you, Judge Reiner. Gentlemen and gentlemen of the jury, my beloved client, Mr. Reiner, is ninety years old. He has already lived two-thirds of his projected life, which means that he has less than thirty short years left to enjoy the pleasures that our wonderful civilization has to offer. I ask you to keep that in mind when you listen to the how the prosecutor wishes our self-effacing client to spend, nay squander, four precious hours of his waning existence."

"Mr. Reiner, the court is ready for you to call your fist witness for the defense."

"Thank you, Your Honor. I call to the stand the esteemed twelve-time Emmy winner, the recipient of the Mark Twain Prize for Humor in 1999 and co-Grammy winner for *The 2000 Year Old Man* recording with his good friend, Mel Brooks, Carl Reiner!"

"Order, order in the court! I warn you, if I have to pound my gavel one more time to silence you, I will clear the courtroom. I have zero tolerance for such outbreaks of cheering and applause—however deserved they were. Proceed, Mr. Reiner."

"Thank you, Your Honor. I could not agree more. Now, Mr. Reiner, would you like to tell the jury in your own words, or words that you and I agreed might be more persuasive, your side of the story?"

"I would like to tell our side of the story. This Saturday, I had planned to join two friends, whose initials are R.C. and S.C.—I don't want to drag innocent, well-intentioned people into my personal messes—but we were going to attend the screening of two films at the Motion Picture Academy, and between the showings, we would dine at a new gourmet restaurant that R.C. and S.C. (Ron and Sheila Clark) had discovered. Your Honor, I love nothing better than good movies and gourmet food, and I was primed to say yes until I checked my calendar and saw that on that same day, I had penciled in an invitation from my son, Lucas, and his wife, Maud, to attend a musicale at their home, where I would see and hear my two darling granddaughters, Livia and Rosie, play the harp and cello, respectively.

"It would have been a difficult dilemma for me, had I not attended an orchestral and a choral concert two nights earlier and saw Livia play the violin and harp beautifully and, last night, at the Broad Studio, I heard Rose singing her heart out as a member of the National Children's Chorus. If truth be told—and that's what I am doing, Your Honor—had there been no flesh and blood involved, watching movies and eating good food would trump harp and cello concerts hands down! And to contradict what my learned counsel has told you earlier, I don't think his projection is correct. I do not have thirty years of life left to spend—more like twenty-five, so I think I had better spend them judiciously and creatively. Here, Your Honor, is what I propose:

"I will see the films at the Academy on the night of the family concert, but the following night or any night of their choice, I will invite Maud, Lucas, and my granddaughters to choose a film they can't wait to see and select food they can't wait to eat.

"Further, if they so desire, I will go with them to view the movie of their choice and accompany them to dine on the food of their choosing—I do so swear!"

"Jury, on the evidence presented, I believe that there are but two verdicts you can render: 'not guilty' or 'not *that* guilty.'"

CHAPTER THIRTY-TWO

Georgetown Revisited or Mining Death for Laughs

I n chapter twenty-five, "Father Walsh: Jesuit/Private Reiner: Non-Jesuit," I gave myself the opportunity of reliving a vivid, sixty-eight-year-old wartime memory. In that piece, I described how by opening my big mouth, I had made myself vulnerable to censure and re-assignment from the comfort of a dormitory at Georgetown University in Washington, DC, to a leaky tent in some muddy battlefield.

Last night—and it was precisely last night—I had the opportunity to recreate a performance from my distant past that I held to be my best ever. Well, I daresay that I not only recreated it, but since I am the only living witness to both events, I think I can say, unequivocally, that I topped it.

The event was held in the auditorium of the Paley Center for the Arts, which, if I drive, is located three minutes from my home, and if I walk, fifteen minutes away. The auspices were GEMA, the Georgetown Entertainment and Media Alliance, who, for whatever reason which I did not choose to question, decided that a symposium that chronicles my days at Georgetown University as a student at their School for Foreign Service was worthy of spending the time, money, and effort to bring to pass.

From all reports—by my daughter, Annie; my manager/nephew-in-law, Georgie; friends Sheila and Ron Clark; nephew Richard Reiner; and my friend, Mel, it was more than worth the effort. I concur.

Before my portion of the event at the Paley Center, the GEMA chairman, Richard L. Battista, and other university dignitaries made some opening remarks and then screened a six-minute clip of some fairly entertaining highlights of my career, which included my days with Sid Caesar, my questioning the 2000 Year Old Man, Mel Brooks, and my wild dancing on legs that moved faster and sillier than any sane dancer would want.

For more than an hour, the distinguished critic and editor of *TV Guide*, Matt Roush and I sat on stage and, respectively and respectfully, asked and answered questions about my days at Georgetown.

I was inspired to write this addendum to the chapter on Georgetown when I realized that I still had the ability to conjure up the voices and the words uttered by my old Jesuit professors and their dean, Father Edmond A. Walsh. This was a situation that I had never before encountered or even contemplated. What was bizarre and ultimately heartening was the reaction I received for my efforts to give voice to those old wartime ghosts. When asked afterward how I remembered those voices and words from the distant past, I said there is nothing that sears itself into one's memory more indelibly than traumatic events—happy traumas provoked by seeing priests almost fall out of a balcony laughing at your antics or frightening traumas that scare the shit out of you!

Even while I was getting laughs back in 1943, I was sure that someone who was not laughing would pluck me out of stately Gaston Hall and drop me behind enemy lines in a European battlefield.

Happily, it turned out that Father Walsh, concerned about the possibility of my further mocking the faculty, had benignly suggested that I produce no more holiday entertainments—and I didn't. That is, until a few days ago, when I again got big laughs by resurrecting Father Walsh's sixty-eight-year-old lecture about "Capturing the Heartland."

Had Dean Edmund A. Walsh known of the pleasure his words engendered from this distinguished assemblage of modern-day Georgetown scholars, I have a feeling he might have been pleased—well, not pleased enough to smile, but perhaps pleased that we are keeping his memory alive.

I, for one, am beholden to Father Walsh and am happy to have had him in my life.

At one point during the Paley Center event, I found myself thinking of my wife and doing what I have been notorious for doing all my performing life: adhering to the premise, "On the mind, on the tongue!"

My mind flashed back to the week my wife passed away, and my tongue related the following story.

The front doorbell rang, and our dear housekeeper, Arlene Brown, signed for a package that was being delivered. Ordering things from catalogues was something Estelle loved doing, and Arlene was aware of that. She sighed and remarked, "Looks like another package for Estelle."

I looked at the label and said, "It's not *for* Estelle, it *is* Estelle!"

Estelle and I had agreed that when the time came, we would be cremated. After she passed away, I called the Neptune Society, whose brochure happened to arrive in the mail that week. When I realized that the Neptune Society would scatter her ashes in the ocean, I had second thoughts about a sea burial and asked for her remains to be delivered to our home. Estelle would get seasick at the thought of getting into a rowboat or catamaran—even in mildly choppy waters. After watching her many bouts of world-class retching, I was not about to condemn her ashes to an eternity of nausea. That cardboard box is now sitting on a stool in her bedroom, next to the microphone and amp she used when rehearsing for her supper-club performances. I covered the box with one of the small, colorful tablecloths she used when entertaining guests in her room.

Here is what I proposed to our children, and they did not object. I told them that when I go, I wished to have my ashes mixed with their mother's, along with some Miracle-Gro plant food and have us interred in our back yard patch of "heirloom" tomatoes.

You will have to take my word for this, but that night, the audience at the Paley Center laughed heartily at what some people might think a sad or even ghoulish story. I asked that they tell no one of our ashes being buried in the back yard, as it could negatively impact the selling price of our house.

Now that I think about it, I may have been wrong to ask them to keep my secret. It may well be that knowing a loving celebrity couple was buried in their back yard might be an incentive for some rich, romantic homeowner.

CHAPTER THIRTY-THREE

My Brush with Five Comedy Icons
(Benny, Jessel, Burns, Green, and Lewis)

ICON #1
Jack Benny

I met Jack Benny for the first time in the commissary at Desilu Studios, where *The Dick Van Dyke Show* was being filmed. Mr. Benny was seated alone at a center table and smiled when I entered. I smiled back, and he beckoned me to come join him. Even though we had never met, I knew he watched and appreciated *Your Show of Shows* and *The Sid Caesar Show*. Sid had once proudly showed us a fan letter he had received from Mr. Benny, saying how much he enjoyed Sid's performances.

I loved Jack Benny, and my folks loved Jack Benny, as all of America did. One of the highlights of our family's Sunday nights was listening to his hilarious radio show that featured his wife, Mary Livingston, his butler-chauffeur, Eddie "Rochester" Anderson, and his announcer, Don Wilson.

As I approached his table, Jack held out his hand, and I shook it. He asked if I had eaten, and if I hadn't, would I like to join him? I was thrilled to be lunching with my idol. I don't remember what we ate, but I will always remember the incident he related to me—one that happened earlier that day. He seemed to be anxious to tell someone about his unexpected adventure. I felt lucky to be in the right luncheonette at the right time.

To fully appreciate what Mr. Benny related, a little background about our star would be in order. It has been said, and so far no one has bothered to disprove it, that the single most prolonged laugh in the history of radio comedy was detonated by Jack Benny in response to a five-word straight line.

To refresh your memory or to give you information you never had, one of the traits of radio's fictional Jack Benny was his miserliness. He was a modern-day Scrooge who never picked up a check but always picked up any coin he saw lying in the gutter.

This was the penny-pinching Jack Benny who, when being held up in an alley and asked by the thief, "Your money or your life!" paused for an interminably long time, causing the impatient thief to shout, "I said, your money or your life!"

To which, Benny shouted back, "I'm thinking! I'm thinking!"

This exchange was followed by many unclocked minutes of prolonged laughter from the studio audience.

Now back to our lunch at Desilu. It seems that Mr. Benny had just flown in to meet with Lucille Ball and Desi Arnaz about their upcoming appearance on his television show. Here now, in almost all of his own words, is the story Jack Benny related to me that day.

"You see, I flew into Burbank Airport, in one of those small planes, and just before we were to land, I told the pilot that I would like to use the toilet. The pilot said we'd be down in two minutes, and if I could 'hold it,' I'd be a lot more comfortable using the restroom in the lounge. He was a nice guy, so I held it while he taxied the plane right up to the terminal.

"I dashed off the plane and made it to the men's room. There were two stalls—pay stalls—it took a dime to open. All I had was a couple of quarters and a nickel. I really had to go, so I got down on my knees and slid under the door. It was a real tight squeeze, but I made it just in time—and I mean just in time! Only problem was that when I was ready to leave, I realized that I couldn't slide out the way I slid in. The booth was tiny—no room for me to lie down flat. The only way out was to climb out, so I stepped on the toilet seat and threw one leg over the top of the door. I was about to swing my other leg over, when three guys walk into the restroom—one guy looks up and sees me climbing out of the booth, he recognizes me, and yells out, "Hey, Mr. Benny—it's only a dime!"

That "one guy," like millions of other Americans, enjoyed seeing stingy, old Jack Benny get caught in a situation that re-affirmed his character's reputation as being the cheapest man alive.

And the real Jack Benny enjoyed telling me that story more than any world-class miser would have enjoyed striking oil.

ICON #2
Georgie Jessel

In 1948, while performing as the leading comedian in a touring company of the Broadway musical revue, *Call Me Mister*, I had the opportunity to meet George Jessel, one of show business's most beloved and talented performers. In his long career, Mr. Jessel had been a headlining comedian on the vaudeville circuit and was the original star of *The Jazz Singer*, which he performed for years on Broadway and on countrywide tours. He was a frequent guest on radio, performing his signature telephone conversation with his mother, which began with his saying, "Hello, Mama, this is Georgie—from the money every month?"

By modern standards, not a very sophisticated line, but Jessel's fans loved the sketch and him.

The third act of George Jessel's life saw him perform as a goodwill ambassador to countries our government felt would appreciate a little witty banter along with our goodwill.

Jessel also became known as the go-to guy when anyone was in need of an effective eulogist. He was capable of bringing a congregation to tears by singing the praises of a dearly departed celebrity, relative, or friend— whether he knew them or not.

I first met Mr. Jessel in his spacious office at Twentieth Century Fox after he had graduated from being an actor-comedian to being the head of production at a major film studio.

The musical *Call Me Mister* had opened the previous night in downtown Los Angeles, at the now-defunct Biltmore Theater, and I had come to Beverly Hills to meet with my new agent, Maurice LaPue. Yes, LaPue was his real name. I had hoped he might find a role for me in some film. I left Mr. LaPue's office in the MCA Building, thinking that they liked me, but not well enough to knock themselves out finding me a job. When I approached the parking attendant's shack and handed the cashier my ticket, LaPue's young assistant tore across the lot, shouting my name. When he reached the shack, he breathlessly told me that the office had just received a call from my wife, Estelle, saying that I should get to a radio immediately, tune in to ABC, and listen to the *Hollywood Reporter's George Fischer Show!*"

I asked the parking attendant if he would please tune his radio to ABC, and he obliged. The words that George Fischer used sixty-four years ago to review my work are lost, but believe me when I tell you that the ones I offer now are less flowery and laudatory than the original. For the record, the four bold, italicized sentences in the midst of George Fischer's review are verbatim. It began:

"Last night, as the guest of George Jessel, I sat in the third row of the Biltmore Theater and watched the musical revue, *Call Me Mister*. On stage, we saw a young man who, Mr. Jessel and I agreed, is destined to become one of Broadway's brightest stars. He is tall, dark, and handsome, he can sing, he can dance, and he is hilariously funny. *His name is Carl Reiner. I'll spell that for you, R-E-I-N-E-R! If you are listening to this program, Mister Reiner, please pick up a phone and call George Jessel's office at Twentieth Century Fox! At this moment, there is a big, fat contract sitting on his desk, waiting for your signature!*"

My agent's assistant convinced the parking attendant that it was okay for me to use their phone.

I followed Mr. Fischer's instructions and dialed George Jessel's number at Fox Studios, and to my utter amazement, I heard the famous nasal voice of one of my childhood heroes saying these words: "Hello, Carl. Look, I don't want to make a big *tsimmis*—but can you come to my office tomorrow at ten?"

"At ten? Yes I can."

"Good!" he said and hung up.

For the uninitiated, *tsimmis* is a Jewish dish made of many mysterious ingredients.

At ten the following morning, I entered the impressively decorated reception room of George Jessel's executive suite at Twentieth Century Fox Studios. Mr. Jessel's secretary pressed the intercom button and informed her boss that I had arrived. She then told me that Mr. Jessel would be right out and to please have a seat.

I sat for a good ten minutes before I saw him and then sat for another ten before he saw me. When he came out of his office, he ignored me, walked directly to his secretary's desk, and asked her to check on his lunch reservation at Chasen's restaurant. He then instructed her to get a larger table, as there would be two additional guests. I had no reason to think that I may be one of the guests, but I did think it. As he walked back his to his office, he passed my chair, and without looking at me, squeezed my arm and said, "See you in a minute, kid!"

I chose to believe that his squeezing my arm and calling me "kid" was a friendly gesture and not a dismissive one.

A few minutes passed. Mr. Jessel entered again, crossed to the receptionist desk, dropped some papers on it, and said, "File these!" As he made his way back to his office, he held one hand above his head as he continued to give her orders. I wondered about why his hand was in the air and quickly found out. He was making certain that we saw him kiss his fingers and then touch them to the mezuzah that was nailed to the doorframe. Since his secretary must be aware of his devotion, I deduced that his kissing the religious scroll was for my benefit.

After kissing the mezuzah, Mr. Jessel bid me enter, so I entered. He greeted me warmly and asked if I would like a quick tour of his personal photo gallery. Without waiting for an answer, Mr. Jessel ushered me to a wall of autographed photographs of every major Hollywood star of the era—then to another wall with signed photos of every United States president that lived during his lifetime and every major senator, congressman, or known military hero. He actually read aloud some of the more personal and complimentary inscriptions. After a tour of the floor-to-ceiling photographs, he invited me to sit in an easy chair facing his desk. He settled into a high-backed swivel chair and picked up an eight-by-ten photo from his desk.

"Would you like to have this?" he asked, handing me a photo of Lana Turner wearing an extremely low-cut dress.

It was a friendly, albeit strange offering, and I did not want to appear unappreciative, so I shrugged and took the photo.

He then snatched it from my hand, grabbed a pen, wrote something on it, and handed it back. On Lana's dress, where her nipples were, he had put two little crosses, and wrote, "Notice the great tits!"

He took back the photo, slipped into a folder, handed it to me, and said, "Enjoy!"

All the while, I had been scanning his desk, which was laden with stacks of scripts and contracts, one of which, hopefully, bore my name and awaited my signature.

Mr. Jessel excused himself at least twice to answer his phone and bark out short answers to long questions. Finally, he was about to give me his full attention, when he received a long-distance call.

"I have to take this," he said, excusing himself. "There seems to be a problem in Paris."

I asked if I should step outside, and he waved me off. "Carl, you should know about these things if you are going to be in the business."

He listened intently while someone was making him privy to some problem. At one point, he put his hand over the mouthpiece and informed me, "I'm talking to fools who can't make decisions!"

After listening a little longer, he said, "If you can't make a decision, I'll make if for you! Shoot both endings!"

He slammed the phone down and started on a long diatribe, excoriating the director and producer of a film being shot in Paris.

"Those assholes can't make a fucking decision on their own. They get good money to make these pictures, and they call me and ask *me* to do what I am paying *them* to do. They've got these two possible endings for this picture, and they can't decide which one to go with…so I had to make the decision for them because they're too stupid to know which is the better one. Schmucks!"

I realized that what I just heard was the head of the studio calling his employers "schmucks" for not knowing which was the better ending for a movie—and Mr. Jessel, having taste and judgment, ordered the director to shoot both endings, then grousing, "I have to make all the decisions!"

I was starting to wonder about the contract I was there to sign.

Where was it? Was it among the papers on his desk? Was it in a drawer? Was it in one of the stack of manila folders in the caddy?

While I was starting to get antsy, Mr. Jessel's phone rang. He snatched it up and said, "Okay, tell me—what are you looking for?"

Mr. Jessel listened intently and then suddenly swung his swivel chair around and looked straight at me. With a triumphant smile on his face, he boasted, "Good you called. You are one lucky director, because I got a guy sitting in my office who is staring at me as we speak. You can stop looking right now. I saw him on stage last night at the Biltmore, and he is sensational. Yes, he's tall, dark, and handsome! This guy can knock the shit out of that part! Hold on, I'll ask him.

"Kiddo," he said, lowering the phone, "how long you going to be in town?"

"For another week," I answered, "then two weeks in San Francisco and I'm free."

With a smile on his face, Mr. Jessel passed the information to his producer, listened for a moment, nodded, and still smiling, said, "Kid, it's not going to work out—he needs someone immediately. Sorry."

With that, Mr. Jessel stood up, shook my hand, reminded me to take my photo of Lana, and then ushered me out of his office and out of his life.

I later learned from one who knew Hollywood well that the only thing that Mr. Jessel had been interested in was the publicity he would receive from George Fischer telling the world how George Jessel, the powerful man who ran Twentieth Century Fox, is also a hands-on discoverer of promising young talent.

ICON #3
George Burns

A year before I had the opportunity to direct George Burns in the film, *Oh, God!*, we had one short but significant exchange. It was at a Hollywood party, where Mel Brooks and I were asked to perform *The 2000 Year Old Man*. At that time, we had no thought of recording it, as it was just something we did at parties to amuse our friends. At one of these soirees, after we had performed and received a goodly amount of laughs, George Burns asked, "Have you boys put this on a record?"

When we said we had not, he puffed on his cigar and said, "Record it or I am going to steal it."

It was excellent advice, and we took it.

I admired many things about George Burns, especially his extraordinary work ethic. When filming *Oh, God!*, besides always being on time, George had memorized his entire role, which allowed us the freedom to adjust our shooting schedule should a problem arise. This is a great gift for any director who works on a tight schedule.

On the last day of shooting, I visited George's trailer to thank him for the extraordinary job he did for us and to have a farewell chat. We had an interesting conversation, and he answered some questions I had been dying to ask.

The following exchange is one that I think all men would be interested in reading...and, on second thought, so may most women.

"George," I began, "can I ask you a personal question?"

"Shoot!"

"You have told me many great stories about your early days in show business, but we never had serious conversations—about other things."

"Like, what other things?"

"Well, I've never heard you talk about your children, George."

"They're nice kids. What else you want to talk about?"

"Well, frankly, George, you always talk about girls, and you're often photographed with a young beauty on each arm…"

"And sometimes on my lap…so?"

"Well, you are eighty now, and I am sixty, and I was just wondering about what nature has in store for me—I mean, as far as being sexually active…"

"You mean, what you have to look forward to?"

"Yes."

"I see…well let me ask you something, Carl," he said, puffing his cigar. "Did you ever try putting an oyster into a slot machine?" He took another puff, winked, and said, "Jot that down!"

It took more than forty years, but as George suggested, I jotted it down.

ICON #4
Jerry Lewis

In 1947, I was an elder statesman of twenty-five when I appeared at Boston's Schubert Theater, playing the leading comedy role in the touring revue, *Call Me Mister!* It was after a matinee, in front of the Shubert Theater where I first encountered Jerry Lewis. In a whirlwind of words, this eager lad of twenty told me how much he enjoyed my performance in the show and how thrilled he would be if I and all the members of my cast accepted an invitation to be his guests for the premiere of his new comedy act at the Latin Quarter. He also dropped the information that he and his partner, Dean Martin, were getting "fifteen hundred a week for the gig."

All of the cast members who accepted Jerry's invitation had no idea that we were privy to be at the birth of one of our nation's all-time great comedy acts. What Jerry and Dean did that night, I could not begin to put into words. You must trust me, and even though Mel Brooks claims that I am given to overpraising movies, performances, and pastrami sandwiches, had Mel been there, he would say that I reported it accurately. The following day, everyone who was at the club the night could not stop talking about how they had died laughing at an act that featured a high-pitched, nasal-voiced, skinny, rubber-bodied comic who was part human and part monkey, who told no jokes or stories that were relatable or quotable.

The only thing we could tell people was, "If you want to bust a gut laughing, catch these two guys at the Latin Quarter!"

In a relatively short time, millions of people worldwide had the opportunity to "catch" Jerry and Dean doing their thing on stage, on television, and in motion pictures. For decades, Jerry Lewis has been deeply involved as a fundraiser and tireless spokesman for the Muscular Dystrophy Association.

More than twenty years flew by after Jerry and I had that first encounter in Boston. Our second meeting came when the two of us had offices at Paramount Pictures. I was getting ready to direct my first film based on an adaptation of my first novel, *Enter Laughing*. Joe Stein had adapted it for Broadway, and he and I adapted it for the screen and had signed on to co-produce the project.

Jerry had read of our film script and called to offer himself as a candidate for the lead, which was that of a seventeen-year-old Bronx delivery boy who aspires to be an actor—a lightly fictionalized version of my young life.

Jerry would have been absolutely perfect for the part, had we made the picture seventeen years earlier when Jerry was seventeen. Joe and I were flattered that Jerry Lewis, a major film star, was interested in doing our low-budget film, and we met with him at his office to thank him for his interest.

At this time, Jerry was about thirty-four years old, and we pointed this out to him. He countered with the fact that he would have no trouble "acting seventeen." We agreed he could act seventeen, but "looking seventeen" was too big a stretch, especially for the audience, who knew him and his history so well.

Alan Arkin played the role on Broadway and won a Tony Award. He also expressed interest in doing the film role, but as he was thirty-two, we remained steadfast about our need to find a younger Jerry Lewis or Alan Arkin for the part.

It was a most pleasant meeting, so pleasant that Jerry was inspired to ask Joe and me and our wives if we would like to join him and his wife, Patty, for dinner at their home that evening. We checked, and both our wives were happy to accept Jerry's invitation. It was about four thirty in the afternoon when we made plans for this eight o'clock dinner. I tell you this because time plays an interesting role in this little pastiche.

At eight o'clock, Joe, Sadie, Estelle, and I were welcomed into the Lewises' beautiful Bel Air home, and after wine and hors d'oeuvres in the den, we retired to their exquisitely decorated dining room and there partook of a delicious dinner and some fine vintage wines. After a choice of desserts and a cup of good coffee, Jerry invited us to accompany him to his screening room. He had a smile on his face that suggested we were in for some sort of treat. What might it be? A rough cut of his new film or a print of his favorite old film…or what? I had no idea and, I daresay, neither would you. Whatever you are guessing, you are wrong!

The first thing Jerry did when we entered the screening room was to assign seats for us. He made a point of asking us to sit on the large, upholstered couch below the projection booth. He escorted Sadie Stein to the left end of the couch, invited Joe to sit next to her, and then ushered Estelle to Joe's left and me at the end next to Estelle.

Jerry started out of the room but stopped after checking his watch. He excused himself and opened a door to a small closet on the right wall of the screening room.

The closet was filled with equipment, which we quickly learned was a satellite transmitter for the FM radio station that Jerry owned and operated—which he proceed to do. He hit some toggle switches, turned some dials, clicked on a standing microphone, and instructed some technician to stand by. He waited a moment, broadcast an announcement of some upcoming event, and then clicked off the mike.

I was aware that he was trying to impress us, and he succeeded. I was impressed that he was capable of doing things that I could not.

Jerry dashed from his radio station to his projection booth, where I imagined he had a projectionist and a feature film ready to roll, and I was half right. The projectionist was Jerry, but he had no feature film to show—just a very special Jerry Lewis short subject.

Suddenly, projected on the screen was a giant-sized Jerry Lewis, wearing what he wore when Joe and I visited him that afternoon. Jerry's image now looked down at the couch where Sadie, Joe, Estelle, and I sat, and he said, "Hi, folks! Patty and I want to welcome you to our home!"

Then, turning his head and eyes to the right, he said, "Welcome, Estelle. So happy you could come!"

He then looked directly at me from the screen and said, "Welcome, Carl. Glad Estelle brought you."

He then turned to where Joe sat and, said, "Hiya, Joe. Hope you enjoyed the free dinner."

Then he looked at Sadie and said, "Sadie! Good you came. My wife, Patty, has a little present for you—and for Estelle."

Patty and an assistant marched into the room, each carrying an elegant set of candlestick holders. Jerry Lewis's image then looked to the right and said, as Patty handed Estelle the candlesticks, "Estelle, accept this little gift from Patty and me—they are not cheap!"

Jerry's image then turned to Sadie, who was receiving her gift from their assistant. "Sadie, sorry candles are not included!" Jerry said, "Hope they fit with your decor!"

He then smiled and said to us all, "Folks, don't be strange! Anytime you're in the neighborhood, drop in!"

How had Jerry done it? It was four thirty in the afternoon when he invited Joe and me to dine with him at eight. In the ensuing four hours, Jerry had quietly commandeered a studio's soundstage, arranged for light and sound crews to shoot him on widescreen film, had that film processed by a lab, and then had it delivered to his home in time for its world premiere!

For the record, I am sorry to say that the Steins and the Reiners did not get the opportunity to "drop in" on the Lewises, but we did appreciate and display the beautiful candlesticks we received from them on that memorable night.

ICON #5
Shecky Greene

Shecky Greene is unique. I think I can say with impunity that, in his day, and his "day" is still current, there was no comedian who has more talent or can be more gut-bustingly funny than Shecky Greene. I do not remember ever laughing as long and hard at any comic as I did when I saw him perform in the lounge at a Las Vegas hotel. For an hour or more, I watched him do a hilarious routine about newspaper critics in general, and about one in particular, a "Ben Asshole," who I assumed he had invented to epitomize the worst of the breed. The more venom Shecky spewed, the more the audience howled. He played the audience like the musical virtuoso he was. At one point during his harangue, Shecky picked up his bass fiddle, strummed it like a guitar, and with a surprisingly legitimate operatic voice, sang a song that skewered his target.

I had never met Shecky, but I went backstage to congratulate him on his performance. He was perspiring and did not seem to be happy to see me. I told him how original I thought his material was and how natural and organic his act seemed. He shook his head and angrily informed me that he was not doing his act. He said that he was too damned mad to do his act because of this "Ben Asshole, the fucking shithead critic" on the local paper who had given him a rotten review for his opening-night performance.

Shecky continued to rant at the "no-talent bastard" and never allowed me to tell him how my sides ached from the laughter he provoked.

At his suggestion, I came back to the lounge the following night and watched him do his regular act, which garnered the same reaction from a convulsed audience as did his extemporaneous diatribe on the hapless newsman.

As of now, Shecky Greene has an open-ended contract with the Las Vegas Sands for fifty-two weeks a year, where he performs two shows a night, seven days a week.

To digress for a moment: A few days ago, I told my beloved manager/ nephew-in-law about the chapter I was writing about Shecky Greene, and a day or so later, George said that he had met Shecky and told him about the chapter I was doing on comedy icons. He said that Shecky was happy to hear that I had placed him in the same category as Jack Benny, Georgie Jessel, and George Burns. I am not so sure he will feel quite as happy when he reads the following story, concerning his behavior as a guest on *The Dick Van Dyke Show*.

It was the third year of the show, and we had invited Shecky to guest as an acerbic, Don Rickles-type of insult comedian. It had been written for Don Rickles, who had agreed to do the part, but a last-minute conflict with his recurring role on *McHale's Navy* left us one player short. Shecky immediately came to my mind as being a perfect replacement. He was happy to get the call, and after two days of rehearsal, it was clear to everyone that he would be terrific. The night before dress rehearsal, and a day before shooting the show in front of a live audience, a distraught Shecky called me at home. His voice was cracking as he told me that when he came home from work that day, he could not get into his house.

"She locked me out," Shecky wept. "My wife changed the locks on all the doors."

It seemed that Shecky and his wife were having marital problems, and she picked this day to tell him she wanted a divorce. He sounded awful and actually moaned when he said that there was no way he could possibly make it to work the following day. He started to apologize profusely, and I told him that his was a real-life crisis, which takes precedence over a theatrical one, which I said we could handle a lot more easily than he can his. I wished him well and went about finding someone to replace Shecky.

At a local theater, attending a performance of *The Billy Barnes Revue*, I became aware of a two talented performers, one a young comic actress, Ann Morgan Guilbert, who later became a regular on *The Dick Van Dyke Show* and the other a versatile comedian named Lenny Weinrib. I contacted Lenny immediately, found him available, and within hours, he was hired to replace Shecky.

Lenny had one day to learn the part, which he did without breaking a sweat. He not only saved the day, but he gave a wonderful performance.

The episode was telecast five weeks after it had been shot, and that night, the first call I received was from Shecky Greene. I was happy to hear from him and started to ask him about his wife and how he was coping, when he stopped me by saying, "Carl, I watched your show last night."

For a brief moment, I thought he was going to comment on how well the show turned out, but before I could ask him what he thought of it, he said, "And that actor you hired to take my place…?"

"Yes, Lenny Weinrib."

"Yeah, Lenny Weinrib— he used my line, you know!"

"Your line?" I asked, not knowing what he meant. "Shecky, he just said the lines in the script that were written for his part."

"Yes and also a line from my act—that I threw in."

"Which line is that, Shecky?"

"Where I told about being introduced at a nightclub and hearing people in the audience say, 'Who? Who did he say?' I wrote that line."

I was taken aback but asked, "How long have you been doing that line?"

"At least a year—or more!"

"Shecky," I said, taking a breath, "in Honolulu Bowl, during the war, about twenty years ago, a young soldier was waiting in the wings to perform his act for five thousand servicemen, and after being introduced, he walked out on stage and said, 'Fellers, I can't tell you what a thrill it is to stand in the wings and hear my name being announced over the loudspeaker, and when I walk out on stage to hear so many of you murmur, *Who? Who's he?*'"

"Was that soldier you?" Shecky asked.

"Yes, Shecky."

To Shecky's credit, he shot back, "Can I use your line?"

And I told him that I bequeath it to him in perpetuity.

I will never understand how a great comic mind who can invent whole routines on the spot would ever be concerned about someone appropriating one of his minor jokes. I started this piece by saying that "Shecky is unique"—and I don't think I misspoke.

CHAPTER THIRTY-FOUR

Jolson Hugs Jessel as Jessel Mugs Jolson

As I thought about the chapter I had written about Georgie Jessel, I was struck by the fact that I had another encounter with him, and it took place twenty years after he had presented me with a photo of Lana Turner and ushered me out of his office. Our second meeting was a short one, and it occurred on a night when I was hosting an annual awards dinner. I am a bit hazy about which guild it was, but I think it was the Writers Guild. I clearly remember, though, that Georgie Jessel performed his famous act as Professor Labamacher and had the audience rocking with laughter. I also recall Al Jolson being in

185

that audience, and after much urging, agreeing to come on stage and congratulate his old vaudeville buddy, Georgie.

I will return to their dramatic meeting after I review for you a short history of the landmark film, *The Jazz Singer,* which was heralded as the first "all talking picture." The movie was based on a long-running Broadway play written by Samson Raphaelson, and it starred George Jessel. After Broadway, Jessel continued to perform the role on a nationwide tour. Georgie Jessel and *The Jazz Singer* were synonymous, and when Warner Brothers secured the rights to the film, it was a foregone conclusion that Jessel would be its star. The Warner Brothers were not all that certain that a filmed version of a stage musical would be successful, but they were sure that the newly designed cameras and the recording equipment would make it a very expensive production. They therefore offered Jessel a much lower salary than he was expecting, and he turned it down. He assumed that the Brothers Warner and his agent would negotiate and they would reach a reasonable compromise. Jessel knew that if he held firm, there were only two other performers in the industry who could possibly do the role, Eddie Cantor and Al Jolson, and he also knew that neither of them would ever dream of co-opting his role. And Jessel was proven right. He learned from Eddie Cantor that the Warner Brothers had offered him the role, and Eddie, true to form, thanked them for the offer and said that there was only one person who should play the part in the film, and that was Georgie Jessel.

George assumed that Jolson would be approached and he would react as Eddie did, and George was half right. The Warner Brothers did offer Jolson the role, but Jolson turned down neither the role nor the salary.

Everyone who had ever seen Jolson perform or had dealt with him personally was in agreement about two things: firstly, he was, hands down, the world's greatest entertainer, and secondly, the world's most hated, egotistical son of a bitch in all of show business.

Soon after Jessel learned of Jolson usurping his role as the Jazz Singer, George told Al that he would never forgive him for what he did and would never speak to him again for as long as he lived.

During the production of *Oh, God!,* I spoke with George Burns about Jolson, and he agreed that Al's reputations as a great entertainer and as a bona fide rat-bastard were accurate. George had witnessed Jolson mercilessly berate fellow actors, stagehands, and underlings.

George Burns also related to me how, when he and his wife, Gracie Allen, were on the vaudeville circuit and happened to be playing in the same town as Jolson, they actually canceled a matinee performance so they might catch the great showman's act—and he said they were not disappointed.

Jolson's signature gimmick was stepping through the curtain after doing a blockbuster show and shouting at the audience, "Where are y'all goin'? Sit down, folks, sit down! Ya ain't heard nothin' yet!"

In 1942, during the war, Jolson—who was then in his sixties—appeared in the Broadway musical *Hold On to Your Hats.* My brother, Charlie, who was on an army furlough, secured tickets for us. I will never forget the show and the standing ovation Jolson got at the curtain call and how, after the curtain was lowered for the last time, he re-emerged from the wings, dragging an easy chair to center stage. He banged on the metal-covered footlights with a cane and ordered the orchestra leader not let his musicians leave.

"These nice people," he shouted, "want to hear Jolie sing a few more songs! Am I right, folks?"

The audience responded excitedly and Jolson launched into a medley of his all-time classic hits, among them, "Swanee," "Toot Toot Tootsie," and "Blue Skies."

That night, he did something that was totally unexpected—at least by me. Before singing his signature songs, he decided he wanted to tell a story, and the following is what he shared with us.

"Folks," he started, "before Jolie sings for you, I just gotta tell you something that happened to me a few weeks ago. I was sitting in my dressing room, putting on my makeup, when a li'l cockroach comes out from behind the mirror, walks up the wall and across the ceiling. Poor fella seemed to be struggling, and when he got right above me, he fell and landed on my makeup table. That little guy is laying on his back and trying to move his legs—he wants to roll over—but he can't, and I saw why. When he hit my metal table, he broke one of his legs—he's got six, you know—I felt sorry for the li'l feller. I could see he needed help, and I knew just what to do. When I was a Boy Scout, I learned that if someone broke a leg, you put it in a splint. And folks, that's just what I did. I straightened out that cockroach's skinny, little leg, and with a piece of straw that I got from a broom, I made a splint, and then with some white thread I got from the wardrobe lady, I tied his broken leg to that splint. He let me do it because I told him, "I am not here to squash you, li'l guy—I'm here to help you."

For the next few days, I dripped milk into his tiny mouth with an eyedropper and hand-fed him teeny pieces of a soda cracker I soaked in water. Every day, he got a little bit stronger, and last night he started to move that leg—and with the splint still on it. Well, just before tonight's performance, I removed his splint, and whaddya know, that little scoundrel took his first steps in over a week."

Jolson then took a breath and announced, with pride, "Folks, I wanna tell you that today, that li'l cockroach is as good as any one of you."

There was at least a five-second delay before everyone in the theater, including my brother and me, burst out laughing. We had all heard shaggy-dog jokes before, but this was the first and possibly the only shaggy-cockroach joke ever told.

Now, back to that Writers Guild Awards dinner where I was standing at the podium and about to invite Jolson to come up on stage to join me and Jessel. The audience members were well aware of the animosity that George Jessel bore Al Jolson and reacted loudly and positively when a smiling Jolson climbed the steps to the stage, ran to Jessel, and bear-hugged him. It was quite an emotional moment, and there was not a dry eye in the house.

I later learned that there were two dry eyes in the house, and both belonged to Georgie Jessel.

Backstage after the show, I told Jessel that it was great to see the two of them hugging and hearing Jolson say, "Thank you, Georgie, thank you!"

I asked Jessel what Jolson was thanking him for, and Jessel said, "Well, I whispered in his ear that to me he was still a rotten bastard and that if I live to be a hundred, I will never forgive him for what he did—and to go fuck himself! I guess he was thanking me for those kind words!"

It is a distinct tribute to Al Jolson that, knowing what a "rotten bastard" he was in life did not diminish my appreciation of the magnificent film biography, *The Jolson Story*, that starred Larry Parks lip-synching to Jolie's incomparable voice.

CHAPTER THIRTY-FIVE

Four Fond Memories of My Funny, Foul-Mouthed Friend, David Burns

D avid Burns and I first crossed paths in the 1950s, when we were cast members of two shows that were bound for Broadway. One was *Alive and Kicking*, an undistinguished musical that came and went from the Great White Way in twelve weeks, and the other, *Pretty Penny*, which never went anywhere, save for tryouts at summer theaters at Bucks County, New York, and at Westport, Connecticut.

David Burns, or *Davey*, as he was called, was a well-known character actor. Among his many major roles on Broadway was that of the peddler in a production of *Oklahoma!* and the lead in Arthur Miller's *The Price*. His last role was in *Seventy Girls Seventy*, where he passed away on stage in the middle of the second act.

Through the years, I have enlivened many a dinner party by recounting some of the outlandish things that the irrepressible Davey sprung on unsuspecting "pigeons."

Davey was a stockily built, balding man in his late forties, who had a puckish face that smiled easily and two devilish eyes that twinkled brightly. His voice was strong, and when he was of a mind to make a point, he would bellow. The world was Davey's stage, and he used it in an inimitably warped way.

First Fond Memory

During the out-of-town tryout of the short-lived musical *Alive and Kicking*, Davey and I found ourselves in Boston and staying at the Bradford Hotel. One of the stars of the show was Lenore Lonergan, a lovely and accomplished young actress. She had been invited to stay at Sarah Siddons Hall, an old, ultra-conservative theatrical boarding house, run by mature women who felt a need to protect and chaperone young, single actresses like Lenore. The only men ever allowed to set foot into the Sarah Siddons conclave were those who had been invited by a member to attend a charity function or a quiet lunch.

On a day there was no matinee performance scheduled, Lenore invited Davey and me to join her for that quiet lunch. Lenore, Davey, and I were seated at a cozy corner table in the impressive turn-of-the-century dining hall. Prominently displayed on the wall opposite us was a life-sized portrait of the founder, Sarah Siddons. Most all of the diners were residents and were quite old. It felt as if the diners had been hired by Central Casting to keep the room looking authentically antique. The room was exceedingly quiet, and so as not to disturb the ambiance, Lenore, Davey, and I spoke little, and when we did speak, we spoke softly.

After eating our first two courses, which consisted of a small cup of clear consommé and a lightly dressed Bibb-lettuce salad, Davey leaned over and whispered something to Lenore just loudly enough for me to hear. What we both heard made Lenore grimace and me suppress a smile. It happened sixty years ago, but I will never forget his words: "Lenore," Davey growled quietly, "do you know what I would like to do, right this minute?"

"No, what?" she asked naively.

"I would like to go up to your room," Davey suggested through clenched teeth, "rip off all our clothes, and have you sit on my face—for half an hour!"

Lenore, who knew Davey well, just shook her head and whispered, "Davey, you are disgusting!"

"I'm disgusting? Davey, bellowed, slamming his fist on the table. "I'm disgusting? You are sitting on my face and you call *me* disgusting?!"

With that, Davey stood up, threw his napkin into Lenore's lap, and stormed out of the dining hall. The ensuing silence was deafening. No one dared move—except me, who high-tailed it out.

In the history of mouth-dropping, stunned silences, the one Davey Burns provoked that afternoon has to be ranked in the top ten.

I concluded that the staid women of Sarah Siddons Hall remained silent for so long because they could not process the thought of a woman sitting on a man's face for one second, let alone, half an hour.

Second Fond Memory

It was at the opening-night performance of the short-lived musical *Pretty Penny* when Davey managed to sabotage an actress's performance by saying something to her a moment before she went on stage. The actress was, in truth, a chorus member who was given a small speaking part by the producer, with whom she was having an affair. Davey was miffed that "the Bimbo," as Davey dubbed her, had stolen the part from another chorus member, a truly talented actress who had been promised the part. The meager lines entailed the actress announcing the entrances of the three military officers who were in the upcoming sketch. Two of the officers, Major General Claude Truxton and Admiral Frank Halsey were being played by Davey and me.

Opening night, seconds before "the Bimbo" was to walk on stage and deliver her first line, Davey, with a theatrical injustice gnawing at him, angrily told "the Bimbo": "Honey, I know you are fucking our producer. Well, I must warn you, he's married to my sister, who has threatened to shoot you! And she's sitting in the first row—with a gun!"

Outlandish as it was, Davey's remarks did exactly what he had intended them to do—unnerve and fluster! "Miss Bimbo" stepped unsteadily onto the stage, and instead of announcing "Lieutenant General Phillip Truxton!" she stammered, "Uh, Lt-t-t-tenant General—Trrrillip P-P-Phuckston," and went on to butcher the names of the other two officers.

Thanks to Davey's sense of fairness and innovative intervention, the talented young actress was given back her part and the extra pay that went with it.

Third Fond Memory

Davey did not like surprises, and he abhorred fumbling a line during a performance. He was very hard on himself and on others if he thought they had fed him a wrong cue.

At the Bucks County Playhouse, during a technical rehearsal of *Alive and Kicking*, a musical bound for Broadway, an incident occurred that illustrates just how deeply Davey felt about his art.

A tech rehearsal is one in which the actors go through the play without wearing their wardrobe or emoting fully. It is done primarily to check for technical problems and the setting and handling of props the actors will use for each scene. There is nothing worse than reaching into your pocket for a gun that isn't there and having to shoot a protagonist with your extended forefinger—which actually has happened more than once. In summer theater, as a youth, I actually heard an actor shout "Bang!" and the villain fall to the floor after being shot by a barehanded hero.

As payment to the dozen or so merchants and townsfolk who lend their furniture and rugs to the production, they are invited to watch the tech rehearsal. During this rehearsal, the actors will deliver all their lines and walk through the staging without expending the energy they would for a regular performance. It was at this rehearsal that I saw a side of Davey Burns that I did not know existed. During our time together, I had seen and heard Davey behave as if he were angry at the world and scream, rant, and curse at all the phony idiot producers, politicians, and directors who did not know that they were idiots. The more he ranted, the more beloved his friends found him. Who would not love a madman who made you laugh?

Davey's unraveling started a few minutes after the curtain rose on the scene in which Davey and I played military officers. For some reason, no one had told Davey that an audience would be present. This alone might not have unnerved him, had he not been unshaven and wearing a faded, short-sleeved sports shirt. His temperature and hackles rose considerably when he stuttered delivering his first line. I could see the vein sticking out on his forehead and hoped he would recover his equilibrium after the next exchange. In the scene, I was smoking a cigar, and I asked General Truxton if he would pass the ashtray. Davey said, "Certainly," picked up the glass ashtray, and with all of his might, smashed it on the conference table. It broke into dozens of slivers and shards, and the miracle was that no blood was let from Davey's hand or my face. The audience gasped, and Davey stood up and bolted from the stage.

The stage manager came on and announced that the performance was canceled. I followed an irate Davey to our shared dressing room and tried to calm him—in vain. He yelled at me and asked me if I knew that there would be an audience out there, and I said I did, which made him angrier at me for not telling him. It was at this moment, when Davey was at his angriest and in an invective-tossing mode, that our director, George S. Kaufman, appeared at the door to our dressing room—accompanied by his elegant wife, Leueen MacGrath.

To refresh your memory or add to your theater knowledge, George S. Kaufman and his partner, Moss Hart, were responsible for some of the wittiest and most successful Broadway shows of the thirties and forties. Mr. Kaufman lent his considerable wit to many early TV game shows and was one of the famous celebrities who traded witticisms while seated at the legendary Algonquin Round Table.

When George S. Kaufman arrived at our dressing room, he was aware that his star actor was having a serious meltdown, so with honest concern, he asked, "Are you all right, David?"

David stood up, shook his head like an enraged bull, and delivered a scatological tirade at one of Broadway's most-respected icons who, at that moment, was an ashen-faced target for vitriol. Davey let loose a machine-gun barrage of "F" and "C" words, of both genders and leveled a goodly amount of them at a gasping Mrs. Kaufman, who cowered at the door. When Mr. Kaufman grabbed his wife's arm and fled from the dressing room, Davey followed them down the hall and continued his filthy-mouthed F- and C-word barrage—adding a slew of "mother-effers, bitch bastards, shit bags, and assholes," until the great theater legend and his wife fled the building.

I had never witnessed such out-of-control behavior from any human being. No doubt, David Burns was a tortured soul and a remorseful one, for as soon as he returned to the dressing room, he plopped down at the makeup table and mumbled, "What did I do? What did I do?!"

That night, he did what we both came to Bucks County Playhouse to do—put on a show. Davey performed well that night, and the audience would never have guessed that, just a few hours earlier, one of the lead actors had completely lost his mind.

Usually, during out-of-town tryouts, the director will come backstage after a show and offer notes to the actors, but following Davey's blow-up, we received no notes and no visits from Mr. Kaufman. I did, however, get a visit from a representative of Actors' Equity. It seems that Mr. Kaufman had contacted our union, leveled charges against Davey, and they had come to investigate. I was cited by Mr. Kaufman to be an eyewitness to the event.

I was asked to read a transcript of the words Mr. Kaufman claimed David had used to insult him and his wife, and asked if I could verify that "Mr. Burns had, indeed, used that offensive language."

Of course, there was no chance that I would ever rat on a pal, and as I read the almost verbatim list of foul words Davey had uttered, I immediately thought of how I might respond without perjuring myself and without incriminating my pal.

With as much incredulity in my voice as I could muster, I said, "I am shocked! David Burns? Are you serious? Do you, in your wildest dreams, think that David Burns, who played Mr. Vandergelder in *The Music Man* and won a Tony Award for it would ever use this kind of vile language in a theater? This is a joke, isn't it?"

David Burns was known as a character, and everyone in the union knew of Davey's predilection to rant and rave for comic effect. It was clear that the union rep was relieved that he would not have to censure one of the most beloved characters in our business. Davey received what amounted to a slap on the wrist and a warning not to curse out any more directors.

Fourth Fond Memory

Davey and I were in Manhattan, walking along Broadway and approaching the southwest corner of Forty-Eighth Street, when we had our contentious discussion about religion and the existence of the Almighty.

Davey had asked me outright if I believed in God, and I told him that I did not—that I was an atheist.

"An atheist," he smirked. "Well, I can go you one better. I am worse than an atheist; I am an agnostic!"

"Davey," I countered, "there is no worse or better—if you are going to use 'better or worse' as a yardstick, you should know that an atheist does not believe a God exists, and an agnostic is not sure whether or not there is a God."

"Right!" Davey agreed. "I am saying that I don't know whether or not God exists, but as an agnostic, I hope that he does exist."

With that, he raised his arms skyward, and on that busy corner, he shouted to the heavens, "God I hope you *do* exist—and fuck you, God!"

David later explained that he was pissed off at God for, among other things, allowing Hitler to kill 6 million Jews and as many non-Jews.

Davey was many things, but what really defined him was his love and devotion to his wife, Toddy. For twenty-five years, he had been happily married to Toddy, a lovely, charming woman with whom he lived on the small Connecticut farm they lovingly tended. Mrs. Burns, a Christian Scientist, had heard stories from some not-so-well-meaning friends about her husband's sometimes outlandish behavior—the likes of which she had never witnessed. When asked by one of these "friends" how she could possibly "live with a man like that," Toddy responded, "If my husband were not the dearest, sweetest, most thoughtful man I have ever known, I would leave him in a minute!"

CHAPTER THIRTY-SIX
The Pony and the Pool Table

W ith your indulgence, I would like to return to the year 1960, when our family first moved from New Rochelle to Beverly Hills. Earlier, when describing some of the noteworthy events that took place, such as our dog's attempt to de-feather a pigeon, I had neglected to chronicle the most noteworthy event of all.

That event, a truly blessed one, triggered an emotional response so powerful that it provoked Robbie, Annie, Estelle, and me to laugh so hard and long that we risked blacking out.

Robbie and Annie who, at the time, were respectively thirteen and eleven, were not at all happy that we had uprooted them from their home in the East, where they had many friends, and transplanted them to a house in the West, where they had no friends.

They calmed down when they discovered that one or two of the "geeky kids" they met at school had the potential of becoming a best friend.

In the course of shooting the film *Gazebo*, I became friendly with Martin Landau, who played a role in the film. I perceived him to be a fine actor, but I was not so perceptive as to foresee that later in his career, he would win an Academy Award for his portrayal of Bela Lugosi in the film biography of schlock director Ed Wood.

Marty and his lovely wife, Barbara Bain, a gifted young actress, became our good friends, and one afternoon, at our house on North Alta Drive, Barbara excitedly informed us that she had just learned that she was pregnant. After much happy hugging and well-wishing, Barbara looked at Estelle and stated flatly, "Estelle, I think you're pregnant too."

Estelle, who I remember looking particularly attractive and svelte that day in her short, black dress and high heels, and sporting the shape and weight she had before giving birth eleven years earlier, laughed, and with happy resignation said, "Barbara, I am afraid those days are over for me."

At that time, Barbara did not know Estelle's age. Most women do not go around telling people how old they are, and Estelle was even less eager to do so, since she had not told our children the truth. When asked, she would say she was a year older than I. She did not relish their blabbing to the world that their mother was almost eight years older than their father. When Barbara made her witch-like prediction, Estelle was forty-five, and neither she nor I was concerned about the possibility of becoming parents again. After twenty-five years, we were finally enjoying a carefree and contraceptive-free love life.

What we did not know, but what Barbara intuited, was that somehow, even though Estelle's periods had intermittently stopped and started some months ago, one healthy egg managed to get itself fertilized. Three months later, we were both surprised and happy to discover that the weight that Estelle had started to gain was not due to the long lunches and large dinners we were eating but because she was growing a baby inside of her.

After her gynecologist suggested we think seriously about bringing the baby to term, pointing out that because of our ages, we might not both be around to see our child go through high school, we opted to take our chances.

Before Estelle started to show, we decided to let our thirteen-year-old son and our eleven-year-old daughter know that they were going to have a new sibling in their lives. We chose to tell them the news one Saturday morning while we were all seated at the breakfast table. Robbie and Annie always liked games, so we thought it would be fun to play twenty questions and see how many it would take for them to guess our little secret. We started by saying, "Mom and I have a surprise for you two."

"Is it something I will like?" Robbie asked.

"I think so," we answered.

"Is it something I will like?" Annie asked.

"Yes, you will."

"Is it something either of us has asked for?" Robbie asked.

"Yes."

This was not a lie. Each, at one time, had asked if we would ever consider having another child. When Robbie was two, he had asked if we would "make an older brother" for him. And Annie, when fed up with Robbie's teasing, asked us to make "a little sister to play with."

To properly appreciate the twenty questions they asked, you should know that, at this time in their lives, Annie was obsessed with the possibility of owning a pony, and Robbie yearned to have a full-sized pool table in our home.

"Is it something that we can keep inside the house?" Robbie asked.

"Yes."

"Can I also keep it outside or in a shed?" Annie asked.

"You might."

"Will my friends like that we have it?" Rob asked.

"I think so."

"Do any of my friends have one?" Annie asked.

"Yes!" (One of Annie's friends owned a pony.)

"Do one of *my* friends have one?" Robbie asked excitedly.

"I am not sure, but I think so."

At this, they both jumped out of their seats.

"A pony, a pony!" Annie yelled.

"No, a pool table, a pool table! Robbie shouted.

"No, a pony, a pony!" Annie insisted.

The two then kept jumping up and down and shouting over and over what they hoped the surprise would be.

Estelle and I were aware that our "surprise" was going to be a big disappointment, but we had to tell them.

"Kids, the surprise is that you two are going to have a new brother or sister. Your mom is going to have a baby."

We never expected that our children would react as they did. On hearing the news, their blue eyes popped, their jaws dropped, and they started to laugh so hard that they slid off their chairs and onto the floor. They attempted to say something, but their uncontrollable laughter blurred their words. Finally, Annie managed to splutter, *"A p-p-pony! M-Mom's going to have a poneeeeee!"*

"No, a p-pool table!" Rob gurgled. *"M-Mom's going to have a pool table!"*

And with tears streaming down their faces, they lay on the floor writhing and repeating through giggles and guffaws what Momma was going to give birth to.

Six months later, at the UCLA Hospital, Estelle delivered neither a pool table nor a pony but a six-pound, eleven-ounce baby boy, who we named Lucas Joseph.

I shall never forget that day and the heart-stopping remark that Estelle and I heard the obstetrician make as he examined our newborn for the first time. He said, "This boy will never walk."

Fortunately, the doctor noticed how his remark sobered the infant's exultant parents, and he quickly added, "I meant that he'll never walk, because he'll always be running! This guy's an athlete! Look at him kick those little legs!"

As you will see, that doctor proved to be prophetic.

At the same hospital, three days earlier, Barbara Bain Landau gave birth to Susie, a beautiful baby girl.

Martin Landau and I had the experience of standing together outside the hospital nursery window and staring proudly at the newest addition to our families. Lying side by side in two plastic containers were one-day-old Lucas and four-day-old Susie.

Seven and a half months after their first meeting, the two diaper-clad pals were crawling about on the carpeted living-room floor of our house on North Alta Drive. Marty, Barbara, Estelle, and I stood by and watched as the tots crawled from the center of our sunken living room toward the two steps that led up to the foyer. Just as they reached the steps, something unexpected took place—Lucas stood up! All of us saw him standing up, and all were properly amazed. He just stood there and behaved as if it were natural for him to be upright. Susie, who was sitting just below him, reached up, grabbed a handful of his diaper, and pulled him down to where he belonged, sitting on the floor with her. Undaunted, Lucas stood up again and took two unsteady steps before Susie pulled him back down. Neither tot seemed to be upset. They were just playing a new game they had invented: "I stand up, walk a step, and you pull me down!"

They played the game until Lucas walked too far away for Susie to grab him.

In thinking about Lucas being an early walker, I realized that another in our family was an early climber. Annie, Lucas's big sister, besides walking when she was but nine months, climbed to unexpected heights when she was less than a year.

In our Bronx apartment, when Annie was eleven months old, my wife and I, who were having breakfast, heard her calling us from our bedroom. When we went to check on her, we found her standing atop a dresser. She held out her arms to us and said, "Mommy, down!"

By pulling open each of the dresser's five drawers, Annie had jury-rigged a stairway and crawled to the top but had not found a way to crawl down.

Happily, all of our three children inherited the coordination genes from their mother and their athletic uncles, Eddie and Sidney Lebost.

As for Lucas and Susie, Lucas is happily married to Maud Winchester for twenty-two years, and they have produced two lovely daughters, sixteen-year-old Livia and eleven-year-old Rose. Susie married Roy Finch thirteen years ago, and the Finch-Landau duo created Aria, a darling three-year-old daughter.

I am also happy to add that the friendship Lucas and Susie began a half century ago, in the UCLA nursery, is still intact.

Estelle with our newborn Lucas Reiner… "Neither a pony nor a pool table"

Being interviewed in Vevey, Switzerland speaking Phony Phrench...

CHAPTER THIRTY-SEVEN

Speaking Phony Phrench phor
Charlie Chaplin's Son

I n chapter eleven, "Nose to Nose, Eye to Eye," I described how I taught the legendary Mel Brooks to speak Phony Phrench, and this morning I awoke with the memory of why, when, where, and how I first learned to speak with my phony French accent and how I came to use it when addressing a huge crowd gathered in a town square in Vevey, Switzerland.

Here now is that "why, when, where, and how" it all came to pass.

One summer, when my wife and I were vacationing at our "petite" home in the South of France, we received an unexpected invitation from Christopher Chaplin, the son of the most admired comedy actor in the history of film. Christopher was inviting us to be his guest at their home in Vevey and requesting that I emcee the town's annual charity event. Naturally, I accepted!

Estelle and I were welcomed into Christopher Chaplin's home and stayed with him and his family for the weekend. His family consisted of his wife, their two children, and his mother, Oona O'Neill Chaplin. It was heartening to see what a normal household it was and how much the Chaplin children behaved like regular kids.

To promote the outdoor rally, I was invited to make an appearance on Vevey's local television station, which I was happy to do.

Upon arriving at the studio, I learned that the host would be speaking French, but he would be happy to do my portion of the program in English. I told the producer that I would prefer they conduct the interview in French.

At last, I thought, *a chance to use the skill the army sent me to Georgetown to learn. I would get a chance to show off my excellent French pronunciation of words like "fauteuil et ecureuil,"* (armchair and squirrel), *and get to toss in clever adages like, "Ca vas sans dire."* (That goes without saying) and *"Chacun a son gout"* (Each to his own taste), or a mundane *J'ai besoin d'une lime a ongle.* (I need a nail file.)

At the studio, a young, French-speaking anchorman introduced me to his television audience by listing my credits. He spoke French too rapidly for me to understand everything he was saying. After struggling to figure out the first questions he put to me, I admitted that he spoke too rapidly for me and suggested that if someone translated his questions into English, I would answer in French.

It worked, but after a few successful exchanges, the simple questions the anchorman asked that begat simple answers were replaced with complex questions about issues that required me to use words I could not translate into French—not without using a dictionary.

One such question was, *"Monsieur Reiner, quelle est votre avis de La Nouvelle Vague?"* (What is your opinion of the New Wave?)

"La Nouvelle Vague," I repeated, *"je crois que 'La Nouvelle Vague' est une developpmente tres interessante—"*

After saying, "I think that the New Wave is a very interesting development," I found myself struggling to find the French words to say something bullshittingly clever, like: **"All new waves in all art forms are noteworthy inasmuch as they tend to reflect the mores of the society they are currently inhabiting."**

Starting with a few French words, *"Toutes Nouvelle blagues dans tous les artes sont,"* I translated "noteworthy" into my Phony French, "nuutwerthie," and continued with, "een soo mooch, zat zey reeeflecttuh, de sociyeeeetyuh zay arre cureenentillee eenhabbiteen."

The interviewer and his staff members found my speaking English with this phony French accent to be amusing, and their good-natured laughter encouraged me to use it again when I addressed the throng of citizens in Vevey's town square.

I explained, in French, that I intended to host the whole event speaking both French and a new language I had recently mastered, Phony Phrench.

"My new language," I continued, "consists of English spoken with an exaggeratedly phony French accent. I will now translate the last sentence I spoke into phony French.

"The words 'My new language' becomes 'Myyyah nuuha lengwaaajuuh'—and the phrase 'consists of English words' becomes 'cohnseests uf Ingehleeesh wuurrhdsa'—and 'spoken with an exaggeratedly phony French accent' becomes 'spohkeeenn wiz eksahjurraytedillee fohnnnee Frehnchuh ecksssenteh.'"

I remember little of what I said at Vevey Square, but I do recall getting lots of laughs and receiving Christopher Chaplin's heartfelt gratitude for helping to raise funds for his charity.

I just had a fleeting thought about contacting someone at *Webster's Dictionary* and offering them the opportunity to publish "The Phirst Phony Phrench Phully Abridged Dictionary."

As I say, it was a fleeting thought—and one of the fleetingest I've ever had.

I do, however, have a permanent memory of the Chaplins' lovely but unusual garden. I still have the photo I took of Estelle standing between a bronze statue of Chaplin as the Tramp, and a twenty-foot-high, shiny silver fork that some witty sculptor had stuck into their lawn.

With Sid Ceasar

CHAPTER THIRTY-EIGHT

Tony Webster Pays His Debt
with "God Almighty"

I met Tony Webster when Max Leibman, the producer of the television series *Your Show of Shows* added him to the staff of brilliant writers who wrote sketches for likes of Sid Caesar, Imogene Coca, Howard Morris, and me. What set Tony apart from our group of New Yorkers was that he was born in the Midwest and was the sole Christian in the room. He rarely smiled, but his quietly delivered acerbic comments would get lots of smiles from us and a goodly share of laughs.

I recall one sketch the writers were working on that was one of the strongest of the season. In it, Sid and I played brothers who were born in Hell's Kitchen and grew up in poverty. Sid became a mob boss, and I, whose bills he paid to send though law school, became a crusading district attorney. He was proud of me and particularly of my achievement as "a good speller," often requesting that I spell the word "magnanimous" for him. In the last scene, Sid, the mobster, was gunned down on the steps of the courthouse, in front of his wife. The mobster's dying request, as he lay bleeding, was that I spell "magnanimous" for him one last time. After tearfully choking out the letters, M-A-G-N-A-N-I-M-O-U-S, the sketch needed a funny final line for the wife, Imogene Coca, to say.

The writers had spent most of the afternoon trying to come up with that elusive tag line. Dozens of funny attempts flew back and forth, but none was deemed worthy. It was Tony Webster who came up with those final words—the ones, all agreed, Coca should say.

After hearing me spell "magnanimous," the mobster dies, and his distraught wife, with tears in her eyes, cries out, "We have *got* to do something about slum clearance!"

The line was greeted by silence. The live audience who viewed the show at the theater that night waited until the lights were fading on the scene before breaking into laughter—and applause.

After *Your Show of Shows* ended its run, Tony and I went our separate ways, and not until I was producing *The Dick Van Dyke Show* did Tony pop back into my life. He paid a visit to my office at Desilu-Cahuenga, and I was so happy to see him. He had been writing episodic television, and I hoped that he might like to write an episode for *The Dick Van Dyke Show*, but he said that he had just come by to "visit and vent." And vent he did. He complained about most television shows being "shitty" and that he had no more interest in writing for it. He seemed to be at odds with himself and the world and just wanted to complain about having nothing to do. I told him that he had no right to complain about having nothing to do. I said actors can complain because they have to wait until someone offers them a job, but a writer who has a typewriter or a pencil and a pad cannot grouse about having nothing to do. With that, I grabbed a note pad and scribbled, "Carl Reiner, IOU One Play!" and asked Tony to sign it, which he did. I tossed his IOU into a desk drawer and told him that when he hands me his new play, I would tear it up.

Tony returned a couple of months later, threw his play on my desk, and barked, "Tear up that damned IOU."

The play he had written was entitled *God Almighty*, and I thought it brilliant. Tony had once described himself as a "fallen Catholic," and his play dealt with man's confused feelings about life and his attempt to understand the Supreme Being.

I attended a staging of the play in Los Angeles, where it was well received by critics and audiences. There was one scene in his play that contained some of the most insightful and humorous discussions man has ever had with his Maker.

His bare stage was lit to suggest that we were in some heavenly limbo where a "Man" who has passed on is meeting his Maker for the first time. The archangels, Michael and Gabriel, are present when God asks Man, "Who are you?" And when Man tells God, "I am Man!", God shakes His head and says, "I do not know you!" to which Man replies, "You must know me, for it was You who made me!"

A puzzled God shakes His head and says that He had no memory of ever making Man. After Man insists that he was told that he was made in God's image, God racks His memory but cannot remember making Man.

"I remember making ants," God recalls. "I was really impressed at how much weight those little creatures could carry—many, many times their own."

God did remember creating flowers, and how much He liked their array of colors and their fragrances. He then reiterated having absolutely no recollection of creating Man, and after looking at Man curiously for a long moment, God asks, "All right, Man—show Me what you do!"

With that, Man launches into a classic soft-shoe routine. Man takes the stage and demonstrates, with ultimate grace and fluidity, all the iconic steps that the likes of Fred Astaire or Gene Kelly might have used.

At the end of the dance, God pauses, gazes at Man for a long moment, and then asks, "Can you teach me to do that?"

The simple question that God asked of Man is the reason I had to write about Tony Webster.

The scene fades with Man teaching a choreographically challenged God how to dance a soft-shoe.

Tony's choosing the soft-shoe was sheer brilliance. The essence of the soft-shoe embodies that which is sweet and loving in humans. It has grace, charm, and good humor, is calming, and the only dance where, when you are watching, you feel that all is right, not only with the person who is dancing, but with the entire world.

Have I gone too far? Maybe. But if I did go too far, who will it hurt?

At the end of Tony Webster's *God Almighty*, a defeated, forlorn God finds Himself standing alone on stage and realizes that after countless thousands of years, wars, disease, greed, murder, rape, poverty, and pestilence still exist. As He contemplates this, the spotlight starts to dim. The Almighty then slowly raises His arms, looks heavenward, and as the light fades, we are left with an image of God looking for God to help Him.

For the record: Tony Webster (1922–1987), inspired by his winning bout with alcoholism, wrote a moving television play, *Call Me Back*, that starred Art Carney.

Besides being a successful writer, Tony was also a loving and successful single father of a loving, successful daughter.

CHAPTER THIRTY-NINE

O.Z. Whitehead Discovers Sex!

O.Z. Whitehead and I met during World War Two. We were both assigned to an army entertainment unit that was stationed in Hawaii on the island of Oahu.

O.Z., short for Oothout Zabriskie, was the scion of a long line of Zabriskies. O.Z.'s direct ancestor, whose forename he bore, was General Oothout Zabriskie, who, during our war for independence served under General George Washington. A bronze statue of General Zabriskie on horseback is proudly displayed in a town square in Ithaca, New York.

My buddy O.Z. stood six feet, four inches tall, weighed about 130 pounds, and sported a head of straight, reddish-blond hair. One might accurately describe him as ungainly, uncoordinated, and scarecrow-skinny. O.Z. began his career as an actor in the Chicago cast of *Life with Father*. In the play, he portrayed one of the many redheaded children of redheaded parents. The family's matriarch was portrayed by the world-renowned silent movie star, Lillian Gish.

In the late thirties, a committee of backward-thinking citizens formed The America First Committee, an organization that, besides harboring an anti-Semitic and pro-Nazi philosophy, somehow attracted famous, well-meaning folk like Charles Lindbergh and Lillian Gish and recruited them to spread the committee's misguided idea of patriotism. Lillian Gish, in turn, recruited her naive and respectful cast member, O.Z., to join her in making stump speeches, praising The America First Committee for the great work they were doing to "misinform" America about who our nation's actual enemies were. It took the sneak attack on Pearl Harbor and Germany allying itself with Japan for O.Z., Lillian

Gish, and others to realize how misguided and dangerous were the hate-spewing America Firsters.

On discovering who the real villains were, O.Z. felt compelled to take immediate action. To undo the harm he had done to his beloved country, he hurried to the nearest recruiting center, and despite being too old to be drafted, volunteered to join the army. As anxious as the recruiters were to add able-bodied citizens to their roster, they could not, in good conscience consider a thirty-four-year-old gangly, six-foot-four, 130-pounder to be able-bodied.

O.Z. would not be daunted and visited a half dozen other recruiting centers in different parts of Chicago. All found him to be unfit for military duty—save for one center, where a reasonable sergeant rejected O.Z.'s list of reasons for fighting the Nazis but fully accepted the five hundred dollars in cash that O.Z. offered him. Had that patriotic sergeant not done what O.Z. paid him to do, I would never have had the pleasure of knowing O.Z.

As a member of our army entertainment section, O.Z. patiently waited in vain to be cast in one of the shows that toured the Pacific. The highlight of his act consisted of an impersonation of Eddie Cantor, a then-beloved star of Broadway, films, and radio. Cantor stood about five foot four and was a dynamo on stage. With his high tenor voice, he delivered his signature song, "If You Knew Susie Like I Know Susie," while clapping his hands, rolling his big, brown eyes, and skipping wildly back and forth across the stage.

None of us had never seen O.Z. do his impression of Cantor until one night in the company's recreation room, he decided to favor us with a sample of his work. It would be fair to say that he exhibited a combination of childlike charm, exuberance, naiveté and grace, not unlike his modern-day counterpart, Pee Wee Herman.

The initial reaction to his singing and dancing of the first chorus was jaw-dropping, but by the time he was into his fourth of five choruses, we were all either holding our sides or looking away and begging for him to stop. We were never sure whether we were laughing *at* him or *with* him, but it did not much matter. We all laughed so hard that one of us is now writing about that hilarious impression of Eddie Cantor that O.Z. did sixty-seven years ago.

For the last few months that I was stationed in Oahu, I spent most of my free hours palling around with O.Z. Whitehead and Lieutenant Leon Kirchner. Leon, who had recently been transferred to our outfit, was a brilliant pianist and composer who, as a composer, had already received multiple awards for his modern compositions.

In the following chapter, I describe how this musical genius risked a court-martial rather than obey his commanding officer's order to write incidental music for a production of *Dracula*.

In 1948, a year after my discharge from the army, I received a note from O.Z. informing me that he had recently moved to Manhattan and would love to have lunch with me. He was most anxious to meet Estelle, whose praises I had sung often and loudly during our days in Hawaii. Estelle was equally interested in meeting the man I described to her as being "kind, sweet, ungainly, and strange." However, I did not expect him to demonstrate *how* strange he was.

Estelle and I were seated in the Algonquin Lounge when we spied a happy, grinning O.Z. all but running across the lobby toward us. Before I could say, "O.Z., say hello to Estelle!" a breathless O. Z. screamed out, "Carl, Carl! I had sex yesterday afternoon for the first time in my life—and I loved it! I just loved it! So many people told me that the first time I do it, I won't like it, but I *loved* it! It felt sooooo good! I can't wait to do it again!"

He then went on to tell me—and everyone in the hotel lobby—that it was not his idea to have his first sexual experience, but his friend's, an actress he was visiting. She was the one who suggested that they "do it."

When O.Z. was a teenager, this well-known stage actress had played his mother in *Life with Father*, and he said that yesterday, while visiting her, she had asked him if he was still a virgin. When he admitted that he was, she told him that she would "have to do something about that."

He described how she escorted him into her bedroom, helped him remove his clothes, and then went about teaching him to do things that made him "smile all over!"

I daresay that decades ago, the witty members of the famed Algonquin Round Table, who were noted for their original and memorable exchanges, never uttered lines more original or memorable than O.Z.'s "I had sex yesterday afternoon for the first time in my life, and I loved it! I just loved it. It felt sooooo good that I can't wait to do it again!"

One last note about Oothout Zabriskie Whitehead: in John Ford's classic 1940 film version of John Steinbeck's novel, *The Grapes of Wrath*, O.Z. was cast as Tom Joad, the driver of the dilapidated truck that transports the Joad family through the drought-stricken dust bowl to California.

O.Z. looked so beaten and lifeless in the film that it inspired Hitler's Nazi propagandists to publish photos of the emaciated, ashen-faced O.Z. and cite him as an example of the decadence in America and how the United States government sucks the life out of its citizens and condemns them to an existence of hellish poverty.

O.Z. was pleased and proud to have played that role in our war effort.

O.Z. Whitehead in "The Grapes of Wrath"

CHAPTER FORTY

Count Dracula Encounters Lieutenant Kirchner

Courtesy of Lisa Kirchner and Paul Kirchner

L eon Kirchner was, at this time, a young, brilliantly talented composer of serious music who had recently been awarded the Rome Prize for composition—one of a myriad of prestigious awards he would receive in his lifetime. Our commanding officer, as I noted earlier, was Captain Allen Ludden.

Nearing the end of the war, Captain Ludden decided that a production of the play *Dracula* that had been adapted from the film and had enjoyed a successful run on Broadway would be something that our servicemen

217

would enjoy seeing. One of the members of our acting troupe was perfect for the leading role. He was tall, dark, and looked like a vampire—and his name was Ken Tanner. I just happily surprised myself by recalling Ken Tanner's name. At my present age, I am happy when I remember to take my vitamins and put in my prescribed eye drops.

The rehearsals and the building of the sets for *Dracula* were progressing well. The set designer for the entertainment section was the talented Fred Fox, the same Fred Fox who was hired by Max Liebman after the war to design sets for *Your Show of Shows*—just another example of the surprising accuracy of clichés like "It's a small world."

About a week or so before *Dracula* was to be performed for members of our Armed Forces, Leon Kirchner groused to O.Z. and me about an impossible request he had received that morning. Captain Ludden had asked him to write some background music for the production, and Leon explained that a serious composer did not write music to be used as background for scenes in plays or films, but wrote music to be heard in concert halls or salons.

Leon's explanation for not accepting the assignment turned into a discussion, which quickly became a heated argument. It was then that the captain reminded Leon that he was his superior officer, and Leon countered that he would not write incidental music unless he was ordered to—and the captain obliged. He ordered Leon to write incidental music!

Leon knew he had a choice: he could write "the damned music" and stay in Special Service or refuse and be re-assigned to the infantry.

In record time, Leon handed in a finished score for *Dracula*—the work containing hundreds of scribbled notes designating which instruments played which parts. Surprisingly, Leon seemed to be in a good mood and suggested that he and I hang around when the copyists transcribed his master score for the musicians. He seemed proud to have done something that he hated doing, and I soon learned why he was smiling so broadly.

Through the barracks' open transom-like windows, we heard a few of the music copyists discuss Leon's orchestration:

"What the fuck is this, a joke?!"

"If it's a joke, it ain't funny!"

"If he thinks it's funny, he's got a warped sense of humor."

"What the hell is this shit he doodled for a time signature?"

218

One of the better-educated copyists started to laugh.

"Those are not doodles. You know what the son of a bitch did—instead of putting in 2/4 or 4/4 for the time, he gave us an algebraic equation to decipher."

"Who the hell remembers how to do algebra?"

Fortunately, one did and went about translating the algebraic equation into numbers. Because Leon's music was modern and complicated, so were his time signs. Few or none of the copyists had ever before noted or played a selection in 5/7 or 2/5 time.

I accompanied Leon to the opening performance of *Dracula*, and Leon, who had groused about being bullied into doing something he had promised himself he would never do, was, for some reason, in a rather upbeat mood.

Leon, who could not do anything musically that was not at least interesting, had managed to add a good deal of excitement to many of the scenes. Particularly effective was the music Leon had composed for the end of an act, when a drooling Dracula approaches the heroine, Lucy, who is reclining on a couch. Leon had orchestrated the violin section to play sustained, discordant high notes when Dracula puts his lips to Lucy's white neck. The instant the vampire bites, the violins hit a tremulous crescendo as a soprano voice screams a hair-raising high note. So blood-curdling was the high-noted scream that every member of the audience, including me, literally jumped out of our seats. Leon had hired an operatic soprano to sit in the string section and deliver a nerve-shattering high F above high C, confident that it would get the reaction that it did. I daresay that, in the history of American theater, no soprano has ever had a shorter, more well-paying role or received a greater audience reaction for her effort.

In later years, Leon never wrote anything that he was not inspired to write. In his life, he composed a great deal of highly lauded compositions, works that were premiered and performed in all of the world's great concert halls.

Estelle and I were thrilled to have attended a number of his premieres, including two memorable ones with the New York Philharmonic Orchestra, when Maestro Dimitri Mitropulous conducted.

Many of Leon's close friends were successful composers who sometimes wrote scores for important films. Leon never felt that there was anything demeaning about their writing music for worthwhile films and being paid handsomely for it, but he never considered that they were writing serious music. I remember Leon saying something to this effect: If one writes music for a film to help make a scene happier or scarier or more exciting or romantic, then you cannot be writing serious music. You are writing music to enhance what someone else has created. You are not allowing yourself to express what is in your head and heart.

Those words are not Leon's, but I believe the thought is. Leon was, among other things, a scholar. He was a voracious reader of books on history, art, politics, science, as well as novels, and was, I recall, a fan of the writings, the mind, and the man who is Stephen Hawking.

Leon Kirchner was, for some reason, always curious about the amount of money certain performers earned. I remember him asking me how much Sid Caesar made and if he was paid more or less money than Jackie Gleason.

"Who is more powerful?" is how he put it. It seemed that Leon, like too many people, equate money with power.

Leon truly admired Sid Caesar's ability and told him so when I invited him and his good friend and fellow composer, Lukas Foss, to meet Sid. At that meeting in Sid's rehearsal hall, Sid, who had heard Leon Kirchner's work and knew of his vaunted place in the music world, did something that I was surprised he would do. He dared to make fun of Kirchner's music. Sid sat down at the rehearsal-hall Steinway and proceeded to satirize a Kirchner-like modern composition. Sid played that piano much like he spoke foreign languages—in double talk. With his fingers flying all over the keyboard, Sid "double-talked" his impression of a virtuoso playing a discordant modern work. He started by pounding the keys wildly, then tinkling them, then running a few glissandos, sweeping his knuckles up and down the keyboard and then raising his leg and striking the keys with the heel of his shoe—sort of a satiric "foot note" to his performance.

All eyes were on Leon as Sid started his recital, and all those eyes had tears in them when he finished. Leon Kirchner, besides being a serious composer, was serious appreciator of good comedians—Zero Mostel and Jack Gilford being two of his other favorites.

One day, while visiting us in our Bronx apartment, he told Estelle and me of the offer he had received from RKO Studios, asking him to score their film of Norman Mailer's *The Naked and the Dead*. Alex North, a friend and fellow composer, had been offered the job but was unavailable, so he recommended Kirchner. Leon, who could have used the money, had no interest in scoring the film but told me that he was going to meet with the producers just to find out how large a sum of money he was not going to be earning.

The following day, Leon asked the producer what was the most he had ever paid a composer to score a film, and when the producer told him, Leon asked if he was willing to pay five times that amount. When the man turned him down, Leon countered with, "In that case, my price for not doing your film is ten times what you originally offered, and that is final!"

One very fond memory I have is of our two-year-old son, Lucas, sitting on the living-room floor of our Bronx apartment and paying rapt attention to Leon, who was sitting next to him and plunking out a tune on Lucas's tiny, red toy piano.

And now, an inevitable and sad addendum.

O.Z., Leon, and I, as I have said, were all members of an army entertainment unit that once boasted scores of talented performers. Last week, Stan Harper, one of the "scores," with whom I toured in *Shoot the Works*, called to inform me that another of our alumni, the brilliant lyricist, Hal David has passed. There remain now but four:

1. Stan Harper: Acknowledged as world's foremost harmonica virtuoso.
2. Guido Salmaggi: Operatic tenor, ninety-eight and still singing.
3. Ray Olivere: Eminent portraitist. Latest commission: Bernard Baruch.
4. Me: Author of *I Remember Me*.

Given the above statistics, it behooves me to type as fast as I can.

CHAPTER FORTY-ONE

My Minor Involvement
with Major Stars

O ne of these stars was Hedy Lamarr who, in her day, was considered to be the world's most beautiful woman. Miss Lamarr, who insisted I call her Hedy, had been invited to appear on a game show, the name of which escapes me. Hedy and I were two of three panelists who sat directly across from the host, who I believe was the talented and ubiquitous Bill Cullen.

Hedy was seated beside me as we all listened to our host give us instructions about the game. From the corner of my 20/20-visioned right eye, I saw Hedy reach into her purse and lift a cigarette from a pack. In those days, the big tobacco companies' ads assured us that cigarette smoking was not only a pleasant way to relax but a healthy one.

I kept my eyes on the host, as my above-average coordination allowed me to see Hedy put the cigarette to her lips. As I answered Bill's questions, I suavely took a pack of matches from my pocket, lit one, and without looking at Hedy, offered her a light.

Hedy, instead of thanking me, looked at the lit match I held beneath her chin and asked sweetly, "Carl, what are you trying to do—light my lozenge?"

What Hedy had put to her lips was not a cigarette but a peppermint Life Saver.

The audience's faces were red from laughter, and mine was that color from embarrassment.

Since writing about Hedy Lamarr, I learned something about the woman that I had not known until reading the Calendar section of today's *L.A. Times*. The headline read, "Screen Beauty's Striking Brain." It seems that the late Hedy Lamarr, besides being beautiful, was also a gifted scientist. She was the co-holder of a patent on spread-spectrum radio, a technology that underlines modern conveniences such as mobile and cordless telephones, wi-fi, Bluetooth, and GPS.

It seems that Hedy Lamarr's beauty was more than skin deep.

Dinah

In 1960, I found myself happily employed as a writer/actor on Dinah Shore's popular variety show, which was aptly titled *The Dinah Shore Show*. Dinah Shore was, by anyone's standards, the loveliest, most charming hostess in all of television. Charley Isaacs, a great comedy writer and I, co-wrote sketches for Dinah and her guest stars, and every second week, besides writing for the show, I also appeared on it. On those alternate weeks, I received an unusual billing that Charley dreamed up. The announcer would say, "And on tonight's show, Dinah's special guest will be, Yves Montand, and her *not*-so-special guest, Carl Reiner."

Dinah and I became good friends during that period. Estelle and I were often invited to her home to dine with her and George Montgomery, her extraordinarily handsome husband, whom she adored. She told us that she had fallen in love with him before they ever met and how after they met, she blatantly pursued him, caught him, married him, and had a lovely daughter with him, Melissa.

Among other things, Dinah was an excellent cook. Her culinary skills were on a par with her singing, and as evidence, she wrote two bestselling cookbooks, from which my wife culled many a fine recipe.

This one lazy afternoon, Dinah and I were on our way to a rehearsal in Studio Two at NBC. To remind those who remember Dinah Shore, and to inform those who were too young to know her, Dinah had one of the best figures in Hollywood—a figure which, on her show, she chose to clothe in dresses, sweaters, and gowns that were designed by one of the reigning fashion designers of that era, Bob Mackie. Dinah's wardrobe did not include anything that was bare, off-the-shoulder, or revealed any appreciable amount of cleavage. Whatever she wore, Dinah always managed to exude a subtle sexiness. In good part, it was due to the fact that she was blessed with an innate calm, a soothing, Southern-accented voice, and an absolutely beautiful bosom—which is the *raison d'etre* for this essay, which I had considered titling, "What Was I Thinking?".

That afternoon, as we strolled down the long hall making small talk, I, for some unknown reason—perhaps because Dinah and I were good friends or because I have a devilish bent—stopped, turned to her, and said, "Dinah, there is something that puzzles me, and maybe you can help me. You do know that you have a smashingly beautiful bosom. I know it! Your fans know it! Your designer knows it! Everyone knows it! It is common knowledge. Well, something just occurred to me—I was thinking that if I had breasts like yours, I would be playing with them all day long—I would not be able to resist fondling them. I just don't understand how you can walk around and completely ignore them. I have never seen you even touch them—let alone fondle them. How can you resist them? Can you please explain that to me?"

Dinah stared at me, thought for a second, and then answered, "No, I cannot explain it, Carl—but I will say that you have given me something to think about—and I thank you!"

She laughed, punched me lightly on the arm, and said, "Carl, you are too much!"

To this day, I have seen many women whose bosoms deserve praising or at least positive comments, but Dinah's were the only non-spouse breasts I have ever openly praised—or ever will. That's the kind of guy I am.

CHAPTER FORTY-TWO

Me and Gregory Peck

I had just been honorably discharged from the army, where for the past year I had toured the Pacific islands, performing as a comedian in an army show entitled "Shape Ahoy." I was now an out-of-work actor and looking for a job on Broadway or in a film. To this end, I visited a small theatrical agency where a lone, sad-looking agent was looking to cast a young actor to play a small role in a film scheduled to be shot in New York. Before sending me to read for a part, he asked if I would recite something for him—just to make sure I didn't stink. I chose to do a monologue I had learned when I was seventeen years old. It was a speech from *Death Takes a Holiday*, a film that starred Frederic March playing the title role of Death. Disguised as the sophisticated, tuxedoed Count Circe, Death visits Earth to discover why its inhabitants feared him so deeply.

In my audition scene, the Count describes how it might impact us all if he, Death, took a holiday.

"Imagine," he declaims, "a world where nothing will decay, nothing will crumble...not a leaf will fall, nor a star from heaven. There will be only life and growth...and a sort of cosmic springtime..."

After proving to the agent that I did not "stink," he made an appointment for me to visit a film producer whose offices were in the Twentieth Century Fox building on West Fifty-Seventh Street. A secretary greeted me in an outer office, handed me some pages from a script, and suggested that I familiarize myself with the scene, in case the producer asked me to read for a part.

By the time I was called, I practically had the scene memorized, and it was good that I did, because the producer who read the other part mumbled so quietly, I could not hear what he was saying. When I said my last line, he nodded his head approvingly, smiled, and told me that I was "a good actor" and that I had given "an intelligent reading."

When he added, "Mr. Reiner, there is no question in my mind that you can do this part and do it well," I thought, *Bingo! I got the part!*

But then he added, "But what we are looking for is a Gregory Peck type."

Shit! I thought. *I'm not a Gregory Peck type!*

With a frozen smile on my face, I thanked the producer for his time, walked out of his office, past his secretary, and into the hall, where I stopped short. A thought struck me, and I strode back to the producer's office, popped my head back in, and asked, "Excuse me, sir—you said you were looking for a Gregory Peck-type actor. I was wondering—what type of actor do you think they were looking for when they found Gregory Peck?"

I did not wait for an answer.

Some years ago, I met Gregory Peck at a party, and he laughed when I told him the reason I had once been rejected for a part in a film. He was so gracious and charming that it was all I could do to keep myself from asking, "Say, Greg, I was wondering: have you ever been turned down for a part because they were looking for a Carl Reiner type?"

Darn, I wish I had asked!

CHAPTER FORTY-THREE

Lucas and *The Greatest Story Ever Told*

I n Hollywood, at 6360 Sunset Boulevard, between Cahuenga Boulevard and Vine Street, there sits a geodesic structure known as the Cinerama Dome. In 1963, I was invited to attend the theater's star-studded premiere of the film, *It's a Mad, Mad, Mad, Mad World*. For me it was a very special event, as I was a party to two separate premieres, the Cinerama Dome's and the film's, in which I had a small role.

Stanley Kramer was the film's director, and he cast every role in the film with a famous comedian or a famous comic actor, be they starring roles, supporting ones, or bit parts. Every funny man in our business eagerly awaited a call from Mr. Kramer, asking if they would join the cast. I was happy to be in this elite group and do a cameo as an air-traffic controller. In the scene, we instruct two hysterical passengers, Buddy Hackett and Mickey Rooney, how to land a small plane that their dead pilot is no longer capable of doing.

As the director-producer of this eagerly awaited blockbuster, Stanley Kramer had worked hard to complete and deliver the final print for the premiere. The Cinerama Dome's landlords, however, were not as diligent about delivering a completed theater for his premiere.

When my wife and I and other guests walked down the hall at the back of the theater, we had to avoid tripping over workmen who were on their knees, trimming and stapling plush, red carpeting into the floor. As we were ushered to our seats, we saw another raft of workers tacking carpeting to the floor of the stage below the Cinemascope screen.

In spite of the delays, *It's a Mad, Mad, Mad, Mad World* was well received by the celebrity audience, and with the help of positive reviews, went on to do huge business. There were a few negative reviews about the film's excesses, but for the most part, the general public enjoyed the premise and the performances of a cast that included Spencer Tracy, Sid Caesar, Milton Berle, Jonathan Winters, Phil Silvers, Peter Falk, Ethel Merman, Edie Adams, "Rochester," Jimmy Durante, the Three Stooges, Dick Shawn, and Buster Keaton.

Though it was not one of my stellar roles, my wife and I thought our young son, Lucas, might enjoy seeing what his daddy did when he was not at home. We were amazed at how patiently our three-year-old sat for a film that was long enough to need an intermission. When it ended, Luke amazed us further by asking when he could see it again. He obviously loved the experience, because he never forgot it.

Two years after attending the premiere of *It's a Mad, Mad, Mad, Mad World* at the Cinerama Dome, Estelle and I were again invited to the Dome to join another elite audience, this time for the premiere of *The Greatest Story Ever Told*. This epic movie contained some of the most spectacular scenes ever filmed and boasted the starriest, star-studded cast ever assembled.

Estelle and I were ushered to our reserved seats in the tenth row of the center section. A couple of seats to our right was Sheldon Leonard, my friend and executive producer of *The Dick Van Dyke Show*. My having created *The Dick Van Dyke Show* brought me the kind of stature that got me invited to such a classy event.

Unlike the premiere of *Mad, Mad, Mad, Mad World*, the theater was ready. The lights dimmed on time as the curtains parted on the massive, 260-meter, curved Cinemascope screen. The opening titles were projected against an orange-hued background, while a very subdued, legato orchestral score accompanied the credits. The very first words scrolled on the screen, in very small print, were "Released Through United Artists." Then, in alphabetical order, in the very, very smallest print any of us had ever seen, were the unreadable names of following stars:

Max Von Sydow, Michael Anderson Jr., Carroll Baker, Ina Baul, Pat Boone, Victor Buono, Richard Conte, Joanna Dunham, Jose Ferrer, Van Heflin, Charlton Heston, Martin Landau, Angela Lansbury, Janet Margolin, David McCallum, Roddy McDowall, Dorothy Malone, Sal Mineo, Nehemiah Persoff, Donald Pleasance, Sidney Poitier, Claude Rains, Gary Raymond, Telly Savalas, Joseph Schildkraut, Paul Stewart, John Wayne, Shelley Winters, and Ed Wynn.

As I think about the small-lettered billing the stars were given, it well may be that the producers of the film were saying that no actor deserves star billing except for the real star of the film, Jesus Christ.

When the film started, we gave it our full attention, but after the first fifteen or twenty minutes, we all sensed that we were trapped watching a long, slow, boringly produced film about a subject that deserved a better fate. The production, the sets, the costumes, the art direction were beautiful, artistic, and lavish, but their magnificence could hold an audience's interest just so long. The invited guests sat quietly, and for almost a half hour, nobody moved a muscle. We all knew that our hosts' eyes were fixed on us, and they would interpret any movement we made as being a negative criticism. Without turning my head, I looked at my neighbor, Sheldon, who sat rigidly, his legs crossed. He kept them way for another fifteen or twenty minutes and then—uncrossed them! The moment he did, every head in my row turned to see who it was that dared to move. It caused a ripple effect, and those in the row behind Sheldon looked to see, as did those in the row behind the row behind Sheldon. Somehow, Sheldon uncrossing his legs gave the audience the freedom to behave as they ordinarily would when in a movie theater. They whispered to each other, they adjusted their clothing, coughed, sneaked a candy, or nodded off.

In the film, there were some all-time, memorably cringe-worthy moments. For me, the most memorable one involved a truly iconic Western star who, like many of the stars, had a very small part. This major box-office draw, John Wayne, had but one line.

Dressed as a Roman warrior, the imposing cowboy star looked upon the body of the crucified Christ, and sounding exactly like John Wayne, delivered the film's last line: "He—truly—was—the—son—of—God!"

There has never been a more

disciplined or respectful audience. There was no audible laughter, thanks to those who stifled it by covering their mouths with their hands or biting their lips.

When the screening ended, it was not difficult for the invitees to find enough praiseworthy things to say about the boring but brilliantly produced film that told one of the greatest biblical stories ever.

A few weeks after its premiere, my wife and I and five-year-old Lucas were driving past the Cinerama Dome. The film, which had received mostly fair to poor reviews, was still playing there, and Lucas, recognizing the theater, asked if we would go in and see, *It's a Mad, Mad, Mad, Mad World* again. When, told it was no longer playing there and that a new one was, he asked, "Can we go see the new one?"

"I don't think you will like this one, Luke."

"How do you know?" he asked.

"Mom and I saw it."

"Didn't you like it?"

"It was all right, but we don't think you will like it."

"What's the name of it?"

"*The Greatest Story Ever Told.*"

"I'll like it!" he shouted. "I want to see the greatest story ever told!"

"It is called *The Greatest Story Ever Told,*" we explained, "but the movie isn't very good."

"Why do they call it *The **Greatest** Story Ever Told,* if it isn't very good?"

It took a lot more explaining, and I was almost tempted to take him to see the four-hour film, so he could see for himself what a dud it was—and how, in the future, he should trust our judgment—but I resisted.

The other day, I told fifty-year-old Lucas that I am writing about when he was five and his wanting to see *The Greatest Story Ever Told,* and our telling him that it wasn't very good and that he would not like it, and he said, "You know, Dad, I saw a little bit of it not too long ago. I kinda liked it!"

I feel that I need a moral for this tale, and only one comes to mind: "*Sobre gustas, no hay disputa!*"

For those thirty-two Americans who do not speak or understand Spanish, *Sobre gustas, no hay disputa* means, "About tastes, there is no dispute."

George Shapiro holding my son, Lucas, the Little League's big leaguer.

CHAPTER FORTY-FOUR

My Son, the Little League's Big Leaguer

I n the summer of 1966, for one full season, Lucas Reiner, who aspired to be a member of his Beverly Hills Little League team, was one month shy of the age required to participate as a player. Lucas told us of one boy who had fudged about his actual birth date, and he wanted to do the same, but my wife and I, who were law-abiding citizens, would not allow him to lie. Poor Luke, who had as much ability as his friend, spent his first season in the league as a mascot for the Beverly Hills Dodgers. He was permitted to wear the team uniform, sit in the Dodgers' dugout, and root loudly.

Even though our son never played during that first full season, my wife and I attended every game and watched a frustrated Lucas sit on the bench and root.

The following season, during the first few practice sessions, it became apparent that Lucas Reiner had the makings of a fine ball player, and his coach, Hy Braun, chose him to play two key positions, shortstop and pitcher.

The Beverly Hills Park Department had furnished our fair city with a beautiful baseball field for the Little Leaguers to play on and two sturdy grandstands for their parents to sit in.

Two six-inning games were scheduled every Saturday and on the season's opening day, Lucas was scheduled to pitch the second game. His best friend, Johnny Zucker, who was a member of the Beverly Hills Pirates, had just finished pitching the first game, and his teammates were congratulating him. When Lucas walked onto the field, Johnny told Lucas that he had pitched a no-hitter. Lucas smiled and said, "That's great! I guess I'll have to throw a no-hitter too."

With his mother, father, sister Annie, brother Rob, cousin Georgie, and friend Billy Persky among the crowd rooting him on, Lucas Reiner not only pitched a no-hitter but a no-hit no-run game. Which means that no one scored, and no one got on base by virtue of walks or errors—a rare thing in Little League.

Lucas was as proficient with the bat as he was with his arm. He had many multi-hit games and powered at least one home run.

Early in his first season, a game I remember well featured Luke's defensive skills. He was playing shortstop, and it was the bottom of the sixth, the final inning of the game. His team was leading by two runs, and the opposing team had the bases loaded and their best hitter at the plate. There were two out, and a big hit would win the game for the opposition. To guard against their ace slugger blasting one over the fence, Hy Braun, the team's manager, instructed his three outfielders to paste themselves up against the four-foot-high fence.

Our pitcher threw a strike, and the batter swung and hit a "Texas Leaguer," a short fly ball over the heads of the infielders. It was not hit hard or high enough to reach the deeply positioned outfielders but hard enough to make it difficult for the infielders to chase it down. From where we sat, it looked like the whole team was racing to catch that soft fly ball.

Lucas, who had spent hours in our back yard, practicing to bird-dog this kind of fly, was ready for the challenge. He and I would stand together at the far end of our back lawn, and I would toss a high lob toward our house. He would take one quick look over his shoulder, judge the height and trajectory of the lob, and take off after it. He would not turn his head until the last second, when he would stick out his gloved hand and make an over-the-shoulder catch. A conservative estimate would be that each time we played catch, we practiced this particular move 50 million times, or at least fifty. We played catch quite a lot, and I was amazed at his ability to throw strikes—fast-ball strikes, curve-ball strikes, and believe it or not, a knuckle-ball strike. For the life of me, as a kid, I could never throw a strike. I was so happy to discover that Luke had inherited his throwing genes from his mother and her brother athletes. Our firstborn, Rob, who is almost thirteen years older than Luke, loved baseball and played Little League in New Rochelle. He was a good athlete and played first base and pitched. For the six years he played, I never missed one of his games or failed to be thrilled about how well he played and comported himself.

Rob, who to this day loves baseball and is almost as knowledgeable about the sport as Vin Scully, once said while watching his kid brother play, "Ah, we now have somebody in the family that we can live through vicariously!"

That Texas Leaguer pop fly I was describing that was hit into no man's land, was falling to earth just as the potential winning runs were crossing home plate. The game was over, or would have been, had Luke not taken one look at the ball's trajectory and dashed, full throttle from his infield position into short center field, stretched his gloved hand out as far forward as he could, and snatched the ball just before it hit the ground. A second after Lucas fell on his face, his teammates fell on Lucas, or more accurately, jumped on Lucas and congratulated him by pounding his back with their gloved hands. It was exciting for the team and the spectators and would have been for my wife and I, had we not been concerned about his being pummeled to death.

Lucas's beloved wife, Maud, had heard this bit of folklore many times and on many occasions when friends and family get together, and she had to assume, as most people would, that when parents sing the praises of one of their children, they are probably exaggerating just an eensy bit.

Maud never accused us of overpraising Lucas, but one day she found herself at the marina and being offered a ride by a good Samaritan. When Maud introduced herself as Maud Reiner, the woman said, "Reiner? I knew someone named Lucas Reiner—any relation?"

On hearing that Lucas was her husband, the woman lit up and proceeded to do what I had done—praise Lucas. The woman had a son who played in the same Little League, and she described how talented a ball player Maud's husband was and in what high esteem he was held by his fellow Little Leaguers.

Maud told me about this meeting and how happy she was to learn that I had no need to embellish the facts about her husband's short career as a major Little League ball player.

In his short baseball career, these are some of Luke's stats:

His combined overall batting average for his career was over .525, yes

.525, mostly line-drive hits. His pitching record one year was eleven wins and no defeats—among them that no-hit, no-run game and a few one- and two-hit games. He pitched his team to a league championship and went on to win an interleague game by hitting a last-inning triple. In that last game, he tired in the sixth inning, and by virtue of his walking two batters and an error by a teammate, the bases were loaded. The manager walked out to the mound and asked Luke how he felt and if he thought he could continue. Lucas asked, "What do I have to do?"

"You have to get three outs," the manager answered.

And that is what Luke did. He struck out the last three batters.

Lucas played Little League baseball for six full seasons, and when being wooed to join a Pony League team, he asked me a question that I did not expect. "Dad," he asked, "how would you feel if I did not go on and play in the Pony League?"

I would have felt awful, but I bit my tongue and asked quietly, "Don't you want to continue playing ball?"

"Not really. I would like to get a guitar and learn how to play it."

He explained that even though he liked playing ball, he did not like the pressure it put on him.

"Luke," I responded, "if that's what you want, I have no objection. One thing, though: if I buy you a guitar, will you promise to take lessons?"

He promised to take lessons, and we bought the guitar. He immediately started to noodle on it and in a short time figured out how to strum a chord or two. When he knew that he needed help, he asked around and found a teacher. By the time he was sixteen, he and his friends formed a rock band they called the Johnnys. The Johnnys played a few small venues in town, one a bowling alley where my wife and I caught their act. Not because Luke was our son, but his mother and I agreed that the Johnnys were "not bad, not bad at all."

I am pleased that Lucas chose not to be a ball player. If he had been a successful one, it would have delayed pursuing his calling to be an artist for at least ten years—ten years being the average length of a ball player's career.

By attending Otis-Parsons, Lucas successfully tapped the fine-art gene he inherited from his mother and with it established a flourishing career as a painter. Fine-art galleries throughout Europe and the United States have exhibited Lucas Reiner's oil paintings and etchings of trees and also his large canvases depicting the aftermath of fireworks.

Displayed on the following pages are examples of his paintings.

I can't tell you how much *nachus* I *shep* from Lucas and all the members of my whole family!

For those who do not know the phrase, *shep nachus*, I should tell you that *shep nachus* or *shepping nachus* is Yiddish for "to derive great pleasure from." One usually *sheps nachus* from a child or grandchild who has drawn a picture that looks like a cat or a dog, or has played his or her first song on a musical instrument, or brought home a good report from their teacher, or hit the proverbial home run in any of their endeavors.

Lucas Reiner 2008, Oil on canvas, 14x12 inches,
Title: On Pico Blvd. #7

Lucas Reiner 2012, Fall 2, Etching, 6x4 inches
Title: VII (from XV Stations)

CHAPTER FORTY-FIVE

Yenemvelt

W hat is Yenemvelt? Yenemvelt is the name of an exclusive social club that came into existence forty-two years ago, and I am proud to be one of its founding members.

In 1980, at the behest of writer/producer Norman Lear, five couples spent a memorable weekend together at a beautiful, five-bedroom home in Palm Springs, California. If laughter and unbridled joy be the yardstick, that weekend had to be the most satisfying, fun-filled one I have spent in my entire life—and so have said the nine other participants.

Since what I am about to tell you may seem like a fairy tale, I feel it fitting that I start with:

Once upon a time…

Or because there was a second fun-filled weekend that equaled the first one, I should say…

Twice upon a time…there were two events of unbridled joy that took place in consecutive years at two magnificent homes that were owned by a Mr. Perleman.

Norman Lear personally knowing Mr. Perleman, and all of us knowing Norman Lear, made it possible for Norman to invite eight dear friends to be his guests at Mr. P's five-bedroom homes. The five fun-couples consisted of Norman and his wife Frances, Anne Bancroft and Mel Brooks, Larry Gelbart and Pat Marshall, Dom DeLuise and Carole Arthur DeLuise, and me and my wife Estelle.

The laughter and gaiety started the moment we stepped across the threshold and into the foyer of Mr. Perleman's La Costa mansion, where we were welcomed by the sound and sight of sixteen violinists descending a marble stairway while playing a lush Viennese waltz. After a rousing ending, the violinists, whom Norman Lear had gone to much expense to hire, marched off and disappeared—only to re-appear later at the dining-room table, where they serenaded us while we ate the first course of a lovely dinner that the Lears had catered. I do not recall what we ate or what was said, but I do remember explosions of laughter and a reluctance to leave the table after we had finished our dessert and coffee.

At one point, someone suggested that "we repair to the living room," and after deciding that the living room "did not need repair but might enjoy a visit," we adjourned to it and continued laughing at the pearls that were dropping from the mouths of at least five of the assembled guests. During an unexpected lull, someone suggested that we play a round of "pass the orange." It may be that I suggested it, for I had, as a youth, worked as a social director at a mountain resort. For the uninitiated, "pass the orange" is played by one person cradling an orange in the crook of his or her neck, and without using their hands, attempting to pass it to another member's neck-crook. It is not as easy as it sounds, considering the differential between men and women's physical height, neck length, apparel, ticklishness, and proneness to giggle. I daresay that the older and more serious the participants are, the greater the appreciation is when an orange is successfully passed from one neck to another. It may seem apocryphal, but underlying this seemingly childish activity, there is a palpable quotient of primal sexuality.

After playing a round or three of "pass the orange," which could just as aptly be named "drop the orange," we segued to a brand-new game, an original one that our group invented and played for almost an hour. We called it "celebrity grapefruit" in honor of the ten celebrities who created it that night. Each couple made up a team, and each team would compete against one other team. For example, say the first match was the Brookses versus the Reiners. Estelle and I would stand about six feet apart and face each other, as would Anne and Mel. Each of us would have a grapefruit in hand. The object of the game was for one partner, on the count of three, to toss a grapefruit to his partner, who was to catch it and toss it back—without hitting your partner's or the other team's airborne missile. The team with the greatest number of catches would be declared the winner. It was one of our group's favorite activities, but sadly, the only opportunity we had to play the game was when we were together at

Yenemvelt. As far as I know, there are but ten people in the world who have had the pleasure of playing "celebrity grapefruit."

After many satisfying rounds of "CG," someone noticed that it was almost two in the morning and way past our bedtime. It was at this point that someone else suggested song, and the song we chose to sing was "My Hero" from Oscar Straus's *The Chocolate Soldier*. A wise choice, as all of us knew most of the lyrics of the chorus and verse:

(The verse:)
"I have a true and noble lover,
He is a sweetheart, all my own,
(something, something, something)

"Oh, happy, happy wedding day,
Oh happy, happy wedding day."

(Then the soaring chorus:)
"Come, come, I love you only,
My heart is truuuuuuueeeeee.
Come, come, my life is lonely,
I long for youuuuuuueeeeeeee.
Come, come, naught can efface you.
My arms are aching
Now to embrace you.
Thou art diviiiiiiiiiiiiiiiiiine!
Come, come, I love you o-o-oonly.
Come, heroooooo miiiiiiiiiiiiiiiine!"

Written in 1908 by Oscar Straus
Lyrics: Rudolph Bernauer & Leopold Jacobson)
(English lyrics by Stanislaus Stange—1909)

We had formed a semi-circle and belted out the lyrics, until some unseen force directed the couples to turn and walk toward their bedrooms. We sang those last few notes of the song with mounting fervor and then backed into our rooms and shut the doors.

You are going to have to take my word for it, but without being cued by anything but our mutual understanding of theater and fun, all five couples quietly started to reprise the song's verse, and after the first two lines, exited our bedrooms singing and slowly made our way into the living room. With Estelle, Mel, and Pat providing the harmony, we finished the verse, and as we reprised the chorus, we all turned and strolled back to our rooms.

This entire musical staging was repeated at least twice before we undressed and made ready for bed. Before we settled in, Norman, unable to resist activating an intercom he found on his bedroom wall, sang softly, "I have a true and noble lover," which triggered an encore performance by the pajama-clad Yenemvelt Opera Company.

That night, as we nodded off, I am sure the members of the company all had smiles on their faces.

After we all fell asleep, Norman's voice came over the intercoms, announcing that breakfast was being served. It was actually three hours that we slept, but it seemed like three minutes. I don't think anyone groused, and if we did, it was a good-natured grouse. Eating, laughing, and "funning" easily trumped sleeping.

It was at the breakfast table that the word *Yenemvelt* was first uttered. Once again, I am not certain which of us said it, but I do know that for my mother, *Yenemvelt* meant "the other world" or "the next world"—a place where poor people would be wealthy enough to own a private home, a car, or whatever luxury their heart desired. My mom would say sarcastically, "Sure, we'll get all those things —in *Yenemvelt!*"

It seems that those of us who had Jewish parents had heard the word spoken in their home, and so Yenemvelt was unanimously accepted as our club's name. It was also agreed that Yenemvelt should have a song to celebrate its existence, and it was Mel, Larry, or Norman who suggested that the music of the German Yuletide favorite, "O Tannenbaum" would scan perfectly.

It took no longer than the time it takes to sing a chorus of "O Tannenbaum" for our resident composers to devise the following lyrics for our anthem:

"Oh Yenemvelt, oh Yenemvelt, oh Yenemvelt, oh Yenemvelt.
Oh Yenemvelt, oh Yenemvelt, oh Yenemvelt oh Yenemvelt.

Oh Yenemveeeeeeeelt, oh Yenemveeeeeeeelt,
Oh Yenemveeeeeeeelt, oh Yenemveeeeeeeelt,
Oh Yenemvelt, oh Yenemvelt,
There is no veeelt—like—Yenem—veeeeeeeelt!"

We were all so pleased with our emotion-filled rendition of our anthem that we could do nothing less than pledge our loyalty to the precepts of Yenemvelt.

I truly believe that it was I who suggested that we do this by sealing our commitment in wax, as our Founding Fathers did when signing the Declaration of Independence. Having no parchment or sealing wax available, I suggested that each founder place the tips of their pinkies into the ears of whoever was seated on either side of them. With no hesitation or discussion, the suggestion was implemented, and there we sat, ten full-grown adults, each with someone else's pinky stuck in their ears. At this point, someone started to sing our anthem and was quickly joined by the rest of us, who rendered a deeply emotional version of "Oh Yenemvelt."

I do not remember the contents of the hilarious, joke-laden exchanges we had during that first Yenemvelt breakfast, but I do remember being angry that I had to miss some of the hilarity by going to the toilet to pee.

During those etched-in-memory Yenemvelt weekends, we took part in two other events that I feel bear noting. One was a spirited and original game of charades and the other a star-studded variety show.

One night, after dinner, someone realized that we had so many wonderful entertainers in our midst and suggested that we ask them "to put on a show for us!"

"But who would they do the show for?" another of us asked.

"For those of us who are not in the show," someone else answered.

"That's a great idea," another chirped up. "Whoever is not performing would become a member of the audience."

And thus, a show was born! Each of us graciously stood up and contributed to the evening's entertainment.

<u>Mel Brooks</u>: Leaped out of his seat and immediately became Fred Astaire! With the aid of an umbrella he had commandeered from a stand, and twirling it like cane, he became Fred Astaire and started to

sing: "I'm puttin' on my top hat, tyin' on my white tie, brushing up my tails!"

Mel then proceeded to tap dance on the parquet floor and punctuated his choreography with smart Astaire-like kicks to every piece of furniture in the room. No easy chair, couch, coffee table, chest of drawers, or lamp stand escaped being jumped upon or kicked.

Anne Bancroft: With her expressive hands and body moving flapper style, the Academy Award-winning actress sang a throaty version of Irving Berlin's "Some Sunny Day":

Some sunny day with a smile on my face,
I'll go back to that place far away...
Some sunny day, I'll be on that express,
Flying away to my little bunch of happiness.

Estelle Reiner: Accompanying herself with the ukulele that I brought from home, she sang: "Dapper Dan was a Pullman porter man on the train that ran through Dixie. Everyone knew Dapper Dan, knew him for a ladies' man..."

Carole DeLuise: A capella, she did a hilarious, spot-on impression of Imogene Coca singing the lament about Jim: "Jim never sends me pretty flowers..."

Dom DeLuise: Did a hilarious but loving impression of his father, a city garbage collector, endorsing his weekly paycheck. Sadly, Papa DeLuise was illiterate but had learned to write his name.

Before picking up his pen, Dom went through a torturous ritual that included a careful clearing of the kitchen table, the continuous wiping of sweat from his brow with the palms of both hands, and the loosening of tension in his upper body by rolling his shoulder sockets in a circle. After unscrewing the top from the pen, Dom illustrated the herculean effort his dad made to write his name on the back of the check, one letter at a time, pausing, sighing, and mopping his brow after each successful effort.

Me: For my contribution, I think I did my standard, fairly humorous impressions of Jimmy Stewart, Ronald Coleman, Charles Boyer, and Akim Tamiroff.

Norman Lear: Gracefully walked into the room carrying a large, three-layer cake that he had commandeered from the kitchen, and asked, "Who'd like a piece of this delicious cake?"

He then dug his bare hand deep into the cake and offered us a wad of the wet goop he had scooped out. Throughout his long and extraordinarily successful career, Norman has always found the time, the layer cakes, and the occasions to delight audiences with his classic pantomime. Gentleman that Norman is, he always offered to serve the ladies first.

Pat Marshall: Strode confidently to the grand piano that stood in a corner of the living room and magnificently accompanied herself as she belted out "Mr. Wonderful," the hit song from the Broadway show of the same name that starred Sammy Davis Jr. and Pat Marshall.

Frances Lear: A businesswoman, who had no known performing talent, she announced that she was going to do her impression of a woman in a current mystery film who had been murdered. Frances then lay down on the floor, face up, and became the corpse. To her credit, she did not breathe or move a muscle for almost a full minute. For her accurate portrayal, she received at least as much applause as any of the seasoned performers.

It was at this point that Larry Gelbart suggested that it might be interesting if a couple of us eavesdrop on the members of the audience and report back what they said about the performers and their performances. Anne Bancroft was the first to volunteer, and she did this by casually moving to where two of us, who were designated as audience members, were chatting. Anne then returned and reported to the others that the audience absolutely loved the show and all the performers, and singled out "the interesting dark-haired girl, Anne Bancroft," saying how thrilled they were to discover that "an Academy Award-winning actress could sing so beautifully and be so gracious and down-to-earth."

Pat Marshall had a similar experience and mentioned that someone wondered if they could get a recording of her singing "Mr. Wonderful" and a copy of Good News, a movie in which she starred with Peter Lawford and June Allyson.

And so it went, each performer eavesdropping on the audience and reporting what was overheard. Every performer had similar story to Anne's, with each being the audience's particular favorite.

Larry Gelbart claimed that he had left the house and visited a local restaurant, where he heard strangers who had wandered into our living room and seen our show report how amazed they were "to see so many big celebrities all in one house—and putting on a show!" He said that they particularly liked Pat Marshall's singing and the hilarious quips her husband delivered. The man couldn't remember his name but said that he wrote most of Bob Hope's jokes and also the play, *A Funny Thing Happened on the Way to the Forum.*

CHARADES:

The playing of charades was, at that time, a favorite after-dinner activity, and during one of these historic weekends, our group played a round of charades with a passion and an outcome that was above and beyond what I believe most people have experienced.

As prescribed, we formed two teams, and to add spice, we decided that husbands and wives would be on opposing teams. Their team, captained by Norman, went into an adjoining room, and ours, led by Larry, went into another room to find subjects that would be both challenging and funny to act out. After coming up with ten good charades, Larry called out, "We're ready to play!" and Norman responded, "We need a few extra minutes!"—which we gave them. After the "few extra minutes," Larry called out again, but this time there was no response. When we went to find out why, we found their room empty, the front door open, and Norman's car gone. We also found their little joke to be mildly funny and a bit mean-spirited. Naturally, we immediately started to discuss what we could do to ensure that they got the comeuppance they deserved. Again, I have no memory of who suggested that we do what we did, but by gum, it was one heck of a brilliant suggestion.

Guessing that their group would soon return feeling smug about their little gambit, we worked feverishly to do something that would make them regret making us feel like dopes.

The "something" we did was go about and strip the cushions and pillows from every sofa and club chair and toss them about the room. We overturned the chairs and sofas, toppled the coffee table, the dining-room table, and a couple of standing cabinets. We pulled the large area rugs from the floor and stacked them in a rumpled mess against a wall. We took the oil paintings off the walls and placed then atop the upended furniture. The larger oils we left on the walls but made them hang askew.

After making the room appear to have been vandalized, the five of us vandalized ourselves by rumpling our clothing, tousling our hair, smudging our faces with fireplace ashes, and disheveling ourselves sufficiently to appear as if we were the victims of violent intruders.

Estelle and Anne, who had been a party to the idea of sneaking out and going off, shrieked in guilty horror when they saw the lifeless bodies of their husbands sprawled about. It was a short-lived guilt, for they quickly realized the truth, but we felt that their few horrified gasps were enough for our charades team to claim a moral victory. We had beaten our loved ones at their own dirty game!

It may be hard to believe, but I contend that the fun and laughter we all had on that first Yenemvelt weekend was equaled the following year, if not surpassed—and you can check that with any member of our club. I am sad to note that, of the five founding couples, one member of each Yenemvelt family has "shuffled off their mortal coil." Anne Bancroft, Estelle Reiner, Dom DeLuise, Larry Gelbart, and Frances Lear are no longer with us, but if you were in a position to check with their mates, you will find that I speak the truth...or something close to it.

CHAPTER FORTY-SIX

Rickles, Kovacs, and Sinatra
(A Warm Story about Cool Celebs)

In 1959, I had the pleasure of going out on the town with the above "cool celebs." At that time, Don Rickles was not yet a "celeb," but Frank Sinatra certainly was, and Ernie Kovacs was a newly arrived one. Ernie's wildly inventive comedy shows were a staple on early television, and at this point in his career, he was being wooed by filmmakers and television producers to star in some prestigious works—one being a *Playhouse Ninety* production of *Topaze*, a classic play by Marcel Pagnol. In an early film version, the character Topaze, a naive schoolteacher, had been portrayed by no less a star than John Barrymore.

I was offered a supporting role in the project and was excited by the prospect of flying to Hollywood and appearing in a film that starred a one-of-a kind comedian whose inventive mind had always intrigued me.

As I recall, neither the play nor the production was very impressive. The production company had reserved suites for us at the Beverly Hills Hotel, which was both convenient and scary. Ernie's driving to and from work every day was the convenient part—the scary part came as we left the hotel driveway each morning. At about sixty miles per hour, he sped from the front of the hotel down a steep hill, past the stop sign at the end of the driveway, made a sharp left turn onto a street, and traveled twenty yards before coming to a screeching halt at the red light on the corner of Sunset Boulevard and Rodeo Drive.

Had another vehicle been coming down the intersecting street Ernie had blindly entered, you would not be reading this book.

After experiencing Ernie's harrowing maneuver, I questioned his judgment and sanity. "Ernie," I asked tactfully, "are you crazy or what? What if someone were driving down that street?"

"I knew there wouldn't be!"

"How the hell could you know that?"

"Because it's a thousand-to-one shot a car would be there. The odds are in my favor."

"Well, my odds could be a five-to one—so I'd appreciate it if we go by my odds."

He compromised and accommodated my urge to live by heeding the stop sign—on most mornings.

One night after rehearsal, Ernie asked me if I would like to join him and Frank Sinatra to catch "this wild new comic, Don Rickles."

Of course I accepted his invitation, and it turned out to be a memorable evening, so memorable that, at this very moment, I am typing it into my computer. Before I get to a conversation I had with Frank Sinatra, I would like to quote some of the less-censorable lines I remember Don Rickles spraying about that night. For those few dozen people who do not know what Don Rickles does, he is a comedian who never fails to convulse an audience by picking on and insulting various members of that audience who have paid money to see him.

Ernie, Frank, and I were seated at a little table in the middle of the club. None of us had ever seen Rickles before, but we had heard that he picked on people. He started by asking questions of and insulting the people closest to his platform. The two quips that have stuck in my head all these years, he directed at two celebrities he was told were in the room. The first was Elliot Roosevelt, President Franklin D.'s oldest son. Rickles wasted no time.

"I'm told that Elliot Roosevelt is with us tonight," he said, smiling. "Elliot, where are you?"

Elliot stood up and embarrassedly waved at Don, who said, "Hi, Elliot! Folks, let's give Elliot Roosevelt a big hand!"

While the audience applauded, Rickles continued, "Say hello to your mother, Elliot. I saw her in Vegas last week—yeah your mom, Eleanor—at the Frontier Hotel. She was in the lobby, standing behind a pole, swinging her pocketbook over her head and yelling, 'Hi ya, sailor, you wanna have a good time? Room 204!'"

At one point, a young girl came to our table and asked Sinatra for his autograph, and this caught the quip master's eye.

"Hey, Frank," Rickles shouted. "You're not going to get rid of those pimples on your face tonight—that broad you're with—she ain't gonna put out for ya!"

And so it went. Everyone was fodder for Rickles's verbal abuse, and strangely, those in the audience whom he chose not to insult were openly disappointed.

After the performance, a smiling, pussycat version of Don Rickles came to our table, fawned over Sinatra, said how happy he was to meet me, and then walked off, chatting with Ernie. For the next half hour, I found myself alone with Frank Sinatra, and during that half hour, we sipped some beer and had a conversation that forever endeared him to me. I don't know how the subject came up, but we found ourselves talking about our parents, generally, and our fathers, specifically. We both seemed to have mothers who were supportive and very proud of us and told us so. My father, I offered, was not very demonstrative but made it clear that he agreed with my mom when she first expressed her view of my performances.

"He's the best one!" my mom whispered out loud when she saw me perform in a school play as a third grader. Mom continued to repeat that mantra throughout my career whenever she saw me perform on Broadway or on television.

Sinatra volunteered that he never knew what his father thought about him or if he ever thought about him. He said that his father was not much of a talker.

"When I was a kid," he said sadly, "I don't think my father said ten words to me."

When I asked how his father felt about his son being the idol of millions of bobby soxers all over the country, he shrugged and said, "I didn't know how he felt, because he sure as hell didn't tell me. All I know is that he got up every morning, went to the firehouse, maybe put out a couple of fires, came home, had dinner, then went to the bar and chatted with his buddies until it was time to come home and go to bed—that was it."

Sinatra said that's how it was for years. When I said that I could not believe that his father was not aware and proud of what his son had accomplished, he told me about this one particular visit he made to his parents' home in Hoboken, New Jersey. He had just returned from a highly successful tour, and all the newspapers were filled with descriptions of the love and adulation he had received from the tumultuous crowds of screaming fans.

His mother welcomed him home with a big hug and kiss, and when he asked where his dad was, his mom told him that he was probably at the corner bar, his off-duty hangout.

Frank said that he went to the bar, but his dad wasn't there. The bartender had a funny smile on his face. "If you are looking for your Pop," the bartender informed him, "he didn't come in today—but he sure paid us a visit yesterday."

Sinatra seemed to be enjoying telling me this story, and it soon became apparent to me why. Frank learned from the bartender that his father came into the bar the day before, and just as he walked in, he heard a customer at the bar ask his friend what he thought of "this Sinatra kid," and his friend made a very derogatory remark about Sinatra's sexuality.

Frank said that the bartender told him that his father pulled the guy off his stool and beat the crap out of him—and gave his buddy a few shots too. Frank was beaming with pride as he related the story. He said that he went to the fire station to pay his Pop a visit and maybe say "thanks for standing up for me." When Frank got to the firehouse, he was told that his father was in the locker room. He went up a flight of stairs and found his father standing at his open locker and reaching into it.

"His back was to me," Frank said, "and I called out, 'Hi, Pop!' and without turning, he slammed his locker shut, then looked over his shoulder at me and said, 'Hi, Frankie. What're you doing here?'"

He said that he and his father had one of their regular, unsentimental exchanges, but the overall effect of that visit changed his feelings about his father and his father's overt disinterest in him or his career.

In the few seconds Frank's father stood in front of his open locker, and before he slammed the door shut, Frank was able to catch a glimpse of dozens of newspaper photos and clippings scotch-taped to the inside of his locker door—and all of them about Frankie Sinatra!

Frank said that those few seconds made him realize that his father did love and care about him but could never allow his son or the world to know that he had a soft side. Those few seconds also allowed Frank to search for new ways to be a dutiful son to a reluctant father.

CHAPTER FORTY-SEVEN

Can a Jewish Kid Be an Irish Tenor?
(And Someday Meet Judy Garland)

John McCormack

W hen I was six years old (and yes, I do remember that day eighty-four years ago), I asked my father that question. To my young mind, it was a perfectly reasonable thing to ask. Among his collection of RCA Victor's Red Seal recordings by Enrico Caruso singing arias from *La Traviata* and *Pagliacci*, were a few songs recorded by the world-renowned Irish tenor, John McCormack. The one I loved was, "The Tumble Down Shack in Athlone." By listening to it over and over and singing along with him, I learned all the words. I did have some difficulty in staying on pitch and keeping proper time, but I was quite pleased with my rendition.

261

I had another compelling reason to feel that I might one day pursue my dream to be an Irish tenor. My father had an old and dear friend named Max Kalphus, who spoke with a distinct German accent. He had a brother who sang on the radio, and every Monday night at seven, my parents would tune in station WOR and listen to a program of Irish songs sung by John Calvin. I had been told that John Calvin's real name was Joseph Kalphus, and he was Max Kalphus's brother.

John Calvin spoke with a charming Irish brogue, and before each song, he would talk about why he had selected to sing it. To introduce "The Tumble Down Shack in Athlone," I heard him say, "I first heard this loovely song, when I was a wee lad, a'sittin on me mither's knee. I c'n still hear her sweet voice a'singin'...*I'm a lang way from hoooome and my thoughts ever roaaam, To 'ould' Erin far over the seeaaa*."

After the song ended, I told my father that when I grew up, I wanted to be an Irish tenor like John Calvin. My father said when I grew up, I could become a singer and sing Irish songs, but I could not become an Irish tenor. When I asked why not, he reminded me that our family was Jewish. I was confused and asked how Max Kalphus could be Jewish and have a brother John who was Irish. My father had the patience to explain that in show business, an actor or a singer can be become anything they want to be. If an Irish man wanted to sing Jewish songs—that would be fine. He pointed out that Al Jolson, who was Jewish, sang songs that black people sang—and he even put on make-up to look like the singers who sang those songs. Whatever my father said to me obviously did not discourage me from pursuing a profession where I was able to attempt— and more times than not, successfully perform—as an Englishman, a German, a Russian, an Italian, a Frenchman, a Japanese samurai, and, for one memorable evening, an Irish tenor.

That performance was memorable, not only for my singing of "The Tumble Down Shack in Athlone," but for singing it to my all-time favorite movie star, the one and only Judy Garland.

In 1960, I was invited to be a guest on a show Judy hosted, and I had the best time sitting beside her and being interviewed by her. In my time, I had sat beside and been interviewed by the greatest hosts, among them Jack Paar, Johnny Carson, Jay Leno, David Letterman, Dick Cavett, Regis Philbin, Merv Griffin, Craig Ferguson, Art Linkletter, Ernie Kovacs, Mike Wallace, Ellen DeGeneres, Joy Behar, Katie Couric, Arlene Francis, and others, but on none of them did I ever have a romantic crush.

On Judy's show, I told her of my desire, as a wee lad of six, to grow up to be an Irish tenor, and to prove to her that a Jewish lad could have become an Irish tenor, I sang for her, and for an unsuspecting public, a creditable, Irish-accented rendition of "The Tumble Down Shack in Athlone."

Judy's smile of approval made my day.

Before that show, at a pre-interview in her dressing room, Judy and I discovered that we were the same age. I confessed to her that when I was thirteen, I was smitten by a girl who sang "Balboa" in the short subject, *Pigskin Parade*. At sixteen, when I saw her play Dorothy in *The Wizard of Oz*, my feelings for that girl deepened.

When we discussed how time had flown and realized that we were now thirty-seven years old, Judy grimaced and said these exact words, "Thirty-seven is a shitty age—don't you think?"

I confessed that I had not really thought about it but asked why she thought it was shitty.

"Because it is!" Judy insisted. "Being thirty-eight would be okay—it's a nice, round number, and it's just two years from forty—and they do say, 'life begins at forty.' I am all for that!" she laughed. "Forty is fine, but thirty-seven is nowhere."

I reminded her of the song, "I'm Just an In-Between" that she sang to a photo of Clark Gable when professing her unrequited love for him.

"That's it," she said with a laugh, "at thirty-seven, I am once again 'just an in-between!'"

Soon after, I was privileged to be invited to guest on Judy's CBS series and chatted with her on the "Tea for Two" segment, where Judy interviewed celebrities.

The thrust I chose for my appearance was to make the case that I was not a celebrity. I went on and listed for her the a few reasons why I was not a celebrity and did not feel like one.

"To start, I said, "I am rarely recognized when I go out in public. Women never shower me with kisses, as they do Sinatra and Vic Damone. No one had ever done a caricature of me. Dick Van Dyke, who is a fine caricaturist, confessed that he is unable to do a satisfactory one of me."

To add fuel to my premise, I told Judy of a cab driver who did not recognize me but boasted about all the celebrities who had sat in the back seat of his cab—among them Eleanor Roosevelt, Jack Carter, Winston Churchill, Buddy Hackett, and Sonny Sparks. Sonny Sparks was a minor celebrity but obviously more well-known to the driver than I was.

The gravely-voiced cab driver, speaking New Yawkese, had asked what I did for a living, and when I said that I was an actor, he asked where he might have seen me. When I told him that I was on *The Sid Caesar Show*, he asked, "Whut did ya do on it?"

"Have you ever seen the show?" I asked.

"Nevuh miss it—I love it. Whut do ya do on it?"

"Well, do you know the sketches with the phony German professor?"

"The German professor cracks me up," he said, checking his rearview mirror. "That ain't you!"

"No, Sid Caesar plays the professor—I'm the guy in the trench coat who interviews him."

"Don't ring no bell. That Caesar is great. What else did you do?"

"Did you ever see the take-offs we do on foreign movies?"

"Yeah, I love 'em—that Caesar guy is a riot, the way he talks in them phony foreign languages!"

"Well, I'm the guy Sid is talking to when he talks in those phony languages."

"You tellin' me that you can speak them phony languages?"

"Maybe not as well as Sid does, but well enough…"

"Which ones you do?"

"All of them, Italian, German, French…"

"Oh yeah, do French!" he ordered.

For the rest of the ride, even though there was no prospect of the driver hiring me for a job, I auditioned all my phony language skills for him.

When we reached our destination he turned and shouted, "Son of a gun, I know who you are! You're that Art Carney!"

When I told him that Art Carney worked on *The Jackie Gleason Show*, and I was Carl Reiner and worked with Sid Caesar, he nodded and said, "Oh, yeah!"

I hoped I had convinced him that I was me, and to let him know that there were no hard feelings, I gave him a huge tip.

He was very appreciative of my largesse, and as I left the cab, he saluted me with the bills in his hand and mumbled, "Thanks, I really appreciate this—and you do crack me up, Mr. Carney!"

I considered that incident a learning experience for both the cab driver and for me. Once again, I learned that I was not a true celebrity, and the driver learned that Art Carney was a generous tipper.

On a second appearance on Judy's show, I related another story about my dubious status as a celebrity. It dealt with an experience I had while lunching at the Oyster Bar in New York's Grand Central Station.

I sat alone at the oval bar and was enjoying a plate of Italian lasagna. Yes, lasagna! I was just as surprised then to find that dish on the menu as I assume you are now.

I was halfway through my meal when a middle-aged couple settled in seats directly opposite me. The clothes they wore suggested they were from out of town—had one of them been holding a pitchfork, they could have been the couple who posed for Grant Wood's painting, *American Gothic*.

They were scanning their menus when the woman stopped and glanced in my direction. She mumbled something to her husband, which made him lower his menu and look at me. They seemed to be in disagreement, and the more they stared at me, the more certain I became that the woman recognized me and was trying to convince her husband that I was, indeed, "that guy on television." Finally, they stood up and made their way toward me. I could all but keep from blurting out, "*Yes, I am! I'm Carl Reiner.*" I restrained myself from taking out my pen and signing their menus. My two shy fans approached, and with their menus in hand and warm smiles on their faces, apologized for disturbing me. I smiled and assured them that they were not disturbing me.

The man uttered the classic line that I had heard many times in my career as a supporting actor: "My wife and I are having a little disagreement, and we made a bet on who is right—and you can settle it for us."

I smiled, and just as I was about to admit that whoever said I was Carl Reiner was correct, the man spoke. "Sir, I am sorry to bother you, but my wife and I were watching you eat, and she is sure that you are having that Italian lasagna, and I said that you are eating the fried oysters..."

While hiding my disappointment, I graciously informed him that his wife was right: I was having the lasagna. The couple thanked me for settling their dispute and left me with further evidence that the long-standing belief in my status as a non-celebrity was intact.

CHAPTER FORTY-EIGHT

Joseph Owens, Guilty
until Proven Guilty

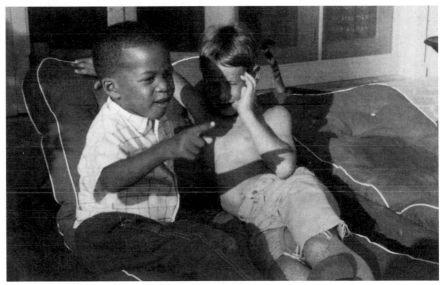

Joseph & Lucas at 6

For six days in August of 1965, there was rioting in the streets of Los Angeles in the area called Watts. The Watts Riots were headline news in every newspaper in the country. At that time, working for us as a housekeeper, was a lovely woman, Amanda Owens, a single mother of two and a resident of Watts. As soon as the riots broke out, my wife and I, concerned about the safety of Amanda and her children—six-year-old Joseph and eight-year-old Nancy—invited them to live in our home until their neighborhood quieted down. Amanda was only too happy to accept our offer, and she and her children moved in. Our son Lucas was three at the time, and he and Joseph seemed to get a kick out of each other. The above photo is of them lounging at our pool.

All was going smoothly until one morning, when I put on a clean pair of pants and went to re-pocket the stuff I had taken from my old trousers the night before and placed on a countertop. The small wad of bills I had put there the night before was now a much smaller wad. It originally held eighty or ninety dollars in twenties, tens, and fives, and what it now held was a ten and two fives. I drew the only conclusion I could—someone in the house had "lifted" some of my money.

I was terribly upset, as was my wife, when I told her what I suspected.

I decided that I could not confront Amanda and suggest that one of her kids was a thief. After some amateur sleuthing, I deduced that it was Joseph who did the deed. He was a wanderer, and he loved roaming about the house. I remembered his mother once admonishing him not to "go around touching things!" I decided that for the boy's sake, his mother must be made aware of her son's behavior.

I started by saying that we liked having her and her children as our guests, and what I was about to tell her about Joseph was for his sake. I said that all young kids, at one time or another, take things that don't belong to them, and they have to be told that it is wrong. I told Amanda about the missing money and made a point of saying that I was not looking to get the money back, but I wanted her to let Joseph know that he might someday get into real trouble if he continued to take things that were not his.

I could see Amanda was hurt. She could not believe her son would do such a thing, but said she would talk to him about it.

The following morning, Amanda told me that she had confronted Joseph and asked if he taken any of "Mr. Reiner's money," and Joseph swore that he had not. She also asked her daughter if Joseph had taken the money, and Nancy said, "Mama, Joseph is dying to buy candy, and if he had that kind of money, he'd go out and buy some!"

I let the subject drop and told Amanda that I was not upset and had faith that she would help Joseph grow up right.

Amanda and her children lived with us for a little over a week before returning to their apartment in Watts. Amanda worked for us for another six months and then left with her children to go back to their home in Georgia. For a short time after, we kept in touch by letter and post card.

It was many years later, I think in 1970, when Joseph and the memory of his deed resurfaced—and in a most unlikely manner.

I was at home, seated at my office desk and typing away on my Royal portable typewriter. I was in the process of attempting to write a major American novel when I stopped typing and idly stared straight ahead at the closed door of an adjoining room. That door was few feet away, at the end of a very narrow alcove.

I had stared at that tiny alcove many times while searching for an idea or considering how to phrase a thought. However, this time, as I stared down at the two small, molded panels that were on either end of the two-foot-wide alcove, I noticed something different about the panels. Stuck in the edge of the panel furthest from me were two thin, inch-long, metal cylinders. The panel closest to me had no such cylinders.

By Jove, I thought, *those metal cylinders are hinges—and there is a small hole in that panel!*

With Sherlock Holmes-like acuity, I deduced, *That small hole may well have held a screw—a screw that once fit into a knob!*

Squatting on the floor of the alcove and digging into the molding with the tips of my ten straining fingers, I succeeded in swinging open a small panel door and in doing so, solving a decade-old crime.

Behind the panel, sitting on two small shelves, was a treasure trove of evidence! Besides the sixty dollars I accused Joseph of taking, the following booty was stashed—booty that I never missed:

+ Two leather passport cases with Mr./Mrs. Carl Reiner printed on them.
+ Seven expired passports.
+ Two broken, strapless wristwatches.
+ One expandable metal watch strap.
+ One beige watch strap.
+ The brass knob that was missing from the panel door.
+ A "short-snorter" (a wartime souvenir of worthless Japanese currency which we collectors had scotch-taped end to end).

I was pleased to have solved the case of my missing money and sad that

I had upset Amanda by accusing her son of being a thief, when he was nothing more than a kid on an adventure. Joseph was an explorer, a collector, a hoarder, and something more—a discoverer, which I most appreciated. It was he who discovered our hidden vault that, in later years, my wife and I used to keep our cherished valuables. A thief had no chance of finding some of the expensive presents I had bought for her— like the very limited-edition gold neck piece designed by the renowned artist, Erte, or the sting of elegant pearls I had gifted my wife for an important birthday, or the heavy, gold charm bracelet that was presented to me by Ralph Edwards on his TV show, *This Is Your Life!*

Except for the pearls and the piece by Erte, all of the above items are still stashed there. I have, since then, added to the stash, items such as a half-dozen of my Pop's hundred-year-old Daguerreotype plates, including the ones he took of my mother nursing my brother, Charlie, and the one of Charlie at two, sitting on a small "toidy." In Joseph's hiding place I have also placed my father's small jeweler's scale and his handwritten formula of the elements that went into creating the dry-pile battery for his pendulum clock that was geared to run a hundred years without recharging. The clock, for which he received a US patent, ran for over sixty years.

And there is more to this tale.

Fifteen years after Joseph and his family had spent that charged week in our home, I received a phone call from a young man who identified himself as Joseph Owens and said that he was on an army furlough for two weeks. He wondered if he might stop off on his way home, to pay us a short visit, and I told him that we were looking forward to seeing him.

Corporal Joseph Owens turned out to be a handsome young man who exuded confidence. After my asking about how his mother and sister were doing, he quickly segued to the reason for his visit. He had come to apologize for the trouble he had caused and was anxious to tell me that he had not taken my sixty bucks and to show me where he had hidden the bills. He was surprised and genuinely disappointed to learn that I had found his hiding place and the money. He so wanted to confess his sin and show us that he had turned out okay. I was able to say, with all honesty, that having the mother he had and the personality he had as a six-year-old, I was fairly confident that he would turn out as he did.

We had offered him a bite to eat, but all he seemed interested in was exploring the house, as he did years ago, and seeing the hiding place he had once discovered.

He did all of the above and got a special kick out of finding that all the booty he had stashed on those shelves was still there. He laughed when I told him that I had spent his sixty-buck "stash."

Joseph left happy, and he promised to drop us a card, which he did.

It occurred to me that if ever Joseph Owens wrote his version of "Joseph Owens, Guilty until Proven Guilty," he might title it. "Carl Reiner, Guilty of Conclusion Jumping."

CHAPTER FORTY-NINE

My Personal Road from Here to There

The year was 1959, and for the important meeting with my representative at the William Morris Agency, I had decided to wear my blue blazer, gray wool slacks, a white shirt, and my regimental tie. My agent, Harry Kalcheim, had set up a meeting with two young writers who had written a pilot script for a situation comedy they thought would be perfect for me. To discuss this possible series and other projects Harry thought would interest me, I had arranged to be at his office a half hour before the young writers were due.

It was a lovely, sunny day when I walked out of the Lombardy Hotel on East Fifty-Sixth Street, so lovely that I decided that a long, brisk, cross-town walk from Fifty-Seventh Street and Park Avenue to my agent's office at Fifty-Sixth and Broadway was just what I needed to get my blood moving. I had ample time to make the trek, unless something untoward happened, and five minutes into my stroll, the untoward happened: a cloudburst. A billowing mass of vapor obliterated the sun, and a hurricane-style gust of wind whooshed my gray fedora off my head and into the gutter. As I ran to retrieve it, a flash of lightning and a clap of thunder heralded the sheets of water that came down on my head and the heads of other hapless New Yorkers.

I was several blocks from my agent's office, but I would not allow a rainstorm to keep me from hearing more about starring in a new situation comedy. I leaned into the wind, and for two long blocks, with water pelting my face, I slogged on as I looked for refuge, which, thankfully I found at Saks Fifth Avenue. My hair was drenched and my clothes so laden with water, I looked as if I had jumped into a swimming pool.

As I stood in the store's lobby and felt the water squishing in the bottom of my wing-tipped shoes, I made a decision that only a man with a healthy assortment of credit cards could make: *I'll go on a shopping spree.* After toweling off in Mr. Saks's men's room, I went and picked out a single-breasted blue suit in a forty-two long and told the salesman that I would only buy the suit if he was able to get the trousers cuffed while I shopped for the rest of my wardrobe. I explained why I was in such a hurry, and luckily the salesman, a former kid actor, sympathized with my dilemma. As soon as he measured my inseam, I was off again, and by the time it took me to buy boxer shorts, a T-shirt, a spread-collared white dress shirt, a new regimental tie, black socks, shoes, and a snappy gray fedora, the accommodating tailor had finished cuffing my slacks.

I looked at my image in a floor-length mirror and saw a much better-dressed man than the one who left the Hotel Lombardy earlier that morning. Wearing my spanking new outfit, I met for the first of two meetings in Harry Kalcheim's office—two meetings that changed the arc of my career.

At the first meeting, the two eager, young writers, who professed to be fans of my work on *Caesar's Hour* and *Your Show of Shows*, presented me with their pilot script. As soon as they left, I read it and found the premise of the show and their writing to be wanting.

My very smart wife read it and concurred. As she put it down, she said, "Honey, you can do better than this. Why don't you write one."

I reminded Estelle that I had never written a situation comedy, and she reminded me that I had never written a novel before writing *Enter Laughing.*

The five words Estelle uttered, "Why don't you write one," were prescient and life-changing!

I have been interviewed many times about writing the pilot for a situation comedy, and I was always pleased to talk about it. Vince Waldron's *The Official Dick Van Dyke Show Book* has it all down accurately, but my writing about the fondly remembered details of the show's genesis still gives me pleasure, so...

One late afternoon, driving home from Manhattan to New Rochelle, on the East Side Drive, I was approaching Ninety-Sixth Street and thinking about a premise for a situation comedy that might suit me. I asked myself a question.

Before I tell you what I asked myself, I want to say that I actually did talk to myself, out loud—and still do. I recommend it highly, especially to intelligent people like yourself. I suggest that an intelligent person asking him- or herself intelligent questions is likely to get intelligent answers.

"Reiner," I asked myself, "what piece of ground do you stand on— that nobody else it the world stands on?"

"Well," I responded, "I live in New Rochelle with my wife and two kids. I work in Manhattan as an actor-writer on a comedy-variety television show.

"That's it!" I told myself. "Write about that!"

And that is what I wrote about. A character who lives in a split-level home in New Rochelle and who, six mornings a week, drives to Manhattan, where he works as an actor-writer in a weekly variety show and, eight hours later, drives back home. While at home, he discusses with his wife the problems that beset him at the office, and while at the office, he unburdens himself to his co-writers about his life in the suburbs with his loving wife and kids.

And thereupon, a pilot arose that I called, *Head of the Family*.

My pilot script was well received, so well that my agent, Harry Kalcheim, arranged for one of his clients, actor Peter Lawford, to finance a pilot. Peter had been looking for a project to produce.

The pilot script had flown out of my typewriter in about four or five days, and when I was told that Peter Lawford had made it a "go" project, I panicked.

I thought, *Hey, if the pilot is sold, and I was to star it in, how in the world would I find the time to get enough episodes written for a series?*

I knew that I would need writers to help me, but I also knew that from my one script, they could not know enough about who and what made these characters tick. To that end, I wrote what I considered to be a "bible" for the show. The bible consisted of the thirteen complete episodes I wrote during our six-week vacation on Fire Island.

Using my wife and me as templates, I wrote about characters I knew—what they thought and how they might behave and interact in any given situation.

Before shooting the pilot, I received a request from my agent to mail a copy of the script to Joseph P. Kennedy, the father of President John

F. I asked "Why in the world would he want to read it?" and I was told that since his daughter, Pat, was married to Peter Lawford, which made Peter a member of the Kennedy clan, Joseph P. wanted to be certain that my script reflected good morals and wholesome values.

We sent the script off to Florida, where the old man resided, and I remember saying to my agent, "Harry, that man, who makes millions as the world's biggest distributor of scotch whiskey, is going to be an arbiter of wholesomeness! That man, who cheated on his wife and humiliated her by having a scandalous affair with his mistress, Gloria Swanson, the star whose movies he financed? He is concerned about my morals?"

As far as I know, the one positive thing Joseph P. Kennedy ever did was not object to his son-in-law financing my pilot.

I liked Peter Lawford. I particularly enjoyed him in the MGM musical, *Good News*, in which he co-starred with one of my all-time favorites, June Allyson—but mostly I appreciated Peter getting my pilot made.

We assembled a fine cast that included Barbara Britton as my wife and Morty Gunty and Sylvia Miles as my co-writers, Buddy and Sally. We shot the pilot, *Head of the Family* in late 1958, at the Gold Medal Studios in my hometown, the Bronx!

The excuse given by some, including me, as to why *Head of the Family* failed was that situation comedies were not selling. It was the year of "the horse and the gun"—and unless the star played a cowboy or a detective, it had no chance of getting on the air. In hindsight, and to be completely honest, *Head of the Family* was a good show but not nearly good enough.

I was disappointed and came out of it a bit bloodied and only slightly bowed. I say *slightly* because I had another iron in the fire that I had not realized I had placed there. It was placed there months earlier, when Mel Brooks and I attended a dinner party given by Broadway producer Joe Fields. Joe was a fan of the *2000 Year Old Man*. He had seen us do our routine many times at the dinner parties he hosted for friends who loved to laugh.

At this one outing at his home in Beverly Hills, we entertained a group of what Hollywood columnist Hedda Hopper once dubbed, "A-list celebrities." After we caused these "A-Listers" to laugh till their sides ached, a number of them came up to shake our hands.

George Burns asked us if we had recorded an album of what he had just heard, and when we said we had not, he said, "Record it…or I'll steal it!"

Edward G. Robinson, sounding like the Al Capone-type character he played in *Little Caesar* said, "Make a play out of that material. I'd like to play that 'Thousand Year Old Man' on Broadway!"

"He's two thousand," I corrected him.

"One thousand, two thousand," he shouted, "I can play either age—just write the play!"

Steve Allen came up to us and made us an offer we did not refuse. He offered us a studio and a live audience to hear us record our 2000 Year Old Man. He wanted no recompense for it, just the pleasure of bringing laughter into the world. It was because of Steve that the 2000 Year Old Man's voice was first heard by the public—and can still be heard in a boxed set containing four newly mastered compact discs.

At that very same dinner party, after the others had left, Ross Hunter, a most successful film producer at Universal Pictures, came up to me and asked if, perchance, I had "an idea for a screenplay."

I asked why he had thought that I might, and he said that from the way I ad-libbed questions, he surmised that I had a might have a story idea in my head. I really had not thought about writing a screenplay but was intrigued by his saying that he was looking for a vehicle for Judy Holliday and that he would be interested if I could come up with an idea for her.

I, like most people who had seen Judy Holliday in her Broadway and film performances in *Born Yesterday* and *Bells Are Ringing*, loved Judy Holliday!

At the time, I did not have an idea, but the thought of working with that great lady sparked one.

I recalled a moment of pique that I had experienced when hosting the game show, *Keep Talking*. It was sponsored by Regimen, a diet product that guaranteed weight loss. It was moments before airtime, and I still had not been made up because the make-up artists were busy fussing with advertising agency reps and their models who had taken Regimen diet pills. During the commercial, each model would step on a scale to check her week's weight loss. It was one minute to airtime when I slid my face in front of one of the models and shouted, "Hey, do me first!"

A second later, the announcer's voice boomed, "Welcome to *Keep Talking*! And here is our host for the evening, Carl Reiner!"

With make-up drying on my face, I dashed on stage, accepted the huge applause that the small audience was instructed to give me, and started hosting.

The day after Ross Hunter asked if I had an idea for Judy Holliday, I found myself thinking about the day, and my wife and I drove with our friends Pat and Larry Gelbart to their home in the country. I was thinking about the day I vied with the Regimen models for the attention of a make-up artist, and it triggered a story idea. I told Larry about Ross Hunter and Judy Holliday and the nub of an idea I had for a film about people in advertising agencies who cared more about marketing their stupid diet product than they did about the contents of the show they were sponsoring.

Working for a couple of hours in Larry's den, he and I managed to bang out a three-page story outline that we thought pretty darn funny. We even had a provocative title for it, *The Thrill Girl*. Sadly, for me, Larry had committed to fly to London and write a film for Peter Sellers and so was not available to continue to work with me on a screenplay.

A couple of days later, with Larry's blessing, I delivered our three-page story outline to Ross Hunter, who liked it well enough to make a deal for me to develop a screenplay for *The Thrill Girl*. He also arranged for me to meet Judy Holliday at her apartment and pitch the idea to her.

Judy lived at The Dakota, a building famous for its celebrity clientele and also infamous as the assassination site of the brilliant John Lennon.

Judy Holliday could not have been more charming and gracious. She knew who I was and seemed sincere when she said that she loved the skits I did with Sid Caesar and Imogene Coca. She asked if I would read to her our short outline of *The Thrill Girl*, and I obliged. She had a big smile on her face as I told her that the part she would be playing was that of a housewife turned glamorous TV spokeswoman who becomes famous and makes more money selling soap than her obstetrician-husband does delivering babies. Judy laughed heartily when I described a scene we had not yet written that entailed her husband unwittingly driving his car into a swimming pool that his wife's sponsor had, unbeknownst to him, constructed in their back yard. Judy found it funny and laughed so hard

278

that she slid off her chair and onto the floor. While lying flat on her back, she complained that she had sprained it laughing so hard.

When I asked if I could help her up, she inhaled deeply and said that she would like to lie still for a while. She smiled and winced as we shook hands to say good-bye.

Very shortly after that extraordinary meeting, we heard that Judy Holliday learned from her doctor that she did not have a sprained back but an incurable cancer that would soon take her life.

As you might expect, all who knew her and loved her were in shock. I lost interest in the project, but Ross Hunter and the Universal front office, shocked and saddened as they were about Judy's passing, had a "go" project on their front burner and a major star available to take over the title role of *The Thrill Girl*. They had been looking for a new project for one of their biggest box-office draws, Doris Day! Her last film, *Pillow Talk*, which co-starred Rock Hudson, was a huge success, and the studio was anxious to find a new vehicle for her.

That vehicle turned out to be *The Thrill Girl*, now re-titled, *The Thrill of It All*, and it also turned out to be the vehicle that launched my moderately successful film career.

CHAPTER FIFTY

Three Fond Memories of Julie Andrews that I Most Happily Recalled after Rummaging through a Large Cardboard Carton of Publicity Photographs and Finding a 1974 Color Picture Postcard Promoting a Show Done in Great Britain and Starring Julie Andrews, Dick Van Dyke, and Myself as the Ghost of Covent Gardens Which Was Performed in Both a Film Studio and Also at the Famous London Produce Market

I feel very lucky and very proud. Lucky to be reminded of something for which I should not have needed a reminder, and proud to have written a title for a chapter that could very well end up in the *Guinness Book of World Records* as the longest title for a chapter in a showbiz memoir, written by an author who has just passed his ninetieth birthday and yet doggedly continues to believe in the goodness of man and the non-existence of an almighty being.

I first met lovely Julie Andrews at Longchamps, an upscale Manhattan restaurant, where a luncheon had been arranged for us by two enterprising theatrical publicists. NBC's *Caesar's Hour* hoped to reap the benefit of this arranged tête-à-tête with Julie, and *The Boyfriend*, an off-Broadway hit, would garner whatever jump-in box-office sales might be engendered by a photo of Julie and me having lunch together.

I found Julie Andrews to be beautiful, shy, charming, self-effacing, and in need of a champion. We spoke of many things—I about my wife and two children, she of getting used to the limelight and being called upon to do things she did not feel comfortable doing. She told of an audition she had for a new musical which the producers and the writers agreed she was perfect to play the lead role. She, on the other hand, thought "they were daft!" She was quite adamant about their having made a big mistake and upset about her agent having his own best interests at heart when he talked her into signing a contract to play the lead in a musical version of George Bernard Shaw's *Pygmalion*.

Julie actually thought that she was all wrong for the part. As I recall, her exact words were, "I am all wrong for the part!"

And I, a practicing thespian and a student of theater, said—and these are my exact words: "Wrong for the part? There has never been anybody righter for that part than you!"

Julie was 100 percent wrong in her assessment, and I, of course, was proven to be 100 percent right!

My wife and I were privileged to attend the exciting Broadway production of *My Fair Lady* and see Julie Andrews not play, but *become* Eliza Doolittle. I had seen many great Broadway performances, but never had I felt or reacted the way I did on the night I saw a glowing Eliza Doolittle glide gracefully down a long flight of stairs while singing "I Could Have Danced All Night!" I had what some people have come to describe as "an out-of-body experience."

I literally felt some part of my being leave my body, float up toward the balcony, and hover there until Eliza sang the final note of her song.

As we applauded, I turned to Estelle and told her of the unusual reaction I had to Julie's singing; she nodded and described a similar reaction.

Apropos the 1974 TV show that I had the pleasure of performing with Julie and Dick Van Dyke, I just Googled the title, *Julie and Dick at Covent Gardens*, and my computer coughed up a clip of the three of us in the scene at the produce market where I, the Ghost of Covent Gardens, meet tourists Dick and Julie. I did not remember any of this when I started this piece, and boy, am I glad I Googled. I actually laughed when I saw myself as a bearded Ghost of Covent Gardens, decked out in Shakespearean doublet and hose and describing how he died and became a ghost.

"I was a young actor playing Laertes in *Hamlet*," the ghost explained, "I was in my dressing room and nervous—I had just opened a bottle of spirit gum, when my dresser, to calm my nerves, handed me a cup of mulled wine, which I drank in one gulp—only it wasn't the mulled wine, it was the spirit gum! I pasted my guts together and glued myself to death!"

He goes on to explain that as punishment for his stupidity, the ghost of this terrible actor was constrained to haunt Covent Gardens for eternity or until he could act better or at least well enough to discourage audiences from booing him and tossing things at him.

And I try. At the very end of our show, so that I might rest in peace, I attempted one more time to "act better." I struck a pose, declaimed, "To be or not to be"—and was immediately met by a barrage of foodstuff.

Without warning me, our devilish director, Blake Edwards, having faith I would come up with a suitable last line, instructed the crew and the vendors to pummel me with as much fruit, tomatoes, and vegetables as possible—and they did! I was really surprised but managed to come up with a button for the scene. I laughed triumphantly and shouted, "My acting has improved. Tonight, much less garbage was thrown at me!"

In that same show, Dick and I did another sketch—a traditional English Christmas pantomime that required us to dress as women. In my years with Sid Caesar, we assiduously avoided wearing women's clothes. Dressing in drag was Milton Berle's domain.

The one thing I learned from that experience is that I made for a very unattractive woman—but, I daresay, a more attractive one than Dick will ever be—and Dick concurred.

At our first meeting at Longchamps, I did perceive that young Julie was right for a particular role, but I never could have foreseen that she would go on to become one of the most celebrated, admired, and beloved performers of our time. Nor did I have an inkling that one day, she and her daughter Emma would become bestselling authors of delightful children's books. I feel that Julie Andrews, had she kept her Mary Poppins umbrella, could, if she chose to, still fly over rooftops.

CHAPTER FIFTY-ONE

I Am Cleveland

At lunch a few months ago, an old friend, Joe Smith, the legendary record mogul and one of the producers and promoters of *The 2000 Year Old Man* album, asked if I had any thoughts of retiring.

"Retire?" I said. "Right now, I am writing a memoir, and recently I played small parts on two very popular television series."

I mentioned too that I had recently performed on a CD as Albert Einstein in *The Universal Properties of Acceleration*, written by my nephew, Barry Lebost.

To play the great mathematician, I wore a wig that a Cleveland toupee-maker had presented to me thirty years ago. When I thought of the two television shows on which I have roles and of Albert Einstein's Cleveland-made wig, a small bell tinkled in my hearing aid. I realized that in this past year or so, Cleveland has become an integral part of my life. Besides donning Einstein's Cleveland-wrought wig, I had a recurring role as Max in *Hot in Cleveland*, and in the animated *The Cleveland Show*, I give voice to Murray.

Albert, Max, and Murray! I have been given the opportunity to portray three distinct and clever, old Jewish men and, as a bonus, one of these old Jews has had the opportunity to kiss Betty White—thrice—and on the lips!

Retire? I may be old but I am not crazy!

CHAPTER FIFTY-TWO
Homer's Major Contribution to Scientology

The Homer referred to in the title is not the revered, epic poet who lived in Greece from 800 BC to 733 BC but the beloved Great Pyrenees-Australian shepherd who lived in California, from 1981 AD to 1992 AD. There is no record of the weight and height of the great Greek philosopher, but the Great Pyrenees stood three feet high and weighed 126 pounds—and from whence did Homer the dog come? Hearken.

I was seated at my desk, poring over the script for *Dead Men Don't Wear Plaid*, a film I was preparing to direct, when Judy Nagy, my then-loyal secretary and still-loyal friend, placed a small, white fur ball on my desk and asked, "Do you want to take this home?"

Judy's friend, Mark Steen, had enlisted her help in finding homes for this fur ball and its three siblings, which he carried in a cardboard box. It seemed there had been eight premature pups born in a stable, and four had been stomped to death by the horse whose quarters had been commandeered by the pups' mom. If any dog deserved a home, Homer did.

At this time, Buffy, a female beagle, was the designated pet at our house, and had not this sweet-faced, white fur ball been so needy and irresistible, I might not have awakened my wife from a nap, placed the fur ball on her chest, and asked, "What do we do with this?"

Her face lit up as she cradled it in her hands, and she said, "We keep him."

I do not know how Estelle arrived at it but, after handling the puppy for just a few seconds, she said, "Homer—he looks like a Homer, doesn't he?"

By God, he did—and thereupon Homer became Homer! We had no idea what breed of dog he was or how big he would grow. My wife pointed out that the size of his paws indicated that we had just adopted a very large animal.

It may sound as if I'm exaggerating, and what I am about to suggest may seem far-fetched, but I have the photos to prove my case. Homer grew so fast that if one had the time and the patience to sit and stare at him for hours on end, one would actually see him grow. A pair of photos says it all—one of Mel Brooks placing a three-month-old, fifty-pound Homer atop the head of his and Anne Bancroft's eight-year-old son, Max, and the other of this puppy trying to sit in my wife's lap.

In less than a year, Homer grew to be a handsome, 126-pound, gentle giant who became a treasured member of our family. My wife, our

children, and I all loved Homer...
not the case with very old beagle,
Buffy, who never warmed to the
idea of an interloper. It was two or
three years before Buffy succumbed
to old age and let Homer become
our sole pet. Except for ole Rinnie,
a goldfish, and a turtle, Homer was
the gentlest pet we ever owned. He
rarely, if ever, barked, and he loved
to be petted or stroked. He was
always happy to accept pats on the
head, be it from family, friends, or
perfect strangers.

Homer had no idea how big he
had grown and continued to act like a pup. After he was full-grown, he
continued to jump up on the couch and attempt to sit in Estelle's lap, and
Estelle never discouraged him from trying.

I return now to "Homer's Major Contribution to Scientology."

One afternoon, I answered the doorbell and was greeted by our
friendly UPS delivery man, who handed me a parcel that was addressed
to me. I did not remember ordering anything. I opened the box, and in
it I found a most impressive-looking leather-bound book. The page edges

sparkled with gold leaf, and on its cover, in raised gold lettering, was the title and author:

DIANETICS
BY
L. RON HUBBARD

The bible of Scientology by the creator himself. I could not for the life of me figure out who would send me this silly science-fiction book. For the last few years, Scientology had been masquerading as a viable, alternative religion—and, sad to say, with more success than is healthy for the untold millions of naive people worldwide. These poor souls were duped into following the cultlike teachings, and many have been convinced to give up their jobs and their earthly possessions—and a few, even more.

There were and are many outraged critics and whistleblowers. One, a Justice Latey of the High Court in London had ruled that: "Scientology is both immoral and socially obnoxious…it is corrupt, sinister and dangerous. It is dangerous because it is out to capture people, especially children and impressionable young people. It is corrupt because it is based on lies and deceit." (*http://londonist.com/2008/05/police_to_prose. php; http://en.wikinews.org/wiki/UK_minor_faces_charges_for_calling_ Scientology_%27cult%27_at_protest*)

Many investigative books have been published on the dangers and possible consequences of becoming a Scientologist. One scholarly work, *Inside Scientology*, is written by Janet Reitman. There are also many websites that carry important information about this cult.

For me, the mystery was, why was this book sent to me? Why was I chosen to be the unwitting owner of a beautiful, Florentine leather-bound copy of L. Ron Hubbard's *Dianetics*?

The mystery was solved when I scanned the first page, and one word jumped out at me—the word "Clear!"

As I read on, I learned that when a young recruit studies Scientology, he spends much time and effort and oftentimes money to reach the ultimate goal. That is to be acknowledged, by the school of Scientology as someone who has become "Clear." *Clear* is the cherished state that all students strive to achieve.

I had inadvertently sent a signal to someone in Scientology that I was one of them! I had done this by virtue of my having once formed a production company to produce the films I wrote or directed.

Years earlier, my company was called Acre Enterprises. It was created by using the first initial of the names of our family members, A for Annie, C for Carl, R for Rob, and E for Estelle. Acre! Devilishly clever, eh?

Sometime later, when we were blessed with our third child, Lucas, we naturally needed to add an L to "Acre Enterprises," but if we did, our company would become "Acrel Enterprises." We guessed that Acrel was not a word, and even if it was, "Acrel" had no flair. "Acre" conjured up something substantial—like a piece of property, a ranch or a farm. Had we placed the L in front of Acre, we would have "Lacre," which conjured up the L.A. Lakers basketball franchise.

I had just completed *The Man with Two Brains*, which starred Steve Martin, and we were in the process of finalizing the opening production credits. With a flash of creative ingenuity, I reconfigured the first letters of our names, Carl, Lucas, Estelle, Annie, Rob, and "Clear Productions" was born.

The enterprising Scientologist must have been excited when *The Man with Two Brains* was released, and he saw the title card, Clear Productions.

My first impulse was to toss the expensively bound Dianetics book into the dumpster in the back alley, but then I remembered something that Mort Dimondstein, a friend and fine artist had once told us about tossing some of his unwanted paintings into the alley. He told us how he overheard the trash collectors discussing his discarded canvases. One was taken by how unlike regular garbage these "nice-colored pitchers" were and how he would feel bad trashing them. He actually selected two of the failed Dimondstein canvases and placed them into the cab of his truck to take home and "hang 'em up—as a present for the missus."

Mort was pleased to hear that someone found his work worthy of hanging, but displeased that bad examples of his art lived on.

Taking a cue from Mort Dimondstein, I worried that if a trash collector saw this magnificent Florentine, leather-covered, gold-leafed book in the dumpster, he would most certainly rescue it and bring it home. The possibility that this man or his wife and children might be seduced by the book's contents upset me. Then I thought about Homer.

At least once a day, our big, healthy animal with a hearty appetite used our spacious back yard as his private commode, and every other day, I used my long-handled Pooper-Scooper to collect Homer's output and deposit it in one of the alley's two dumpsters—the blue one for recyclables and the green one for all other garbage.

And so it was into the green dumpster that I placed L. Ron Hubbard's *Dianetics*. To assure that Mr. Hubbard's philosophy did not damage any more psyches, I dropped two days' worth of Homer's healthy output from my Pooper-Scooper onto its gold-leafed pages. Using the scooper, I closed the book and covered the front and back cover with the remains of my dog's detritus—thus insuring that at least this copy of Mr. Hubbard's book will do no harm.

CHAPTER FIFTY-THREE

Piling It On, Ad Infinitum

Within the last thirteen days, I have been honored to within an inch of my life. These lovely floggings were inflicted at two separate events, in two separate locations—the first at the Hollywood Egyptian Theater and sponsored by American Cinematheque, the second at the auditorium of The Academy of Television's Arts and Sciences, and sponsored by the Television Academy.

At these events, I saw faces from the distant past, the recent past, the present, and gratefully, I saw no scythe-toting, black-hooded faces from my future. All their faces were smiling as they said nice things to my face and also into microphones, so everyone could hear how they thought I had done a great thing by creating *The Dick Van Dyke Show*.

If I were a blusher, I would have easily unseated the world titleholder of the MFWRTAB Award ("My Face Was Redder than a Beet").

A stream of performers, writers, and directors whom I held in great affection found their way on stage and onto the couch on which I had been placed. I will not try to remember or set down what was said to me or about me, or what I responded, but I will say that there was little that did not get a positive response—often in the form of raucous laughter or honest chuckles.

I considered listing the names of the faces I remembered looking at me and embarrassing me, but I fear embarrassing myself by the omission of someone who did not deserved to be "omitted."

Therefore, I will not mention Billy Perksy and Garry Marshall, who, with their recently departed partners, Sam Denoff and Jerry Belson, had written memorable episodes of *The Dick Van Dyke Show*. Nor will I mention

Lily Tomlin, whom I had the opportunity to direct in *All of Me*, and who sat next to me on the couch and described how much she loved listening to my wife's superb jazz albums and watching her perform at the Gardenia Supper Club. Nor will I mention how much trouble comedian Garry Shandling went to making a tape telling how he was too sick to attend my event and then showing up to play that tape, or what a tremendous laugh he got by telling me how uncomfortable it was for him to be "sitting next to an old Jew on a couch and not paying him three hundred dollars for the session."

Neither will I mention Steve Martin's difficult decision about not attending the Academy event for me or the recorded message he sent to explain his dilemma. It was apparent, as we watched his tape, how very tortured he was about having to miss my big night.

It was a genuinely heartsick Steve asking that we understand his valid reason for not showing up. He explained, sadly, that our event was scheduled to be held at the exact time he had would be eating his "dinner at the restaurant next door."

Of course I understood, as did everyone in the auditorium. Steve Martin did not get to be Steve Martin without doing for Steve Martin what Steve Martin required he do for his own best interests: make everyone laugh as hard as I did.

For fear of my seeming self-aggrandizing, I will steer clear of mentioning any of the questions put to me by doting members of the audience, which, I must say, were answered honestly and to great, noisy reactions. I truly feared that the audience members who were screaming with laughter might do physical harm to their internal organs.

One gentleman, who caught me completely off guard and whose identity I have no intention of divulging, was the last guest to walk on stage and sit down next to me. He is an extraordinarily handsome actor, a selfless humanitarian, and someone I have worked with in the films *Ocean's Eleven, Twelve,* and *Thirteen.* If you are guessing it was Brad Pitt, Matt Damon, or Don Cheadle, you would be way off base. I don't mean to be a tease, but his initials are G.C. Some of you may have concluded that Glenn Close is the name I am keeping from you, and to those of you who guessed George Clooney, all I can say is that you may be right, but as I said, I have no intention of divulging G.C.'s true identity or how magnificently he performed in his Oscar-worthy performance in *The Descendants.*

This last unnamed guest said some very complimentary things about me, but I interrupted him to gush about his dedication to making this world a better place for everybody. G.C. and his dad Nick Clooney's humanitarian efforts to ameliorate the suffering in Somalia and the starvation in Darfur went beyond what anyone would expect a private citizen to even attempt.

One thing I'd like to share with you is something Billy Persky reminded me that I did a long, long time ago—something I had completely forgotten.

During the early days of *The Dick Van Dyke Show*, a young network assistant visited our production office. He had come to offer suggestions that he felt would help our then-successful show become even more successful—and funnier. This hot shot breezed in, plopped himself down in an easy chair, and put his feet up on our coffee table. Present and exchanging quizzical glances were staff members Garry Marshall, Jerry Belson, Bill Persky, and Sam Denoff.

With his ultra-shiny shoes resting atop my coffee table, the young lion took out a slip of paper and proceeded to read aloud some of the funny ideas he had jotted down. None of us could believe what we were hearing. Our fresh-faced exec did not have a clue as to what was funny or what audiences might find funny. Since it was my office and on my coffee table that he rested his feet, I concluded that it was my duty to act. So immediately after he told another lame joke and asked, "Now, don't you think that's funny?" I said, "You wanna know what I think is funny?" and then walked to him, pulled off one of his shoes, and threw it out an open window. "*That*, I think is funny!" I then turned and left my office.

It was not long after I left my office that someone at the network asked Mr. Hot Shot to leave his office.

At one point in that evening at the Television Academy, a thought flickered through my mind—actually it was a revelation. My family, friends, close acquaintances, and co-workers had handed me a rare gift. They had given me the privilege to not only attend but actually hear what will likely be said at my memorial service.

If the speakers wax this eloquently when they look at me sitting on a couch, how much more laudatory, forthcoming, and emotional will they be when they look at my urn?

Not much more, I'll bet.

CHAPTER FIFTY-FOUR

The End

I have told many people about the final minutes of my beloved wife's last hour of her last day, and I would like now to tell it again.

Estelle had been bedridden for almost a year, and except for her inability to walk, was in complete control of all her mental faculties. We often invited our good friends, Sheila and Ron Clark, Terry and Sandra Marsh, and our oldest and dearest friend, Mel Brooks—to dine with us in her beautiful, airy, five-windowed bedroom.

Her last day, at the age of ninety-four, our family—which included Robbie, Annie, Lucas, Georgie, and me—were at her side, helping her to say good-bye.

Earlier that week, she had individual conversations with each one of our children and discussed with them her feeling that she had not done as good a job of mothering as she would have liked. One by one, they shot down her arguments and convinced her she was nothing less than an exceptional and inspiring mother whom they loved and appreciated.

As the hours passed, her breathing became more and more shallow, but she seemed to be in no pain. She was still responding to our conversation but spoke less and less. The hospice workers were in the room and ready to help if needed. She had difficulty keeping her eyes open but seemed to be aware of what was being said to her but had stopped speaking or trying to speak. Her breathing was now very shallow, and a quiet moan suggested that she was experiencing a low level of pain. To alleviate this, the hospice nurse suggested I place a drop of a prescribed anti-pain medication under her lip.

Her nephew George told her how much he loved her and that if she wanted to go, she should feel free to do so.

I had the thought of playing a song from one of her CDs. I chose *Grown Up Songs for Kids*, the last recording she did, at ninety. I turned up the volume and hoped that she could hear herself singing, "A, you're adorable, B, you are so beautiful, C, you're a cutie full of charm."

There was no visible reaction from her, and we had no idea that she heard herself singing. The small, intermittent breaths she took were almost imperceptible. I sat beside her and held her hand as we listened to her sing. One of the hospice nurses quietly remarked, "What a lovely, sweet voice she has."

Lucas heard the comment, and with his face three inches from his mother's, he said, slowly and clearly, "Ma, the nurse said that you have a lovely, sweet voice."

We would not have known that Estelle heard what Lucas said, had she not just before expiring, mouthed the words, *"Thank you."*

CHAPTER FIFTY-FIVE

There Is No End for the Living

I titled the preceding chapter, "The End," and then I thought that it was not really "the end"—not for those of us who are still alive—like me.

If it were the end, I would not be thinking about how much I miss my wife and how much she is still with me during the day—and at night before I fall asleep—and in my dreams—and in my writing. This thought came to me while I was driving to our neighborhood Whole Foods to buy some Chilean sea bass for my dinner. While in my car, my wife is always beside me; that is, her sweet voice is. It floats out of the car's multiple speakers, and during the ride, I am able to hear a few of the 137 songs she recorded.

I remember the combination of excitement and anxiety she felt when we drove to the Wilder Brothers Studio to record some of the songs. In particular, I recall a problem we encountered when she recorded one of my favorites, "When the Red Red Robin Comes Bob Bob Bobbin' Along." The problem presented itself when she sang the line, "I'm walking through fields of flowers…"

Having been born and raised in the Bronx, Estelle pronounced the word *walking* as "waawking," as any bona fide New Yaawker would. We redid the track, and she corrected all of her mispronunciations—all but one, I am happy to say. I am still able the hear her sing the lyrics, "I'm waawking through fields of flowers," and I often replay that section just to hear her taawk her Bronx way of taawking. Nothing tickles me more than listening to Estelle strum and sing on "Ukelele Mama 1" or "Ukelele Mama 2." I challenge you not to melt when you hear her sing the old standards, "Blue Skies," "It Had to Be You," "Goody Goody," "Ain't She Sweet," or "Lover Man," which only Billie Holiday sang an iota better.

I believe that her last album has the power to soften the hardest of hearts. To people who have friends or relatives whose hard hearts they have unsuccessfully tried to soften, I recommend that you sit them down and have them listen to Estelle Reiner sing, *Grown Up Songs for Kids.*

I say again that there is "No End for the Living" if you can enjoy memories of a life partner who physically is not there but spiritually is everywhere! There is "No End for the Living" if you awaken each morning and think seriously about what to eat for breakfast. Here now are some twenty random entries in what, I imagine, will be a growing list.

There Is No End for the Living if I Can Look Forward To…

- A morning shower.
- A visit with my children, Robbie, Annie, and Lucas.
- Seeing grandchildren, Jake, Nick, Romy, Livia, and Rose.
- Spending time with daughters-in-law Michele and Maud and their husbands.
- Nightly visits from Mel Brooks.
- Reading Annie Reiner's psychoanalytic books.
- Listening to Annie Reiner sing.
- Viewing Lucas Reiner's oil paintings and etchings and hugging him.
- Attending a screening of a new Rob Reiner film.
- Watching Rob's *This Is Spinal Tap, A Mighty Wind, The Princess Bride,* and *A Few Good Men.*
- Right-wing senators and congressmen losing their seats.
- Lunching at Bier Beisel, an Austrian restaurant that features Weisswurst.
- A sushi lunch with sushi-loving friends.
- A daily, brisk walk with George Shapiro.
- Political programs hosted by someone who shares my views.
- Hearing a great new joke, laughing at it, and then passing it along.
- Hearing Livia play her harp or violin.

- Hearing Rose play her cello and sing Filipino, Peruvian, and Indian songs.
- Watching *Jeopardy, Password, Family Feud,* or good vintage game shows.
- Hearing Estelle Reiner sing, "I've Grown Accustomed to His Face."
- Viewing new films at the Academy of Motion Picture Arts' theater.
- Nightly visits from Melvin Kaminsky.

And finally, there is no end for the living if I can look forward to:

This book entertaining the dozens of loyal readers I have worldwide.

Start YOUR list!